COMBAT AIRCRAFT PROTOTYPES
SINCE 1945

Combat Aircraft Prototypes

since 1945

Robert Jackson

ARCO/PRENTICE HALL PRESS
New York

An Arco Aviation Book
Published 1986 by Prentice Hall Press
A Division of Simon & Schuster, Inc.
Simon & Schuster Building
1230 Avenue of the Americas
New York, New York 10020

First published 1985
by Airlife Publishing Ltd.

Library of Congress Cataloging-in-Publication Data

Jackson, Robert, 1941-
   Combat aircraft prototypes since 1945.

   1. Airplanes, Military—Prototypes.   I. Title.
UG1240.J32   1986   623.74'6044   85-18725
ISBN 0-671-61953-5

Printed in England.

Contents

Introduction

This is the story of combat aircraft that never were. It is a story of hope, and endeavour, and frustration and bitter disappointment; of brilliant technical innovation which, for various reasons, never reached full fruition.

The story begins in 1945, when the Allied powers captured thousands of tons of German research documents and learned, for the first time, of the advanced aviation projects that had been set in motion in the Third Reich — projects whose technological refinement far outstripped anything envisaged in Britain, the United States or the Soviet Union.

Almost overnight, the possession of this mass of detailed knowledge brought about profound changes in the development of military aviation in both east and west. There followed a spate of experimentation, some of it based on shaky foundations, and even concepts that appeared sound in the light of available knowledge sometimes foundered as test aircraft nosed into and beyond the then uncharted realms of transonic flight. Experimental flying, between 1945 and 1955, was marred by a series of appalling accidents in which some of the world's most experienced test pilots lost their lives.

Out of it all there emerged a new generation of combat aircraft which went on to form the mainstay of air forces in both east and west throughout the late 1950s and 1960s. This work is not concerned with them, except in the fact that their success often played a part in the demise of other combat aircraft projects that might otherwise have gone on to equip the world's air combat squadrons in their place.

Whether the shapes of today's military aircraft would have been much different if those projects had reached production status is open to conjecture, but the pattern of operational concepts might have altered appreciably — as might the pattern of world-wide military aircraft exports, with all its associated political undertones.

This book is intended to give an insight into some fascinating possibilities. What, for example, would have been the shape of today's Strategic Air Command if Northrop's giant YB-49 jet flying wing bomber had proven a more successful design than the Boeing B-52? And would military aerospace collaboration within Europe ever have become a reality if an isolationist Britain had proceeded with TSR-2, P.1121 and other projects in the early 1960s?

The reader is left to judge for himself. But is should not be forgotten that, in the wake of every successful combat aircraft, there fly the shadows of a dozen unsuccessful ones which nevertheless have played a vital part in the shaping of modern aviation technology.

Chapter One
The United States, 1945-55: The German Legacy

1. Quest for the Global Bomber

At the end of the Second World War, the most powerful and effective bomber aircraft in the world was the Boeing B-29 Superfortress, the aircraft that had ushered in a new and terrible era of warfare with the atomic destruction of Hiroshima and Nagasaki. Yet even the B-29 was limited in its effectiveness by considerations of range; during its early operations against Japan, operating from bases in mainland China in 1944, it was able to carry only a relatively small payload, and it was not until the Americans captured the Marianas and built airfields on them that the B-29's full potential as a strategic weapon against Japan was realised.

As early as April, 1941, the USAAF had issued a specification calling for an advanced bomber aircraft capable of carrying a 10,000-pound payload over 5,000 miles, or a 72,000-pound load over shorter ranges; it was to have a top speed of between 300 and 400 mph at a ceiling of 35,000 feet, and be able to operate from runways 5,000 feet long. Among the companies that produced designs to meet this specification was Convair, whose project envisaged a massive, heavily-armed bomber with a 230-foot wingspan and powered by six 'pusher' engines; it was designated XB-36, and on 15 November 1941 the USAAF signed a contract for two prototypes. Early development was slowed down by the war, but the XB-36 programme was stepped up when, in 1943, heavy bombing attacks on her home islands seemed the only way of striking hard at Japan, and on 23 July

that year 190 production aircraft were ordered. The prototype Convair XB-36 first flew on 8 August 1946. In all, 154 B-36s were built before production ceased in 1954, and the huge bomber was the mainstay of Strategic Air Command's long-range nuclear striking force until the service debut of the Boeing B-47 jet bomber.

The other principal contender for the wartime USAAF heavy bomber contract was Northrop Aircraft Incorporated, who based their project on a flying-wing design. John Northrop's experience in flying-wing development stretched back as far as 1927, and the first aircraft using this formula, the N1M, had been delivered to Muroc Army Air Base for evaluation by the USAAC in July 1940. This machine, powered by two Franklin pusher engines, made more than 200 test flights by September 1941, and the results encouraged Northrop to submit a design for a four-engined, long-range bomber to the USAAF in a bid to meet the new specification.

In November 1941, a prototype was ordered under the designation XB-35, a week after Convair received a similar order for their prototype XB-36. Both designs benefited from the experience gained with an earlier design, the Douglas B-19, which in effect became a flying laboratory for the new generation of heavy bombers.

Detail design work on the XB-35 started at the beginning of 1942, with the help and co-operation of the Wright Field Engineering Division, and construction of a prototype was approved on 5 July. As Northrop were heavily involved in the development of the P-61 Black Widow night-fighter, the final design of the XB-35's wing

BOEING B-29. The aircraft that gave Boeing the technical edge over their competitors in post-war bomber design: the B-29 Superfortress, seen here over Korea in 1950. The Russians similarly based their post-war strategic bomber designs on a B-29 copy, the Tupolev Tu-4.

NORTHROP XB-35. A four-engined flying-wing bomber, the XB-35 flew on 25 June 1946, and was powered by four 3,250 hp Pratt & Whitney R-4360-17/21 radial 'pusher' engines.

and the installation of the engines were allocated to the Glenn L. Martin Company of Baltimore, Northrop undertaking the aerodynamic research as well as the building of the undercarriage, control systems and surfaces, and ancillary equipment. In a bid to accelerate the programme, personnel from the design department of the Otis Elevator Company, New York, were also drafted in to help with the design of the wing structure.

While design work on the prototype continued, four scale models were built to test the flight characteristics of the all-wing formula, continuing the programme where the N1M had left off. They were also to serve as training aircraft for the pilots who were destined to fly the full-scale machines. The first two models, designated N-9M, were powered by two 275 hp Menasco engines while the third, the N-9M-A, was fitted with 300 hp Franklin motors. The fourth machine, the N-9M-B, was similarly equipped, and like the other had a 60-foot wingspan.

Construction of the XB-35 began in January 1943, the aircraft bearing the serial 42-13603, and at the same time a second prototype (42-38323) was ordered. Before the end of the fiscal year, this was followed by an order for thirteen pre-series YB-35s, which were allocated serial numbers from 42-102366 to -102378. Finally, the Glenn Martin Company received an order for the construction of 200 series-production B-35As. The advent of the jet engine in operational service towards the end of the war, however, changed everything; the order for the 200 production aircraft was cancelled, and on 1 June 1945 the decision was taken to convert the second and third YB-35 (42-102367 and -102368) to YB-35Bs, the four piston engines being replaced by eight Allison J35-A-5 turbo jets.

The piston-engined XB-35 prototype flew for the first time on 25 June 1946, test pilot Max Stanley flying it from Hawthorne to the test centre at Muroc. It was an impressive machine, its huge all-metal wing spanning 172 feet and having a root chord of 37 feet 6 inches. The leading edge was swept at an angle of 28 degrees and had a lower surface dihedral of 1 degree. Directional control surfaces were fitted at the wingtips, with the elevons fitted between these and the outboard engine nacelles. Large flaps extended along the trailing edge from the outboard engines to the central fuselage nacelle. All control surfaces were hydraulically assisted, and leading-edge slats, which opened automatically when the aircraft approached stalling speed, were fitted near the wingtips.

The fuselage nacelle, which was fully pressurized and of monocoque construction, normally housed a nine-man crew consisting of pilot, co-pilot, bombardier,

Designation: Northrop XB-35.

Role: Strategic heavy bomber.

Engines: Four 3,250 hp Pratt & Whitney Wasp Major radials.

Span: 172 ft.

Length: 53 ft. 1 in.

Weight: Loaded 209,000 lb (max.).

Crew: 7.

Service ceiling: 36,000 ft.

Max range: 2,500 miles.

Max speed: 350 mph at 16,400 ft.

Weapons: Provision for two MGs in rear fuselage cone; up to 20,000 lbs. payload.

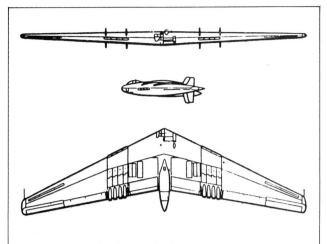

Designation: Northrop YB-49.

Role: Experimental Strategic Bomber.

Engines: Eight 4,000 lb.s.t. Allison J35-A-5 turbojets.

Span: 172 ft.

Length: 53 ft. 1 in.

Weight: Empty 89,600 lb. - Loaded 216,600 lb.

Crew: 7.

Service ceiling: 40,000 ft.

Range: 2,800 miles with 10,000 lb. payload.

Max Speed: 520 mph at 30,000 ft.

Weapons: Double .5-in MG installation at rear of fuselage cone.

navigator, flight engineer, radio operator and three air gunners. The aircraft was also equipped to carry a reserve crew, and six folding bunks were fitted for this purpose. The pilot's cockpit was situated slightly to the left of the centreline under a bubble canopy; the bombardier's station was buried in the wing on the right, with forward vision through windows built into the leading edge. Because of the B-35's relatively modest speed, the aircraft carried heavy defences, the gunners — housed in blisters above and below the wings — controlling six turrets

armed with .5-inch machine-guns. One four-gun turret was positioned above and one below the fuselage nacelle; the other four, each with quadruple guns, were fitted above and below the wing, outboard of the engines. In addition to these sixteen machine-guns, four more could be fitted in the tail cone of the fuselage nacelle, depending on operational requirements. On the XB-35 prototype, these weapons stations were represented by metal blisters.

The XB-35 was powered by four 18-cylinder Pratt and Whitney Wasp Major air-cooled engines, three of which drove eight-bladed co-axial Hamilton Standard propellers. The fourth, port outer, engine was fitted with a six-bladed propeller, and retained this throughout testing. Large air intakes were fitted in the wing leading edge and the wing fuel tanks had provision for up to 18,000 gallons. The aircraft had a tricycle undercarriage, the main units retracting forwards and the nosewheel laterally, and the landing gear was electrically operated.

Empty weight of the XB-35 was 90,500 lbs, rising to a fully-laden take-off weight of 164,700 lbs. However, maximum permissible overload weight of the aircraft was 212,544 lbs, a figure that reveals the astonishing potential of the flying-wing formula. Estimated maximum speed of the XB-35 was 393 mph at 34,650 feet, and economical cruising speed was 183 mph, this giving the aircraft a range of 8,125 miles, which was equivalent to a non-stop return flight from New York to Paris with a 16,000-lb bomb load. When the range was reduced to 725 miles, the aircraft could carry a bomb load of no less than 51,500 lbs. The XB-35 was able to reach a cruising altitude of 35,000 feet in 57 minutes, and had an operational ceiling of 40,000 feet.

Right from the beginning, difficulties were experienced with the aircraft's propeller governing mechanisms and engine reduction gears, and after only a few flights testing was suspended until the problem was sorted out. It was eventually decided to fit simplified four-bladed propellers of a type specially adapted for the B-35, but so that flight testing might continue while Hamilton Standard were working on these, the XB-35 was

NORTHROP YB-49. The thirty YB-49s ordered by the USAF were cancelled after two mid-air disasters and further development of the Northop flying-wing bomber series was abandoned.

CONVAIR YB-60. Designed to the same requirement as the Boeing B-52, the Convair YB-60 was developed from the B-36 and originally designated B-36G. It had a sharply swept wing and tail surfaces and was powered by eight Pratt & Whitney J57-P-3 turbojets mounted in four underwing pods.

temporarily equipped with Curtiss Electric propellers of the type destined for Convair's B-36.

In 1947, the second XB-35 was delivered to Muroc together with the first pre-series YB-35 (42-102366) and shortly afterwards the latter was 'winterized' for Arctic trials, being re-designated YB-35A. The second pre-series YB-35 (42-102367) flew on 21 October that year, and it was this machine that was converted to take eight Allison turbojets; known initially as the YB-35B, its designation was changed soon after to YB-49. The jet engines were closely mounted in two clutches of four at about one-third span, each clutch being flanked by vertical fins that extended well clear of both upper and lower trailing edges and were intended to improve directional stability. The crew was reduced to seven men, there now being only one gunner in command of a twin-gun turret positioned at the rear of the central fuselage cone. Empty and loaded weights of the YB-49 were 89,600 lbs and 216,600 lbs respectively, and there was provision for a bomb load of 37,400 lbs. More usually, a bomb load of 10,000 lbs would have been carried over a range of 2,800 miles at a cost of 16,700 US gallons of fuel.

Although the jet-powered YB-49 showed a considerable speed increase over the B-35 (520 against 393 mph) its reduced range was a considerable drawback, being only about half that of its piston-engined predecessor. Moreover, the YB-49 proved to be a poor weapons release platform because of an instability factor that proved seemingly impossible to correct. Two YB-49s were built and flown, and flight testing quickly revealed

the type's inherent unsuitability as a strategic bomber. However, during an endurance test, one of them remained airborne for 9 hours 30 minutes, covering a distance of 3,458 miles at an average speed of 382 mph and an altitude of between 35,000 and 40,000 feet, and this seemed to lend weight to the idea that the aircraft might find an application in the strategic reconnaissance role. In fact, in February 1948 it had already been decided to produce thirty examples of a reconnaissance variant, the RB-49A; nine of the pre-series YB-35s were to be converted to YRB-49A standard for evaluation, this work being carried out under sub-contract by Convair. To increase the range, the reconnaissance version was to have six turbojets instead of eight.

In April 1949, however, the RB-49A order was cancelled and conversion work was stopped, although one YRB-49A (the eleventh YB-35, 012376) was completed and made its first flight from Hawthorne to Edwards Air Force Base, as Muroc was now known, on 4 May 1950. This aircraft had six Allison J35-A-19 turbojets, four of which were buried in the wing and the other two suspended in pods beneath it. The YRB-49A carried a six-man crew and its equipment included the latest high-altitude cameras, situated in a compartment at the rear of the fuselage nacelle and protected from icing by a special air-circulation system.

Meanwhile, the final nail had been driven into the coffin of the YB-49 jet bomber project. On 5 June 1949, the first YB-49 exploded in the air without warning over Muroc, killing all five crew members, and exactly the

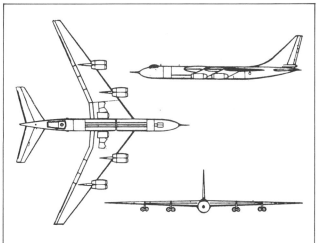

Designation: Convair YB-60.

Role: Prototype Strategic Heavy Bomber.

Engines: Eight 8,800 lb.s.t. Pratt & Whitney J57-P-3 turbojets.

Span: 206 ft.

Length: 171 ft.

Weight: Loaded 300,000 lb. - Max Loaded 360,000 lb.

Crew: 10.

Range (Max): 8,000 miles.

Max Speed: 520 mph at 45,000 ft.

Armament: Two 20-mm cannon in tail barbette.

same fate overtook the second YB-49 on 15 March 1950. Before this, one of them had laid a claim to fame by appearing in the film version of H.G. Wells' classic *The War of the Worlds*, in which it dropped an atomic bomb on the invading Martians (without, it must be said, much appreciable result!)

Another interesting project in the Northrop flying wing programme was the EB-35B, which was to have been fitted with Turbodyne XT-37 turboprops. The XT-37 was a Northrop design and the company had received a contract to build two prototype engines on 1 July 1943; the first was bench-tested in December 1944 and was the first American turboprop to be run with propeller fitted. The Turbodyne had an eighteen-stage compressor and a four-stage turbine, and its development was undertaken by a joint company formed between Northrop and the Joshua Hendy Iron Works. The XT-37 had originally been intended as a potential powerplant for naval aircraft, but when the US Navy lost interest in the project in 1945 development continued under a USAAF contract.

In 1948, Northrop acquired Hendy's shares and formed a new company, the Turbodyne Corporation. Work on the new turboprop went on, and in 1950 the engine, now rated at 10,000 shp, passed a fifty-hour bench test without failing. At the end of that year, all assets of the Turbodyne Corporation were absorbed by the General Electric Company, who continued with the work of advanced engine testing for a time, but then the whole project was abandoned following a spate of

CONVAIR XB-46. Designed in competition with the North American B-45, the Boeing B-47 and the Martin XB-48, the highly streamlined Convair XB-46 flew for the first time on 2 April 1947, powered by 4,000 lbs thrust GE J35-C-3 turbojets housed in pairs in underwing pods.

MARTIN XB-48. Designed to the same requirement as the B-47, the Martin XB-48 experimental jet bomber flew for the first time on 22 June 1947, powered by six GE J35-A-5 turbojets mounted in three-cell underwing pods.

unforseen teething troubles and the EB-35B never flew.

By the end of 1950, the YRB-49A was the only one of Northrop's huge flying wings still in existence, the two YB-49s having been accidentally destroyed and the others scrapped. The YRB-49A was scrapped in its turn in October 1951. By that time, the mighty Convair B-36 — a far better aircraft all round, except perhaps aesthetically — had already been in service with Strategic Air Command for four years.

The demise of the B-35/49, however, was not quite the end of the Northrop flying wing story. In 1948 the company built a small all-wing jet research aircraft, the X-4 Bantam, which flew in December and was powered by two Westinghouse J30-WE-1 turbojets; it was followed by a second aircraft, and both machines were used in an extensive high-speed research programme by the NACA. The X-4 had a maximum level speed of 630 mph at 10,000 feet, and could reach Mach 0.95 in a shallow dive. Although not strictly a military prototype, the information gathered by the X-4 on the flight characteristics of swept-wing tailless aircraft at high subsonic speeds was put to use in the design of operational types such as the Chance Vought F7U Cutlass and the Douglas F4D Skyray.

Returning to the strategic bomber question, the failure of the YB-49 effectively removed Northrop from the running in the race to provide the USAF with a heavy jet bomber capable of delivering nuclear weapons into the heartland of the West's potential enemy, the Soviet Union. One of the main problems with Northrop's design, perhaps, was that it had been ahead of its time; two other contending companies, Boeing and Convair, starting virtually from scratch with jet bomber studies at

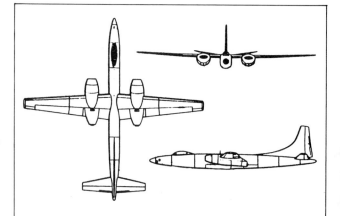

Designation: Convair XB-46.

Role: Prototype Medium Jet Bomber.

Engines: Four 4,000 lb.s.t. General Electric J35-C-3. turbojets.

Span: 113 ft.

Length: 105 ft. 9 in.

Weight: Empty 48,018 lb. - Normal Loaded 91,000 lb.

Crew: 3.

Service ceiling: 40,000 ft.

Range: 2,870 miles with 8,000 lb. payload.

Max Speed: 545 mph at 15,000 ft.

Weapons: (Defensive) Two .5-in MGs in radar-directed tail barbette: (Offensive) 8,000 lb normal bomb load, 22,000 maximum (single large store).

the end of the war, were able to benefit from the wealth of advanced aerodynamic research material that had come out of defeated Germany.

Despite determined efforts by the Germans to destroy it, such material still remained intact in large quantities at locations all over Germany in May 1945, and became the object of an Intelligence-gathering race between the Allies. It was a race won by the Americans, mainly for geographical reasons. In the closing months of the war, most secret German research faculties had been removed from the north to the more secure mountainous regions of central and southern Germany, which placed them precisely in the path of the main American advance; it was therefore hardly surprising that the bulk of the material was destined to fall into American hands.

Before the end of the war, too, every branch of the US armed forces had formed its own team of technical specialists, tasked with ferreting out secret material and the scientists responsible for it. The USAAF team was led by a Lieutenant Morton Hunt, who in May 1945 went into the Dessau area of central Germany with orders to remove everything of aeronautical research value before the territory became part of the Soviet occupation zone. In less than a week, Hunt and his men removed a staggering quantity of documentation, as well as a number of key scientists and their entire households. The whole operation was to have a profound effect on the course of high-speed aerodynamic research in the immediate post-war years, and was to give the United States a lead which it would never lose.

In April 1945, the USAF issued a requirement for a new jet-powered heavy bomber to replace the Convair B-36, which was then in the advanced development stage. Boeing, with a vast amount of bomber experience through the B-17/B-29 line, originally proposed a swept-wing, turboprop-powered design, and this still remained a possibility when two prototypes were ordered in September 1947. Design and performance problems, however, resulted in a considerable revision, and the decision was taken to equip the new design with eight turbojets. The first prototype, the XB-52, began ground testing on 29 November 1951, and on 15 March the following year it was joined by the second prototype, the YB-52. It was this machine that was the first to fly, on 15 April 1952.

Convair's answer, meanwhile, revolved around a straightforward swept-wing development of the B-36, and was intended to give Strategic Air Command an aircraft with the same range and load-carrying ability as the B-36 but with a greatly improved performance. Originally designated YB-36G, the aircraft was re-designated YB-60 in 1950 and Convair received a contract for two prototypes on 15 March 1951. The first of these flew on 18 April 1952, powered by eight Pratt and Whitney J57-P-3 turbojets in four paired underwing pods. The prototype's designation was YB-60-CF and its serial number 49-2676. Three-quarters of the YB-60's structure was similar to that of the B-36, but it had a revised undercarriage and its fuel capacity was greater. Its wing span was 206 feet, the wing being swept at an angle of 35 degrees at the leading edge. Plans called for the production version to be powered by an uprated version of the J57 engine developing 10,000 lb.s.t., which would have given the bomber a maximum speed of 550 mph at 55,000 feet, but the Boeing B-52, which had flown three days earlier than the Convair design, proved superior on almost every count and the YB-60

programme was abandoned. The two prototypes were used on research and development work for some time before being withdrawn from use.

2. Medium and Light Jet Bombers: First Generation

In April 1944, the USAAF invited design tenders for a medium bomber possessing a tactical radius of 1,000 miles, a maximum speed of at least 500 mph and an operational ceiling of 40,000 feet. Four companies — Boeing, Convair, Martin and North American — went to work on the idea and submitted their proposals in December of that year.

The Boeing Company's thinking crystallized, in September 1945, into the design of a strategic jet bomber designated Model 450. The project had undergone many changes since its conception the previous year, and after assessing German research data the Boeing design team decided to adopt a configuration that was a radical departure from conventional design, featuring a thin, flexible wing — based on wartime German aerodynamic work with 35 degrees of sweep and carrying six turbojets in underwing pods, the main undercarriage being housed in the fuselage. A full-scale mock-up was completed in April 1946, and a month later the USAF ordered the construction of two prototypes under the designation XB-47. The first of these, now named the Stratojet, flew on 17 December 1947, powered by six Allison J35 turbojets.

The Stratojet, which was to become the mainstay of Strategic Air Command's nuclear strike force in the early

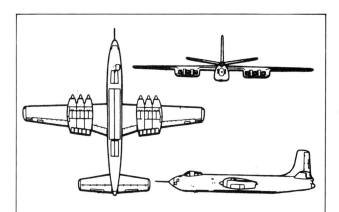

Designation: Martin XB-48.

Role: Prototype Medium Jet Bomber.

Engines: Six 4,600 lb.s.t. General Electric J35-A-5 turbojets.

Span: 108 ft. 4 in.

Length: 85 ft. 9 in.

Weight: Empty 58,500. - Loaded 102,200 lb.

Crew: 3.

Service ceiling: 43,000 ft.

Range: 2,500 miles with 8,000 lb. payload.

Max Speed: 495 mph at 15,000 ft.

Weapons: (Defensive) One radar controlled 20-mm cannon in tail barbette: (Offensive) 8,000 lb. normal bomb load, 20,000 lb maximum.

1950s, was a triumph of engineering skill, and its bold conception a tribute to the confidence of Boeing's designers. As it was one of aviation's biggest successes, it does not come within the scope of this book; but some projects that were evolved from it deserve mention. The first of these, conceived in 1948, involved a proposal for a derivative of the basic B-47 design, with greater wing span and length and a higher all-up weight. Originally known as the Model 474, and later as the XB-55, the aircraft was to have been powered by four Allison T40-A-2 turboprops driving contra-rotating propellers. The XB-55, however, never left the drawing board, and neither did a parallel project, the YB-56, which was also known as the YB-47C. This envisaged a much uprated version of the basic B-47 powered by four 9,700 lb.s.t. Allison J35-A-23 turbojets which would have given the aircraft an estimated maximum speed of 633 mph at sea level and a range of 4,800 miles.

A turboprop-powered B-47 did actually fly, although it was purely an engine development aircraft and not a military prototype. In 1955, two B-47B Stratojets (51-2046 and -2103) were adapted as flying test-beds for the Wright YT49-W-1 turboprop; 51-2103 began flight trials on 26 August 1955 with one of these powerplants replacing each paired inboard turbojet nacelle and driving a four-bladed Curtiss turbo-electric propeller. The outboard turbojets were retained. Both aircraft, designated XB-47D, were extensively tested at the Moses Lake Flight Center, Larson Air Force Base, and reached a maximum speed in level flight of 597 mph.

The design submitted by Convair in a bid to meet the USAF medium bomber requirement was the XB-46, which followed a conventional formula but which was aerodynamically one of the cleanest aircraft ever to take to the air. Powered by four 4,000 lb.s.t. Allison-built General Electric J35-C-3 turbojets mounted in pairs in large underwing nacelles, the prototype, 45-59582, flew for the first time on 2 April 1947, and after initial flight trials went to Wright Field for service evaluation early in 1948. During the course of these trials, the XB-46 reached a maximum speed of 491 mph at sea level and 545 mph at 15,000 feet, and showed its ability to reach a cruising altitude of 35,000 feet in nineteen minutes. The bomber carried a crew of three, the pilot and co-pilot being seated in tandem and the navigator/bombardier in the extreme nose. The XB-46's flight trials revealed excellent handling characteristics, but the type's performance was considerably outclassed by that of its rival, the B-47, and it was not ordered into production.

The Glenn Martin Company's submission, the Model 223, also fell short of performance requirements. Bearing the USAF designation XB-48 and powered by six Allison-built General Electric J35-A-5 turbojets mounted in clutches of three under the wings, the prototype, 45-59585, flew for the first time on 22 June 1947. The XB-48 was of conventional design and carried a three-man crew; like the XB-46, it was designed to carry an 8,000-pound bomb load, although its range of 2,500 miles was less than that of the Convair type. On shorter-range missions, the bomb load could be increased to

DOUGLAS XB-42. Of unusual configuration, the Douglas XB-42 Mixmaster attack bomber had two 1,800 hp Allison V-1710-125 engines in the rear fuselage, driving contra-rotating 'pusher' propellers mounted aft of the cruciform tail unit.

DOUGLAS XB-42A. *XB-42A was a variant of the XB-42, having auxiliary turbojets mounted under the wings.*

20,000 lb. Service evaluation of the two XB-48 prototypes soon revealed the type's performance shortcomings in comparison with the B-47, and no production order was placed.

North American Aviation's design, the XB-45, was regarded as an interim aircraft from the beginning. Its configuration was deliberately kept conventional to avoid any pitfalls that might emerge in advanced aerodynamic design, and the idea was that it would yield valuable information that would permit the designers to develop more advanced construction methods and operational techniques. Similar thinking prevailed in the design of Britain's Vickers Valiant, the first of the V-Bombers to enter production for the RAF; yet in service, both types enjoyed a success that was quite unforeseen. The North American B-45 Tornado went into production for the USAF and entered service in 1948, thereafter carrying out a lengthy tour of duty with USAFE — but in the tactical bombing and reconnaissance role, rather than as a strategic bomber.

The USAF's requirement for a post-war successor to Tactical Air Command's A-26 Invader in the high-speed

DOUGLAS XB-42A.

DOUGLAS XB-43. *The XB-43 was a jet-powered variant of the XB-42 with two GE J53-GE-3 engines, the first of two prototypes flying on 17 May 1946.*

attack role produced two interesting designs, the first of which was the Douglas XB-43. This machine, in fact, was developed from the XB-42 Mixmaster, an unorthodox wartime design that employed two 1,800 hp. Allison V-1710-125 engines installed in tandem in the fuselage and driving contra-rotating propellers mounted behind a cruciform tail unit. Two prototypes were built, and the second aircraft, the XB-42A, had auxiliary turbojets mounted under the wing. The XB-43, unofficially named 'Versatile', was a straightforward turbojet-powered conversion and was fitted with two General Electric J35-GE-3 engines buried in the fuselage and fed via lateral air intakes positioned in the fuselage sides just aft of the cockpit. The XB-43, which made its first flight on 17 May 1946, had a conventional fin and tailplane but was unusual in having two cockpit canopies, situated side by side, under which the pilot and co-pilot sat. The third crew member was housed in the glazed nose. The aircraft could carry a maximum bomb load of 8,000 lb, but no defensive armament was incorporated.

The first XB-43 (44-61508) was followed by a second prototype, 44-61509, which had a 'solid' nose. Both machines were evaluated at the USAF Flight Test Center during 1947, where they showed performance figures that included a maximum speed of 503 mph at sea level and a service ceiling of 38,200 feet. The aircraft, which had a span of 71 ft. 2 in. and a length of 51 ft. 5 in, had a maximum range of 1,400 miles and 1,100 miles with an 8,000-lb bomb load. Flight testing, however, also revealed some undesirable qualities, including instability at certain points of the flight envelope, and the XB-43 was not ordered into production. The second prototype, however, went on to play an important part as an engine test-bed from 1948, assisting in the development of the J47 turbojet.

The design submitted by Glenn Martin, the Model 234 XB-51, was far more radical. Originally designated XA-45, it had a thin, variable-incidence wing swept at an angle of 35 degrees and was powered by three General Electric J47-GE-13 turbojets, two mounted in pods under the forward fuselage and the third in the tail. The tail surfaces were swept, the tailplane being mounted on top of the fin, and the aircraft had a tandem-wheel undercarriage. Two prototypes of the XB-51, 46-685 and

DOUGLAS XB-43.

MARTIN XB-51. Originally designated XA-45, the Martin XB-51 was designed to replace the B-26 Invader in the high-speed tactical bombing role. Two prototypes were built, powered by three GE J47-GE-13 turbojets, two mounted in pods under the fuselage and a third in the tail.

46-686, were ordered in June 1946; the first flew on 28th October 1949 and the second on 17 April 1950. The XB-51 was fast — its top speed was 645 mph at sea level — and its maximum range was 1,613 miles. The operational version would have been very heavily armed, with a battery of eight 20-mm cannon in the nose and up to 10,400 lb of bombs (over 1,000 miles range). The crew consisted of pilot and navigator. The handling characteristics of the XB-51, however, left a lot to be desired, and further development of the type was eventually abandoned when the Martin B-57 — the licence-built version of the English Electric Canberra — was found admirably suited to Tactical Air Command's requirements.

3. Fighter Development, 1945-55: Towards Mach Two

Towards the end of the Second World War, the USAAF, drawing on its combat experience, began to draw up specifications around four quite different fighter requirements. The first involved a medium-range day fighter that could also serve in the bomber escort and ground-attack roles; the second, a medium-range high-altitude interceptor capable of destroying any bomber a potential enemy could conceivably deploy over the next fifteen years or so; the third, a long-range 'penetration' fighter to fulfil the dual role of bomber escort and interdiction; and the fourth, a night and all-weather fighter.

The medium-range day fighter requirement was issued in 1944 and was met by North American Aviation, who at that time were working on the design of the XFJ-1 Fury naval fighter, a turbojet-powered machine of conventional design. North American's initial reaction was to offer a land-based version of the XFJ-1, minus its naval equipment but similar in most other respects; a contract for the building of three prototypes was received in May 1945 and a mock-up of the aircraft, designated XP-86, was approved in June.

During the months that followed, the basic design underwent radical changes as advanced German aerodynamic research material became available. This, together with independent research carried out into high-speed aerofoils undertaken by the National Advisory Committee for Aeronautics, persuaded North American's design team to give their fighter a wing swept at an angle of 35 degrees and also swept tail surfaces. The finalized design that eventually emerged, and resulted in a production contract from the USAF, was the F-86 Sabre, one of the most celebrated fighter aircraft of all time.

The Sabre more than adequately covered the first of the USAF's requirements and also — thanks to the seriously outdated nature of Russia's strategic bomber forces in the immediate post-war years — was sufficient to meet the second, giving the USAF time to reshape its medium-range interceptor requirement and call for an aircraft that would be missile-armed and incorporate an advanced fire-control system.

In the bid to meet this requirement, Convair was first off the mark with the design of a supersonic mixed-power interceptor. Drawing heavily on the results of wartime German research, the Convair design team decided to employ a delta wing, a concept in which they received invaluable help from Dr. Alexander Lippisch, designer of the revolutionary Messerschmitt Me 163 Komet rocket fighter. The Lippisch factory at Wiener Wald had been overrun by US forces in 1945 and its contents, together with Lippisch himself, taken to the United States; one of his designs, the DM-1 delta-wing research glider, was subjected to extensive wind-tunnel testing by the NACA and the information made available to Convair. As a result, Convair, in consultation with Lippisch, decided to build a flying delta-wing model of the proposed interceptor.

The latter, known to Convair as the Model 7, had been allocated the USAF designation XF-92. The flying scale model, designated Model 7-002, used the component parts of five other aircraft in an effort to save time and money. Powered by an Allison J33-A-23 turbojet, it made its first flight on 18 September 1948. The aircraft had a 60-degree delta wing with a thickness/chord ratio of 6.5 per cent, with elevons extending along the whole of the straight trailing edge to provide lateral and longitudinal control and a large vertical fin to provide stability.

While testing of the Model 7-002 got under way, work proceeded with the development of the XF-92, which was to be powered by a 1,600 lb.s.t. Westinghouse 130 turbojet for cruising flight and landing, additional power for take-off and combat being supplied by a 6,000 lb thrust four-chamber Reaction Motors LR-11 bi-fuel

rocket engine. On 3 June 1949, however, further development was cancelled and the Model 7-002 was turned over to high-speed research work, being allocated the designation XF-92A. In 1951, the aircraft's original J33-A-23 turbojet was replaced by a J33-A-29 with reheat; this raised the XF-92A's loaded weight to 15,000 lb, but it reached speeds of up to Mach 0.95 at altitudes of over 45,000 feet.

In 1950, meanwhile, the USAF had held a design contest for an integrated interceptor fire-control system that included air-to-air missiles. The contest was won by Hughes Aircraft, and in 1951 the USAF invited proposals for a fighter design that would accommodate the new equipment and weapons. Convair, whose XF-92A had by that time been extensively tested throughout the flight envelope and produced some excellent results, naturally used it as the basis for the design of a new fighter aircraft, which was known as the Model 8. The new interceptor was in fact a scaled-up XF-92A, and its airframe was designed around the powerful twin-spool Pratt &

CONVAIR XF-92A. The first of jet-powered aircraft of delta-wing configuration to fly, the Convair XF-92A owed much to the wartime work of Dr. Alexander Lippisch and was the forerunner of the F-102 Delta Dart. Powered by an Allison J33-A-23 turbojet of 4,600 lb thrust.

CONVAIR XF-92A.

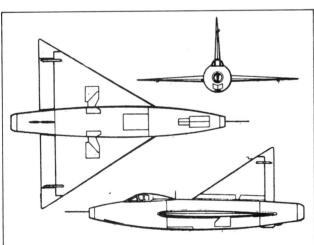

Designation: Convair XF-92A.

Role: High-Speed interceptor R & D aircraft.

Engine: One 6,800 lb.s.t. Westinghouse J33-A-29 turbojet.

Span: 31 ft. 3 in.

Length: 42 ft. 5 in.

Weight: Empty 10,500 lb. - Loaded 15,000 lb.

Crew: 1.

Service ceiling: 50,000 ft.

Range: 500 miles approx.

Max Speed: 630 mph at 45,000 ft.

Weapons: None.

Whitney J57 turbojet, which was then in an advanced stage of development. The USAF adopted the Model 8, which, after various refinements that included the installation of a still more powerful engine that enabled the machine to fly supersonically in level flight, eventually entered service as the F-102 Delta Dagger.

The other competitor in the design contest for a high-altitude, missile-armed interceptor was the Republic Company, who in 1949 were heavily engaged in the production of the F-84 Thunderjet and the development of a swept-wing successor, the F-84F Thunderstreak. Designated XF-91, Republic's interceptor design, unofficially dubbed 'Thundercepter', was unusual in that it had a variable-incidence swept wing with inverse taper and thickness — in other words, the chord and thickness were greater at the wingtip than at the root. This arrangement, coupled with leading edge slots, produced more lift at the outboard wing sections and consequently reduced the danger of low-speed wingtip stall, while the variable-incidence wing allowed a higher angle of attack for take-off and landing. Because of the unusual wing design, the XF-91's main undercarriage, positioned at mid-point, retracted outwards into wells situated at the wingtips.

The XF-91 (46-680) flew for the first time on 9 May 1949, powered by a General Electric J47-GE-3 turbojet. Like Convair's original XF-92 fighter design, the XF-91 was of mixed-power concept, additional power for take-off and combat being obtained from a Reaction Motors

REPUBLIC XF-91. The Republic XF-91 was designed as a high-altitude interceptor. The aircraft was powered by a 5,200 lb thrust General Electric J47-GE-3 turbojet, augmented by a Reaction Motors XLR-11-RM-9 rocket in the rear fuselage.

LOCKHEED XF-90. Developed to meet a USAF requirement for a long-range 'penetration' fighter, the Lockheed Model 153 XF-90 flew for the first time on 4 June 1949, powered by two Westinghouse J34-WE-11 turbojets.

XLR-11-RM-9 rocket engine fitted in the rear fuselage; the rocket motor had four tubes, two above and two below the tailpipe. In December 1952, using both jet and rocket power, the XF-91 exceeded Mach 1.0 in level flight. Later, the aircraft's swept tail surfaces were replaced by a 'butterfly' tail unit, the central fin being deleted. No production order for the XF-91 was placed, and the sole prototype was used for some time on research and development work, mainly at Edwards AFB. It is now in the Air Force Museum at Wright-Patterson Air Force Base, near Dayton.

During its wartime operations over Germany, the

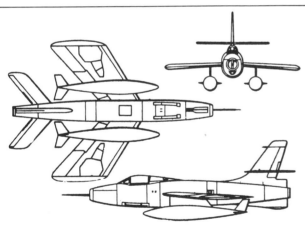

Designation: Republic XF-91.

Role: Prototype High-Altitude Interceptor.

Engines: One 5,200 lb.s.t. General Electric J47-GE-3 turbojet and one Reaction Motors XLR-11-RM-9 rocket engine of 6,000 lb. thrust.

Span: 31 ft. 3 in.

Length: 46 ft. 8 in.

Weight: Empty 19,000 lb. - Loaded 30,000.

Crew: 1.

Service ceiling: 55,000 ft.

Range: 800 miles approx.

Max Speed: 730 mph at 35,000 ft.

Weapons: AAMs.

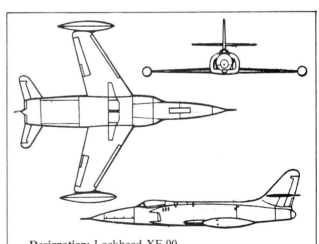

Designation: Lockheed XF-90.

Role: Prototype Penetration Fighter.

Engines: Two Westinghouse J34-WE-11 turbojets developing 3,600 lb.s.t. and 4,200 lb.s.t. with reheat.

Span: 40 ft.

Length: 56 ft. 2in.

Weight: Empty 26,000 lb. - Loaded 33,000 lb.

Crew: 1.

Service ceiling: 45,000 ft.

Range: 2,300 miles maximum.

Max Speed: 685 mph at sea level.

Weapons: (Proposed): Four 20-mm cannon and six .5-in MGs.

USAAF had learned, the hard way, the bitter lesson that bombers could not hope to penetrate deeply into enemy territory in daylight without suffering appalling losses. Consequently, in 1946 Strategic Air Command originated a requirement for a so-called 'penetration fighter', primarily to act as an escort for the mighty B-36 bomber. The idea was that such an aircraft should be capable of sweeping ahead of the bombers and blasting a path for them through the enemy fighter defences.

The Lockheed Aircraft Corporation, whose F-80 Shooting Star — America's first operational jet fighter — was then in full production, immediately initiated a design to meet the requirement. Known as the Model 153, and bearing the USAF designation XF-90, it was a graceful, aesthetically pleasing aircraft with a wing swept at 35 degrees and was powered by two Westinghouse J34-WE-11 turbojets with short afterburners. To conform with its role, the XF-90 carried a substantial fuel load in internal and wingtip tanks, the latter being jettisonable, and this gave the fighter a combat radius of about 1,100 miles — sufficient to penetrate as far as Kiev from bases in Western Germany. The XF-90's planned armament was formidable, comprising four 20-mm cannon and six .5-inch machine-guns.

Two prototypes of the XF-90 (46-687 and -688) were built, and the first of these flew on 4 June 1949. Trials, however, showed the aircraft to be seriously underpowered, with a maximum speed of only Mach 0.9 at sea level and Mach 0.95 at 40,000 feet, and this fact — together with a shift in the USAF's requirement — led to the type being abandoned in 1950.

North American, whose F-86A Sabre had begun to roll off the production line in 1948, proposed a variant to meet the penetration fighter requirement. Designated F-86C, it had an increased wingspan and a larger fuselage cross-section to accommodate a 6,250 lb.s.t. centrifugal-type Pratt & Whitney XJ48-P-1 turbojet with reheat, this being fed via NACA-developed flush air intakes fitted into the fuselage sides beneath the cockpit. The nose section was completely redesigned and equipped with all-weather radar. The undercarriage was also redesigned and twin-wheel main units were installed to support the fighter's 25,000-pound loaded weight. The F-86C bore little resemblance to its stablemates, and was allocated the new designation of YF-93A, the prototype flying on 25 January, 1950. A second prototype was also built and flown, and the USAF placed an order for 118 production F-93As. This, however, was cancelled following the change in requirement and the penetration fighter idea was shelved.

The demise of the penetration fighter requirement also killed another project, originated by McDonnell, although this time there was to be a more fortunate outcome. On 20 June, 1946, McDonnell began detailed design work on a heavy, long-range jet fighter designated XF-88, and the construction of two prototypes (46-525 and -526) was begun in 1947 under a USAF contract. The first prototype XF-88 was powered by two 3,000 lb.s.t. Westinghouse XJ34-WE-13 turbojets, mounted side-by-side and exhausting just aft of the wing trailing edge under a stepped up rear fuselage. This aircraft made its first flight on 20 October 1948, and in 1950 it was followed by the second prototype, which was equipped with 3,600-lb.s.t. XJ34-WE-22 engines with short afterburners, boosting the thrust to 4,000 pounds for combat manoeuvres. The XF-88 had a very thin wing swept at 35 degrees and spanning 39 feet 8 inches; the length was 54 feet 1½ inches.

The first prototype XF-88 reached a maximum speed of 641 mph at sea level and could reach an altitude of 35,000 feet in fourteen and a half minutes. Range, however, was 1,737 miles, a good deal less than that of the

McDONNELL XF-88. Designed as a long-range penetration fighter, the SF-88 was the forerunner of the F-101 Voodoo.

McDONNELL XF-85 GOBLIN. Designed as a 'parasite' fighter to be carried on a trapeze in the forward bomb-bay of the Convair B-36, the diminutive, egg-shaped XF-85 was one of the most unconventional aircraft ever built. Powered by a 3,000 lb thrust Westinghouse J34-WE-7 turbojet, the prototype was launched from an EB-29B on 23 August 1948.

Lockheed XF-90, and operational ceiling was only 36,000 feet. The XF-88 development programme was cancelled in August 1950, when the USAF shelved its long-range heavy fighter plans, but the first prototype was used as a test-bed for supersonic propellers. Redesignated XF-88B, it flew in its modified configuration on 14 April 1953 with an Allison XT38 turboprop mounted in the nose. During subsequent testing, the XF-88B flew with no fewer than twenty-seven different configurations of propeller, ranging from four to ten feet in diameter and with varying numbers of blades.

Meanwhile, in 1951, the USAF had resurrected its long-range fighter escort requirement as a result of the lessons that were being learned in Korea, where B-29 bombers were suffering heavily at the hands of MiG-15 jet fighters; it was obvious that the Russians now had interceptors that were capable of posing a serious threat to Strategic Air Command's B-36 fleet, and even to the radical Boeing B-47 Stratojet, which was then just beginning to enter SAC service. McDonnell therefore adopted the basic XF-88 design as the basis for a completely new aircraft, lengthening the fuselage to accommodate two powerful Pratt & Whitney J57-P-13 turbojets — engines that gave the new fighter a top speed of over 1,000 mph and a ceiling of 52,000 feet — and increased internal fuel tankage. In its new guise, it became the F-101A Voodoo — an aircraft that served the USAF well for many years in the tactical support and reconnaissance roles, even when the penetration fighter requirement was cancelled yet again.

It was McDonnell, too, who initiated the most unorthodox of all escort fighter designs, the XF-85 Goblin. The project was actually originated in 1942 as MX-472, and revolved around the notion of a 'parasite' fighter that could be launched and retrieved by the bomber itself. By 1944, the USAF requirement was more specific in that it called for a parasite fighter that could be carried by the existing B-29 and the proposed B-35 and B-36, and McDonnell Aircraft submitted four separate proposals under the Company designation of Model 27 in the autumn of that year.

The problems involved in successfully launching and recovering an escort fighter were severe enough — the Russians had made a lot of experiments in the field in the 1930s, and had failed to come up with a workable combination, or at least one that could be translated into operational use — but in January 1945 they were compounded even further by a revised USAF specification that required the parasite fighter to be completely housed inside the parent bomber. No designer in the world could have produced a fighter small enough to be buried inside a B-29, but the mighty B-36 was quite a different matter, and the McDonnell design team, led by project engineer Herman D. Barkey, set about revising the Model 27 to meet the new demand.

The extraordinary aircraft that gradually evolved resembled nothing so much as a large egg fitted with flying surfaces. A Westinghouse J34-WE-7 turbojet occupied almost the whole of the egg; the pilot sat astride the engine and was virtually surrounded by tanks containing 112 gallons of fuel, enough for about half an

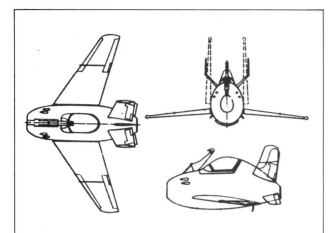

Designation: McDonnell XF-85 Goblin.

Role: Prototype internally-stowed escort fighter.

Engine: One 3,000 lb.s.t. Westinghouse J34-WE-7 turbojet.

Span: 21 ft. 1½ in. (5 ft. 4¾ in, wings folded).

Length: 14 ft. 10½ in.

Weight: Empty 3,740 lb. - Loaded 4,550 lb.

Crew: 1.

Service ceiling: 50,000 ft. (est.).

Range: Limited to 30 minutes' endurance in free flight.

Max Speed: 664 mph at sea level (est.).

Weapons: Four .5-in MGs.

hour's flying. Also packed into the nose of the egg were four .5-inch machine-guns. The XF-85's wings were swept 37 degrees at the leading edge, had an anhedral of four degrees and folded vertically upwards for stowage inside the parent aircraft. The tail assembly was complex, with no fewer than six surfaces. The pilot was equipped with a small ejection seat that was operated by a charge of cordite, an oxygen bottle and a ribbon-type parachute, designed to withstand heavy shock loadings at high speeds.

The XF-85 mock-up was approved in June 1946, and in March the following year McDonnell received a contract for the construction of two prototypes. At the same time, the USAF instructed Convair to modify all B-36s from the twenty-third production aircraft to mount a trapeze for the parasite fighter in the forward bomb-bay, the requirement now being for thirty operational F-85's to be purchased during 1949. Two schemes were mooted for the operational use of the F-85; one involved a single fighter to be carried by each B-36 and another suggested that an attacking force of B-36s, should be accompanied by a small number of specially-modified B-36s, each capable of carrying three F-85s.

In August 1947, following a change in strategic requirements, the USAF cancelled the order for thirty production F-85s. Work on the two XF-85 prototypes continued, however, and a bomber — the EB-29B 'Monstro' (44-8411) — was fitted with a trapeze to engage the little fighter's retractable hook. The first XF-85, 46-523, was flown in a C-97 transport to the Ames Laboratory at Moffatt Field for wind tunnel tests and suffered an immediate mishap when it was dropped from a crane, but by June 1948 it had been repaired and taken to Muroc for flight testing together with the second XF-85, 46-524.

On 23 August 1948, after making five captive flights, the second XF-85 was taken aloft by the EB-29B for its first free flight, with test pilot Edwin Schoch at the controls. At 20,000 feet, with the trapeze fully lowered, Schoch started the XF-85's engine and successfully unhooked himself from the parent aircraft, diving away to carry out a series of manoeuvres at speeds of between 180 and 250 mph. Attempts at hooking-up, however, presented severe problems because of turbulence, and on the fourth attempt Schoch overshot, striking the trapeze and shattering his canopy. With his helmet and oxygen mask ripped away by the airflow, he had no alternative but to dive sharply away and head for Muroc, where he touched down successfully at 160 mph on the steel skid fitted beneath the XF-85's fuselage.

Schoch spent the best part of the next two months practising approaches to the EB-29B in an F-80 Shooting Star before taking the XF-85 into the air again on 14 October 1948. On this occasion he successfully engaged the trapeze on his second attempt and was hoisted aboard the parent aircraft. Two more flights, made on the following day, were also successful, but then a new problem arose. Until now, the XF-85 had flown with its hook extended all the time, the well into which it was recessed on retraction being faired over. With the fairing removed, the aircraft proved to be so unstable due to turbulence around the well that a hook-up was impossible.

Flight testing was temporarily suspended while modifications were carried out; these included the fitting of vertical surfaces at the wingtips to improve stability, and a metal fairing along the sides of the hook well to smooth the airflow. On 18 March 1949, after two captive flights, Schoch and the second XF-85 were launched in free flight again, but trouble struck immediately when part of the trapeze fouled the XF-85's nose and broke

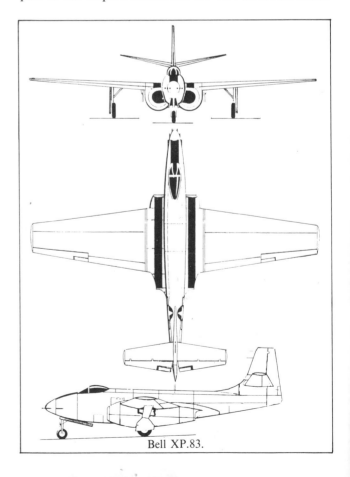

Bell XP.83.

BELL XP-83. An experimental long-range fighter, the single-seat Bell XP-83 flew for the first time on 25 February 1945. The two prototypes built were powered by two 4,000 lb thrust General Electric J33-GE-5 turbojets.

away. Schoch took the XF-85 back to Muroc for yet another hair-raising skid landing on the dry lake bed. It was the last time the second XF-85 ever flew.

The first XF-85, which returned to Muroc in March 1948 after modification, was destined to make only one flight. This took place on 8 April, the aircraft flying back to Muroc after three unsuccessful attempts to hook on. Further testing of the type was suspended, at least until the trapeze had been redesigned, both the USAF and McDonnell quite rightly believing that if a pilot of Schoch's experience was unable to achieve a successful hook-up, the average fighter pilot would stand little chance of doing so. In the event the XF-85 never flew again, although McDonnell proposed a more conventional development capable of a speed of Mach 0.9. The second XF-85 was eventually presented to the Air Force Museum at Wright-Patterson AFB, while the first went to the Air Museum at Orange County Airport, Santa Ana. Between them, the two aircraft had accumulated a total flying time of 2 hours 19 minutes, the highest recorded speed being 362 mph. It would have been interesting to see whether the XF-85 would have been capable of coming anywhere near its rather optimistically estimated maximum speed of 664 mph at sea level.

The USAF requirement for a long-range night and all-weather interceptor originated out of a need to replace the Northrop P-61 Black Widow, which was the USAF's standard specially-developed night-fighter at the end of the Second World War. Among possible candidates for

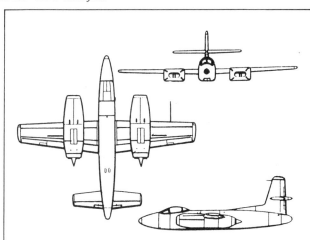

Designation: Curtiss XP-87 Nighthawk.
Role: Prototype Night-Fighter.
Engines: Four 3,000 lb.s.t. Westinghouse XJ34-WE-7 turbojets in paired nacelles.
Span: 60 ft.
Length: 62 ft.
Weight: Empty 25,930 lb. - Loaded 37,350 lb.
Crew: 2.
Service ceiling: 40,000 ft.
Range: 2,000 miles.
Max Speed: 585 mph at 35,000 ft.
Weapons: Four 20-mm cannon.

the role among the early jet-powered designs was the Bell XP-83, which began life as a single-seat, heavy, long-range fighter and flew for the first time on 25 February, 1945, powered by two 4,000 lb.s.t. General Electric J33-GE-5 turbojets. Two prototypes were built and extensively tested, their performance figures including a maximum speed of 567 mph at sea level and 525 mph at 45,000 feet, together with a range of 1,730 miles at 30,000 feet. The proposed armament for the XP-83 was six .5-inch machine-guns, with either four 20-mm or four 37-mm cannon as alternatives. The XP-83's airframe had the potential for conversion to a two-seat configuration and the inclusion of AI radar, but there would have been a substantial weight penalty and the existing engines were not powerful enough. This, together with the fact that XP-83 was outclassed by later designs, led to development being abandoned.

As an interim measure, pending the development of a suitable jet-powered night-fighter, the North American F-82 Twin Mustang replaced the Black Widow in the night-fighter squadrons of Air Defense Command from 1947. Meanwhile, three American aircraft companies,

Curtiss, Northrop and Lockheed, were busy working up designs to meet the USAF requirement, which called for a two-seat radar-equipped aircraft armed with either cannon or machine-guns and possessing a top speed of at least 600 mph and a ceiling of 40,000 feet.

The design submitted by the Airplane Division of the Curtiss-Wright Corporation, the XP-87, was the first multi-seat jet combat aircraft specifically designed for the radar intercept role at night. Developed from an earlier wartime project, the XA-43 attack aircraft, it was powered by four Westinghouse XJ34-WE-7 turbojets, installed in pairs in two nacelles, and was armed with four 20-mm cannon. Provision was also made to install the .5-inch machine-guns in a remotely-controlled dorsal turret, but this was never fitted. The XP-87 prototype, 49-59600, flew for the first time on 5 March 1948, and work began on a second aircraft, the XP-87A (46-522) which was intended to have two General Electric J47-GE-15 engines. The first aircraft was known as the Nighthawk, the second as the Blackhawk. However, the second machine never flew, and an order for eighty-eight J47-powered production aircraft was cancelled to release

CHANCE VOUGHT XF5U-1 – FLYING PANCAKE – An experimental carrier-borne fighter, the XF5U-1 had an unusual circular-planform wing and was developed from the earlier V-173 'Flying Flapjack'. Fitted with two 1,350 hp Pratt & Whitney R-2000 Twin Wasp engines, the XF5U-1 was rolled out in 1946, but was never flown.

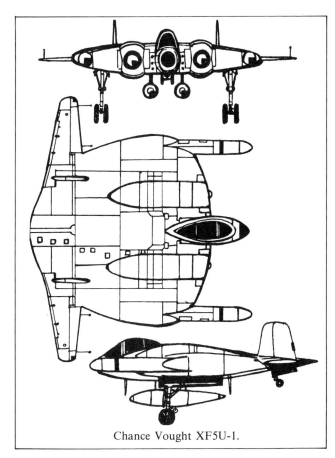

Chance Vought XF5U-1.

4. Aircraft for the Navy: Carrier-Borne Prototypes, 1945-55

Oddly enough, it was a night-fighter project — the Grumman XF9F-1 — that indirectly led to the design of the U.S. Navy's first really viable carrier-borne jet fighter, the F9F Panther. Before that, however, at the end of the Pacific War the Navy was still considering replacing its standard fighter types, the Hellcat and Corsair, with more advanced piston-engined fighters, designed around a specification that was dictated by operational requirements in the Pacific. One such aircraft, for example, designed specifically to undertake long-range operations against Japan, was the Boeing XF8B-1, a multi-purpose machine intended to act as a general-purpose fighter, interceptor, light bomber and torpedo bomber. Designed early in 1945, the prototype XF8B-1 flew in 1946 powered by a 2,500 hp Pratt & Whitney R-4360 radial fitted with contra-rotating propellers. Its maximum speed was 432 mph, service ceiling 37,500 feet and range 3,500 miles. The aircraft, which had a span of 54 feet and a length of 43 feet, could be armed either with six 20-mm cannon or machine-guns and could carry up to 6,400 pounds of offensive stores. A promising aircraft, the XF8B-1 nevertheless appeared too late, and a production order was cancelled.

In 1943, the Ryan Aeronautical Corporation had begun the design of a new naval fighter known as the Model 28. With the Service designation XFR-1, the prototype flew for the first time on 25 June 1944, and first delivery of an operational FR-1 was made to Navy Fighter Squadron VF-66 in March 1945. The FR-1, named Fireball, was the first aircraft to enter service in which a piston engine was combined with a turbojet, the aircraft using both powerplants for take-off, climb and

funds for the development of two more promising designs that were eventually to give the USAF a truly potent night — and all-weather — fighter capability; the Lockheed F-94C Starfire and the Northrop F-89 Scorpion. The XP-87 passed into aviation history as the last combat aircraft produced by Curtiss-Wright.

CHANCE VOUGHT F6U-1 PIRATE. One of America's earliest carrier-borne jet fighters, the Chance Vought F6U-1 Pirate flew for the first time on 2 October 1946, powered by a 3,000 lb thrust Westinghouse J34-WE-22 turbojet.

XFJ-1 FURY. The North American XFJ-1 Fury was designed as a naval fighter. Design work started in 1944.

combat and having the ability to fly and land with either engine shut down. Only sixty-nine Fireballs were built, including four prototypes, and the fighter's operational career was very short, the last examples being retired at the end of June 1947. The XFR-2, XFR-3 and XFR-4 were proposed variants with different engine installations, and a redesigned version, the XF2R-1, flew in November 1946 with a General Electric XT31-GE-2 turboprop in place of the piston engine.

The Ryan XF2R-1 did not enter production. In the early days of the Ryan Corporation's design work on the XFR-1, however, the Bureau of Aeronautics had been sufficiently impressed by the composite-power idea to allocate funds for the development of a larger, more heavily-armed fighter using the same principle. The design contract for the new machine was awarded to the Curtiss-Wright Corporation, and on 7 April 1944 three prototypes were ordered under the designation XF15C-1.

F-86D. By fitting the XFJ-1 Fury with swept flying surfaces, and making use of captured German aerodynamic knowledge, North American evolved the F-86 Sabre – and captured the world lead in fighter development. Shown here is the all-weather F-86D.

DOUGLAS XF5D-1 SKYLANCER. A development of the F4D-1 Skyray, and originally known as the F4D-2N, the XF5D-1 Skylancer had limited all-weather capability and a greater range than its predecessor. The first of four prototypes flew on 21 April 1956 and all four machines were powered by a 10,800 lb thrust Pratt & Whitney J57-P-8 turbojet.

The fighter was powered by a nose-mounted Pratt & Whitney R-2800-34W radial engine rated at 2,100 hp and driving a Hamilton Standard four-bladed propeller, while a 2,700 lb.s.t. de Havilland H-1B turbojet, built under licence by Allis-Chalmers, was installed in the rear fuselage aft of the cockpit. The jet engine exhausted beneath a stepped-up tail unit, the tailplane being mounted on top of the fin.

The XF15C-1 had an interesting performance range. On the power of its piston engine only, the aircraft reached a speed of 322 mph at sea level and 373 mph at 25,000 feet, but with both engines operating these values were increased to 432 and 469 mph. The aircraft, which had a wingspan of 48 feet and a length of 44 feet, had a range of 1,385 miles and an operational ceiling of 41,800 feet. Testing of the three XF15C-1 prototypes, however, revealed a number of aerodynamic problems; the prototypes were handed over to the US Navy for engine trials in November 1946, and further development was abandoned.

By the standards of the day, the mixed-power fighters were fairly unorthodox — but not nearly as unorthodox as a piston-engined naval fighter design, the XF5U-1, revealed by Chance Vought in 1946. Based on the design of a low-powered predecessor, the V-173, the XF5U-1 had a roughly circular wing platform and was powered by

DOUGLAS XF5D-1 SKYLANCER.

McDONNELL FH-1 PHANTOM.

two Pratt & Whitney R-2000 Twin Wasp engines, buried in the wing and driving large four-bladed propellers via extension shafts. The blades were specially articulated, like those of a helicopter, so that at high angles of attack they would move forward at constant pitch and flatten out to enable the machine to hover. The very low aspect ratio wing also housed the fuel tanks and armament, the pilot's cockpit being situated in the extreme nose. It was claimed that the XF5U-1 possessed a speed range of between 40 and 450 mph. The prototype was rolled out in July 1946 amid much publicity, but it never flew and was eventually scrapped. Its predecessor, the V-173 (Bu 02978) is in the Smithsonian Institution's National Air and Space Museum, Washington DC.

Although its operational career was short and it was ordered only in small numbers, North American's FJ-1 Fury nevertheless had the distinction of becoming the US Navy's first operational jet fighter, serving from 1947 to 1949. The XFJ-1 Fury prototype, however, was beaten into the air by another jet design, the Chance Vought XF6U-1 Pirate; the first of three prototypes flew on 2 October 1946, seven weeks before the North American aircraft. The XF6U-1 was powered by a 3,000 lb.s.t. Westinghouse J34-WE-22 turbojet, later replaced by the 4,200 lb.s.t. J34-WE-30A, and carried an armament of four 20-mm cannon. Thirty production F6U-1s were ordered, but the first of these did not fly until July 1949, by which time the FJ-1 Fury had already been in service for eighteen months. The Pirate, which had a wingspan of 32 feet 10 inches and a length of 37 feet 7 inches, could reach a maximum speed of 555 mph and had a range of 1,000 miles with external fuel tanks, but it was clearly inferior to more modern naval jet fighters like the McDonnell F2H Banshee and the Grumman F9F Panther, and no further aircraft were built.

McDonnell, whose name was to become synonymous with naval jet fighter development in rivalry with Grumman, entered the field with the XFD-1, a design

that originated in 1943. The prototype XFD-1, the first American jet aircraft specifically designed to operate from aircraft carriers, flew on 25 January 1945, powered by two Westinghouse J30 turbojets. On 21 July 1946 a pre-series FD-1 carried out the first US jet aircraft carrier trials, and as a result of these a production order for 100 aircraft — later cut to 60 — was placed. On 15 May 1948, Fighter Squadron 17-A, with sixteen FH-1 Phantoms, became the first carrier-qualified jet squadron in the US Navy, operating from the USS *Saipan*. The FH-1 remained in service until July 1950.

When the Korean War broke out in 1950, the McDonnell Banshee and the Grumman Panther formed the backbone of the US Navy's fighter-attack units. Only four years later, however, the Navy was beginning to receive fighters with a truly supersonic capability. The first of them was the radical Chance Vought F7U Cutlass, which in its day was the heaviest single-seat carrier fighter in service with any Navy; it entered service in April 1954, four months after Navy squadrons began to equip with the North American FJ-2 Fury, a subsonic navalized version of the F-86E Sabre. McDonnell's follow-on from the successful F2H Banshee, which had performed sterling work in Korea, was the F3H Demon, which entered service in 1956, while the Douglas Aircraft Company produced the F4D Skyray, a delta-wing design going back to 1948.

The Skyray entered service with the US Navy and Marine Corps in 1956, by which time Douglas were proposing a supersonic successor, the F5D-1 Skylancer. Originally designated F4D-2N, the first of four Skylancers flew on 21 April 1956 and was followed by the second on 30 June. The aircraft was virtually a scaled-up Skyray, but a higher fuselage fineness ratio and a reduced wing thickness-chord ratio produced a greatly improved performance, the F5D-1 reaching a speed of Mach 1.5 at 40,000 feet under the power of a Pratt & Whitney J57-P-8 turbojet. Whereas the Skyray had been a short-range interceptor, the Skylancer was intended to have a limited all-weather capability, and production aircraft were to have been fitted with the latest AI radar, fire control system, four 20-mm cannon and AAMs. The Skylancer, however, never went into production, and the four aircraft that were built were passed to NASA for research purposes.

Meanwhile, Grumman, whose successful F9F Panther had been followed by the F9F-6 Cougar, a development of the F9F-5 with swept flying surfaces, had been experimenting with an advanced variable-geometry naval fighter, the XF10F-1 Jaguar. Conceived in 1948 as a successor to the Panther, the original XF10F-1 design featured a delta wing, but a US Navy requirement for a greater fuel capacity, together with the installation of advanced electronic equipment led to a formidable increase in weight and the Grumman design team eventually opted for a variable-incidence wing that could be swept at angles of up to 40 degrees.

The idea was not new. Much research into the variable-geometry idea had been carried out by the Germans during the war, and shortly afterwards the USAF awarded the Bell Aircraft Company a contract to build a VG research aircraft, the X-5. The design of the Bell X-5 was closely related to that of a German fighter project, the Messerschmitt P.1101, which had been in an advanced stage of construction at the war's end. While the prototype X-5 was being built, the project came under the joint sponsorship of the USAF and NACA, and Bell received a contract to build a second machine. Both

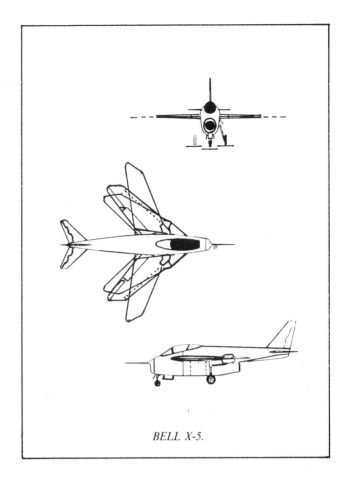

BELL X-5.

BELL X-5. A variable-geometry research aircraft whose design owed much to the wartime Messerschmitt P.1101, the Bell X-5 flew for the first time on 20 June 1951, powered by a 4,900 lb thrust Allison J35-A-17 turbojet.

GRUMMAN XF10F-1 JAGUAR. The Grumman XF10F-1 Jaguar variable-geometry carrier-borne fighter was designed as a successor to the F9F Panther. Powerplant was a 7,200 lb thrust Westinghouse J40-WE-8 turbojet.

aircraft were to have a wing that could be swept at angles of between 20 and 60 degrees, and their design was to conform to full USAF tactical fighter requirements so that they could be used for armament trials at a later date.

The first X-5 flew on 20 June, 1951, powered by a 4,900 lb.s.t. Allison J35-A-17 turbojet, and its wings were swept in the air for the first time during its fifth flight. Changes in sweep were electrically actuated, and to minimise trim change, which would have resulted if the centre of pressure had moved aft with sweep variation, the wing was translated forward in such a way that its centre of pressure retained a near-constant relationship with the aircraft's centre of gravity. To achieve the two basic motions of rotating and translating the wing, the latter was supported on rollers which moved along tracks located on the inboard ends of the wing panels, and sweep from 20 to 60 degrees required only thirty seconds to complete. The principle worked in practice, the X-5 requiring no trim change at 60 degrees sweep. Both X-5s were extensively flight tested by the USAF and NACA, one of them eventually serving as a chase plane until it was retired in October 1955. The prototype X-5 is in the Air Force Museum at Wright-Patterson AFB.

Grumman, benefiting from the experience gained by NACA in testing the X-5, redesigned the wing of their XF10F-1 in 1950, incorporating a two-position configuration with a sweep angle of 13.5° for take-off, cruise and landing and 42.5° for high-speed flight. The change increased the aircraft's weight in landing configuration by 2,200 pounds, but resulted in a dramatic decrease in landing speed from 115 to 95 knots. In addition to the Jaguar's very advanced wing, the aircraft was fitted with a highly evolved power control system in which movement of the control column mechanically operated a small triangular surface which protruded in front of the all-flying tailplane, actuating the latter and giving enhanced longitudinal control at transonic speeds without excessive stick forces. Spoilers were also fitted for lateral control.

Grumman, however, had seriously underestimated the amount of engineering work involved in perfecting the Jaguar's innovations, and when the prototype eventually flew on 19 May 1953 it was three years behind schedule.

The aircraft was tested at Edwards Air Force Base, and problems soon developed with the all-flying delta tail assembly, even though the Jaguar reached a speed of Mach 0.8 with wings fully swept during this phase. It was therefore decided to replace the delta tailplane with a more conventional swept one, and this brought about some improvement in the aircraft's directional stability.

Meanwhile, a second XF10F-1 prototype had been built, although this machine never flew, and the US Navy had awarded Grumman a production contract calling for a total of 112 Jaguars. Grumman themselves, however, realising that the design would need much more

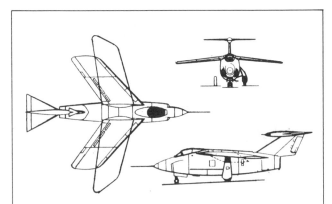

Designation: Grumman XF10F-1 Jaguar.

Role: Prototype Naval Fighter.

Engine: One 7,200 lb.s.t. Westinghouse J40-WE-8 turbojet (11,600 lb. with reheat).

Span: 50 ft. 7 in. (36 ft. 8 in. at maximum sweep).

Length: 55 ft.

Weight: Empty 25,000 lb. - Loaded 33,000 lb.

Crew: 1.

Service ceiling: 45,000 ft.

Range: 700 miles (est).

Max Speed: 722 mph (est).

Weapons: Four 20-mm cannon.

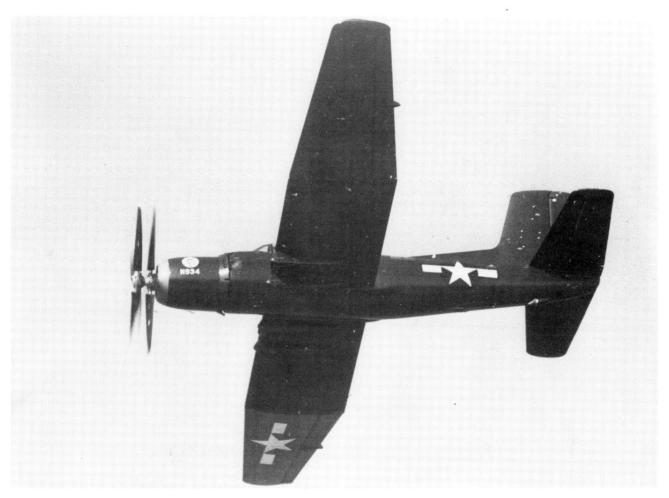

DOUGLAS XTB2D-1. Known as the Devastator II or Skypirate, the XTB2D-1 was a large 3/4 seat carrier-borne torpedo bomber. Two prototypes were built and flown early in 1945, both powered by a Pratt & Whitney XR-4360-8 radial engine developing 3,000 hp.

development — and much more expenditure — before it reached operational status, terminated the contract and the Navy orders were cancelled. The prototype XF10F-1 went to Johnson Naval Air Station, Philadelphia, where it was eventually destroyed in crash barrier tests, and the second aircraft was used as a gunnery target at the Aberdeen Proving Grounds — a sorry end to what was potentially one of the most advanced combat aircraft of its day. Ironically, the one feature of the Jaguar that was truly revolutionary, the VG wing, never gave any trouble.

XTB2D-1.

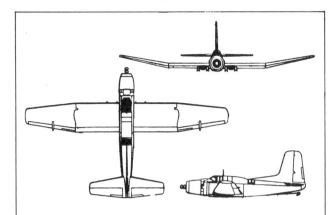

Designation: Douglas XTB2D-1.

Role: Prototype Torpedo-Bomber.

Engine: One Pratt & Whitney XR-4360-8 radial rated at 2,500 hp.

Span: 70 ft.

Length: 46 ft.

Weight: Empty 18,405 lb. - Loaded 34,760 lb (Max).

Crew: 3/4.

Service ceiling: 19,000 ft.

Range: 1,450 miles.

Max Speed: 247 mph. at sea level.

Weapons: Four fixed .5-in MGs plus 2.5-in MGs in dorsal and one in ventral positions (in production version); up to 8,000 lb. of offensive stores.

In the words of the Jaguar's test pilot, Corwin H. Meyer:

"With regard to the variable-sweep wing, I never hesitated to use it under any condition, and it was reputed to be able to unsweep itself if the hydraulic power failed. Fortunately, we never had this problem. There was no question that when the wing was swept and unswept, it had the theoretical effect."

So, with the demise of the Jaguar, the US Navy lost the chance to be the first Service in the world to operate a variable-geometry aircraft. It was not until twenty years later that the Navy had its VG fighter, and that was designed by Grumman too: the F-14 Tomcat.

For a decade after the Second World War, the standard US Navy carrier-borne attack aircraft was the Douglas AD Skyraider, originally conceived in 1944 for use in the projected invasion of Japan. It stemmed, however, from a design that bore little resemblance to it: the Douglas XTB2D-1. Designed in July 1944, the XTB2D-1 prototype 36933, flew for the first time on 18 March 1945 and was followed by a second aircraft, 36934. Powered by a 2,500 hp Pratt & Whitney XR-4360-8 radial engine driving contra-rotating propellers, the XTB2D-1, known as the Devastator II and also the Skypirate, was a 3- or 4-seat aircraft armed with four fixed forward-firing .5-inch machine-guns in the wings; production aircraft were also to have had two .5s in a dorsal turret and another in a ventral position. The aircraft, which had a maximum speed of 247 mph at sea level, could carry four torpedoes or four 1,000-pound bombs under the wing roots.

The Douglas design was in direct competition with an aircraft which, curiously enough, bore a greater resemblance to the Skyraider than did the XTB2D-1. This was the Kaiser-Fleetwings XBTK-1, which flew for

the first time in April 1945. It was considerably faster than the XTB2D-1, having a top speed of 342 mph at sea level, but it carried only one torpedo and eight 5-inch rockets as well as a built-in armament of two 20-mm cannon. Two XBTK-1s were built and flown, a third aircraft being used for structural testing, but the end of the Pacific war ruled out any production orders. An order for twenty-three Douglas TB2D-1s was also cancelled, but the first XBT2D-1 served as the prototype of the AD-1 Skyraider, which, is 1946, entered US Navy service in greatly modified form.

Not long after the Skyraider entered service, Douglas embarked upon the design of a turboprop-powered successor, the XA2D-1 Skyshark, which was intended to make use of as many existing Skyraider components as possible. Powered by an Allison XT40-A-2 turboprop, consisting of twin Allison T38 engines mounted side by side and driving co-axial contra-rotating propellers, the prototype Skyshark flew for the first time on 26 May 1950, and during trials reached a speed of 492 mph at 27,000 feet; maximum speed with a 2,000-pound bomb load was 442 mph. Constant troubles were experienced with the Skyshark's contra-prop gearing, and a second prototype was re-engined with an XT40-A-6, but even then the type was plagued by frequent engine failures and a Navy production order was cut back to ten aircraft, these being used for a variety of engine trials. One of these, 125485, is now in the Air Museum at Ontario International Airport.

The troubles with the Skyshark led to the US Navy seeking another airframe in which to house the XT40 twin turboprop, and the Republic Aviation Corporation came up with a possible solution in the form of a turboprop-powered version of its RF-84F Thunderflash. Republic received a contract to convert three aircraft under the designation XF-84H: two of them were to go to

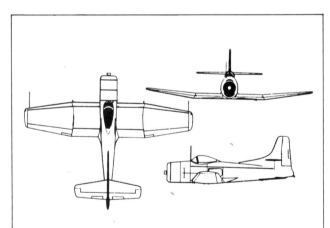

Designation: Kaiser-Fleetwings XBTK-1.

Role: Prototype Naval Torpedo-Bomber.

Engine: One 2,100 hp Pratt & Whitney R-2800-34W radial.

Span: 48 ft. 8 in.

Length: 38 ft. 11 in.

Weight: Empty 9,959 lb. - Loaded 12,728 lb. (normal).

Crew: 1.

Service ceiling: 33,400 ft.

Range: 1,250 miles with torpedo.

Max Speed: 342 mph at sea level.

Weapons: Up to 5,000 lb. of bombs, torpedoes or rockets; two 20-mm cannon.

DOUGLAS XB2D SKYSHARK. Designed as a successor to the AD-1 Skyraider and using many of the earlier type's components, the XA2D-1 Skyshark flew for the first time on 26 May 1950, powered by an Allison XT40-A-2 twin turboprop driving co-axial contra-rotating propellers.

the USAF for tests with various supersonic propellers, and the third was to be allocated to the Navy for trials with the XT40. The first XF-84H, 51-17059, was sent to Edwards AFB for ground tests, and a spate of problems soon developed with the XT40 engine. Apart from that, the supersonic propeller, developed by Aeroproducts, set up severe vibrations and resonance that caused acute nausea in anyone standing nearby.

Despite all this, the XF-84H finally took to the air on 22 July 1955, but engine troubles persisted and the project was dropped by both the Navy and Air Force. A second XF-84H was built, but never flew, and in the end the US Navy's requirement for a Skyraider replacement in the attack role was met by a turbojet-powered aircraft that turned out to be an all-round winner — the Douglas A-4 Skyhawk.

Chapter Two
Great Britain, 1945-55: The Adventurous Years

1. The Forging of a Rapier: Blueprint for the V-Force

In 1939, Great Britain enjoyed a substantial lead in the design and operational use of strategic bomber aircraft. Yet only six years later, when two atomic bombs devastated the Japanese cities of Hiroshima and Nagasaki, that lead had undisputedly passed to the United States.

The reason lay in the different requirements of the RAF and USAAF. Whereas the Americans needed a bomber that could deliver a substantial tonnage of bombs over the long ranges dictated by the geography of the Pacific Theatre of Operations, the RAF required an aircraft that could carry a very heavy bomb load over medium ranges. The only way in which the USAAF could meet its Pacific bomber requirement was to call on the US aircraft industry to design a completely new and ultra-modern machine, and the industry responded magnificently with the Boeing B-29; the RAF's requirement, on the other hand, could be adequately met by developing existing, well-proven designs to lift a greater tonnage of bombs. The result was that in 1945, the latest bomber that was just beginning to enter service with the squadrons of RAF Bomber Command was the piston-engined Avro Lincoln, a straightforward development of the famous Lancaster — and this at a time when the USAF was only three years away from having a four-engined jet bomber, the North American B-45 Tornado. The Lincoln was still Bomber Command's only strategic bomber in 1950, when eighty-seven B-29s were loaned to the RAF to plug the gap — but by this time, the Soviet Union's strategic bombing forces were also equipped with a B-29 derivative, the Tupolev Tu-4, and USAF Strategic Air Command had already taken delivery of its first B-47 Stratojets.

Nevertheless, RAF Bomber Command ended the war with a strategic weapon whose striking power, in conventional terms, was second to none. Its bombing techniques were also highly developed, as were its radar and countermeasures systems. The Air Staff realised that all this experience could well be embodied in a new jet bomber design that would be capable of carrying an atomic bomb, and so in 1946 they conceived a new strategic jet bomber specification, B.35/46, which called for an aircraft capable of carrying a single 10,000-pound store over a still-air range of 3,350 nautical miles at 500 knots, and with a ceiling of 50,000 feet over the target. The new bomber would have a five-man crew housed in a jettisonable pressure cabin, and would be equipped with the latest navigation and bombing system, developed from the wartime H2S radar.

The specification was issued in January 1947, and proposals to meet it were submitted by Armstrong Whitworth, Avro, Bristol, English Electric, Handley Page, Shorts and Vickers. Shortly afterwards, in August 1947, the Air Staff issued a second specification, B.14/46, which called for a more conventional jet bomber to be built as an insurance against the possible failure of the other aircraft. B.14/46 was much less demanding than B.35/46; the bomber was required to have the same range, but its over-the-target ceiling was reduced to 45,000 feet and its maximum speed to 390 knots.

Of the companies that submitted proposals to meet B.35/46, several sought to find an ideal solution in an all-wing design, just as Northrop had done in the United States. In the case of Armstrong Whitworth, the company had already accumulated a good deal of experience in all-wing design, having embarked on a major project to investigate all-wing aerodynamic characteristics in 1943, and in March 1945 had flown a small two-seat research glider, the AW.52G (RG324); this was followed by two jet-powered AW.52 prototypes, which were to serve as aerodynamic test vehicles for a full-scale bomber design. One was powered by Rolls-Royce Nene turbojets and the other by Derwents; the latter aircraft first flew on 13 November 1947 and crashed on 30 May 1949, its test pilot, Jo Lancaster, making the first-ever British emergency ejection as the AW.52 broke up around him during a letdown for a landing at Bitteswell, near Rugby.

The Armstrong Whitworth bomber design was not selected, but the AW.52's flying control system was used in an all-wing bomber design, the Type 698, which was proposed by A. V. Roe and Company. Avro's design, evolved by a team under Roy Chadwick, used a delta wing that was almost a pure triangle; after much redesign, it was to develop into the Avro Vulcan, which would form the mainstay of Britain's nuclear deterrent during the 1960s.

As the Type 698 slowly took shape on the drawing-boards of Avro's project office at Chadderton, Manchester, the Ministry of Supply decided in 1948 to order two one-third scale research aircraft to test the behaviour of the delta-wing configuration at various speeds and altitudes. One of the research aircraft, the Avro Type 707, was to be powered by a single Rolls-Royce Derwent turbojet and was to carry out low-speed handling trials, while the other, the Type 710, was to be fitted with two Rolls-Royce Avons for work at higher speeds and altitudes. In the event, the 710 was abandoned, and the high-speed, high-altitude research programme was undertaken by a modified 707, the 707A.

The first 707, VX784, flew from Boscombe Down on 6 September 1949, with Avro test pilot Flight Lieutenant Eric Esler at the controls. On 30 September, however, for reasons which were never fully established, the 707 crashed near Blackbushe and Esler was killed. Work continued on the second Type 707, VX790, which was fitted with an ejection seat and had modified elevators and air brakes; it was also fitted with the nose section that

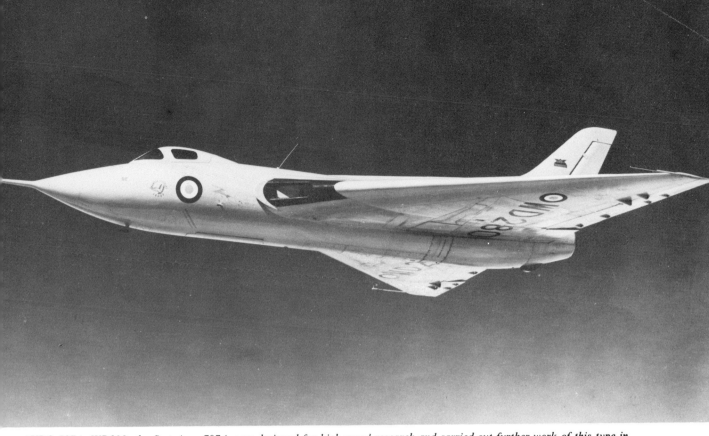

AVRO 707A. WD280, the first Avro 707A, was designed for high-speed research and carried out further work of this type in Australia after 1956. It is now preserved in Melbourne.

had been intended for the Avro 707A high-speed research aircraft, and in this guise it was redesignated Avro 707B. Piloted by Wing Commander R. J. 'Roly' Falk, who was later to test the prototype Vulcan, the 707B made its first flight on 6 September 1950, and after appearing at that year's Farnborough Air Show it began systematic flight trials at speeds of 80 to 350 knots. During the weeks that followed, the little aircraft amassed a good deal of

information that resulted in some structural changes being made to the full-size Avro 698 design, although a lot of time was lost while modifications were made which were of relevance only to the research aircraft's performance.

The high-speed variant, the Avro 707A (WD280), flew from Boscombe Down on 14 July 1951 and was much closer in configuration to the full-scale Type 698 bomber

AVRO 707B. The Avro 707B, VX790. was the second in the series and was designed for low-speed trials.

Avro's little research deltas and their massive stablemates, the two Avro 698 Vulcan prototypes.

having similar ailerons and elevators as well as servo tabs and balances, all of course to scale. It carried out some 92 hours of research work in the United Kingdom before going to Australia for further aerodynamic research in 1956; it was subsequently preserved and put on display in Melbourne. Meanwhile, a second Avro 707A had flown on 20 February 1953; this aircraft, WZ736, was used for automatic throttle development trials by the Royal Aircraft Establishment. It was withdrawn from use in 1967 and went to the aircraft museum at RAF Finningley near Doncaster. The final aircraft in the Avro 707 series was the two-seat 707C, WZ744, which flew on 1 July 1953 and was used by the RAE in the development of power control systems and electronic equipment. It was also withdrawn in 1967, and went to the air museum at RAF Cosford. Neither of these aircraft made any contribution to the development of the Avro 698 Vulcan, the prototype of which had already flown in August 1952, but some of the systems they tested had a direct application to other military programmes.

The Bristol Aircraft Company's proposal to meet the B.35/46 bomber requirements was the Type 172, which featured a wing sharply swept at an angle of 45 degrees; this was ten degrees greater than the optimum angle of 35 degrees, and revealed all too clearly the shortage of advanced German aerodynamic research material that had been made available to British designers for the simple reason that most of it had been siezed by the Americans. Preliminary design work on the Type 172 began in October 1946, and was abandoned two years later.

Handley Page, with a vast amount of heavy bomber design experience behind them, had been interested in the all-wing configuration for a long time, and in 1943 had built and flown an experimental tailless aircraft, the HP.75 Manx. Immediately after the war, Handley Page was fortunate in obtaining a considerable amount of German high-speed research material, most of which came from the Arado Company, and armed with this the firm's design team at Cricklewood set about designing a jet-propelled, tailless bomber with wings swept at 45 degrees and tipped by vertical fins and rudders. This design anticipated B.35/46 by several months, so when the Ministry specification was eventually issued in January 1947 Handley Page used their original studies as the basis of a more refined design that was intended to meet the Air Staff requirement.

Handley Page's solution was to take a delta and a swept wing and combine the two, and the result was a wing with three varying degrees of sweep, curving in a crescent from root to tip. The idea was not new, for Arado had designed just such a wing in 1944. The sharpest sweep was at the inboard section — 53 degrees — and this was reduced to 22 degrees at the tip. By the end of 1947, the Handley Page design to B.35/46 had altered somewhat, the earlier all-wing project being

HANDLEY PAGE HP.75.

modified to include a long fuselage surmounted by a tall, swept fin and rudder topped by a crescent-shaped tailplane. Like the Avro 698, it was to have a crew of five but was to be powered by either Metrovick F9 or Rolls-Royce AJ65 turbojets instead of Bristol BE.10s.

The design was given the type number HP.80, and a prototype ordered by the Ministry of Supply. At the same time, Handley Page sought and obtained the approval of the Ministry of Supply for the building of two scale models — one a radio-controlled pilotless version with a ten-foot wing span, and the other a piloted one-third-scale variant — to test the HP.80's radical crescent wing and T-tail configuration. The radio-controlled model, designated HP.87, crashed on its first flight at Farnborough and was totally destroyed, but work proceeded with the manned aircraft, which bore the designation HP.88. The aircraft, designed to specification E6/48, was actually produced by three different companies, and at one point carried three separate designations. Handley Page, the designer, knew it as the HP.88; Blackburn Aircraft, who built it at their Brough factory, called it the YB.2; while Supermarine, who made available the fuselage of their Type 510 experimental fighter, knew it as the Type 521.

HANDLEY PAGE HP.88.

HANDLEY PAGE HP.88. The Handley Page HP.88 was built to test the crescent wing planform employed in the design of the Victor bomber. The HP.88 research aircraft flew for the first time on 21 June 1951, powered by a Rolls-Royce Nene turbojet.

Powered by a 5,100 lb.s.t. Rolls-Royce Nene 102 turbojet, the HP.88 flew for the first time on 21 June 1951 from Carnaby, near Bridlington, with test pilot G. R. I. Parker at the controls. The aircraft, serialled VX330, went on to make thirty flights from Carnaby, but on 26 August 1951, during a high-speed low-level run along the main runway at Stansted, the machine suffered a failure of its slab-type tailplane's servo-control system, producing severe oscillations that subjected the airframe to intolerable 'g' forces and caused it to break up. The HP.88 crashed and killed its pilot, D. J. P. Broomfield. The tragedy was that the HP.88 had contributed nothing at all to the design of the HP.80, for by the time the research aircraft flew in 1951 the bomber prototype was in an advanced stage of construction. What was doubly tragic was that, in an almost carbon-copy accident on 14 July, 1954, the prototype HP.80 — by then known as the Victor — crashed during a low-level high-speed run at Cranfield with the loss of its crew when the horizontal tail assembly started to flutter and then broke away. Nevertheless, the Victor went on to be a highly successful aircraft in RAF service, and as these words are being written still performs a vital operational task as a flight-refuelling tanker, thirty years later.

The bomber design evolved by Short Brothers was originally intended to meet specification B.35/46, but because of its conventional nature it was quickly realised that it would be more suited to the less demanding specification, B.14/46. The design's wing, which was uniform in taper from root to tip, was mounted in the high shoulder position on a deep fuselage, while the completely conventional tail unit comprised a single fin and rudder and a tailplane with 13 degrees of dihedral. It had originally been intended to fit the aircraft with a jettisonable nose section to form a safety capsule for high-altitude escape, but tests with models revealed that severe tumbling would occur before the supporting parachutes could deploy, so the crew was housed in a normal pressure cabin. In fact, the only unconventional thing about the design, which was named the SA.4 Sperrin, was the arrangement of its four Rolls-Royce Avon turbojets, which were mounted in vertical pairs in nacelles that hugged both upper and lower wing surfaces.

Two Sperrin prototypes, VX158 and VX161, were built using production jigs, and the first aircraft was taken into the air by test pilot Tom Brooke-Smith at Aldergrove, Northern Ireland, on 10 August 1951, and after company trials west to the Royal Aircraft Establishment to carry out operational testing of new high-altitude radar navigation and bombing equipment that would later be incorporated in the RAF's new generation of V-Bombers. The second prototype, VX161, flew on 12 August 1952 and was subsequently employed in aerodynamic weapons testing, dropping concrete 'bomb shapes' mainly in connexion with the development of Britain's first operational atomic bomb, the 10,000 lb. MC.Mk.1 'Blue Danube'. It continued flying until 1956, when one of its undercarriage doors was 'borrowed' to replace one that had broken away from VX158 over the sea. VX161 never flew again, and was scrapped at Sydenham early in 1957.

VX158, meanwhile, after its stint with the RAE, had

SHORT SA.4 SPERRIN. Designed to specification B.14/46, the Short Sperrin was built as an insurance against the failure of the Vickers Valiant. The first prototype flew on 10 August 1951, powered by four 6,500 lb thrust Rolls-Royce Avon RA.3 turbojets.

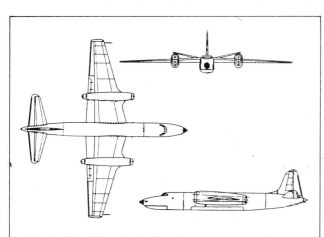

Designation: Short SA.4 Sperrin.

Role: Prototype strategic jet bomber.

Engines: Four 6,500 lb.s.t. Rolls-Royce Avon RA.3 turbojets (second prototype: 7,500 lb.s.t. R-R Avon RA.7s).

Span: 109 ft.

Length: 102 ft. 2½ in.

Weights: Empty 72,000 lb. - Loaded 115,000 lb.

Crew: 5.

Service ceiling: 45,000 ft.

Range: 3,860 miles.

Max Speed: 564 mph.

Weapons: Up to 20,000 lb of free-fall bombs.

returned to Aldergrove in the spring of 1955 to be adapted as a flying test-bed for the 15,000 lb.s.t. de Havilland Gyron turbojet, first flying in this new configuration on 7 July that year. In 1957, however, the Gyron engine project was cancelled, and VX158 was scrapped at Hatfield in 1958.

Had the need arisen, there is no doubt that the Short Sperrin could have been rushed into production very quickly, for very few problems were experienced during its test phase and after, and it would certainly have proved a very viable weapons delivery system, having shown its ability to release payloads of up to 10,000 lb from an altitude of 40,000 feet and a speed of Mach 0.78. The fact that it was not adopted for production was due solely to the higher all-round performance prospects of another conventional design, the Vickers Type 660.

Vickers' last design before the end of the war had been the Windsor, a four-engined heavy bomber; three prototypes had been built and flown, four more were in hand and 300 production aircraft on order. Then had come the war's end, cancellation, and a halt to piston-engined bomber development. Under the direction of their new chief designer, George Edwards, Vickers had evolved a conventionally-configured jet bomber to meet B.35/46, but it had fallen short of the requirement and been rejected in favour of the more futuristic Avro and Handley Page designs. In 1948, however, it was decided to go ahead with the development of the Type 660 as an 'interim' design, and a new specification, B.9/48, was written around it.

The problem with the development of the new V-Bombers, designed to give the RAF a formidable medium-range nuclear strike capability in the 1950s, was that the time-scale was all wrong. After the war, the new Socialist government in Britain had assumed that there would be no major war threat in Europe for at least another decade, and everything, including the British military aircraft development programme was geared to that surmise. But in 1948, with the Russians blockading Berlin, there was a sudden pressing need to bring advanced aircraft into service far more rapidly than had been envisaged, and so the Vickers 660 was selected to fill the bomber gap.

Just how adequately it did so is a matter of aviation history. For several critical years, from 1955 until the service debut of the Vulcan and Victor, it was the Vickers Valiant that formed the mainstay of Britain's nuclear deterrent; it was the only one of the three V-Bombers to drop nuclear test weapons, and — until the Vulcan went to war during the Falklands crisis — the only one to drop bombs in anger. It went on serving until 1964, when the V-Force went low-level to get under the enemy's radar, and fatigue cracks developed in its main spar, causing it to be prematurely retired.

The sad fact was that a derivative of the Valiant might have continued in service for much longer, if the right decisions had been taken. On 4 September, 1953, Vickers flew the prototype Valiant B.2, WJ954, which differed substantially from its predecessors and from production Valiant B.1s. The fuselage forward of the wing was lengthened by four and a half feet, the whole airframe strengthened, the fuel tankage increased and the geometry of the undercarriage radically altered, the main units retracting into pods that protruded from the wing trailing edges. The Valiant B.2 was, in fact, designed for high-speed operation at very low level, and its makers claimed that it would have a maximum speed of 665 mph at sea level, although during trials the aircraft only reached 552 mph. Nevertheless, this was a good 50 mph faster than the B.1, and there is little doubt that the B.2 would have been a formidable addition to Bomber Command's striking power. In the mid-1950s, however, no-one envisaged that the bomber would soon have to penetrate enemy defences 'on the deck' in order to survive, and the promising Valiant B.2 development programme was abandoned.

In 1951, there were strong indications that the Soviet Union was on the point of carrying out some kind of military operations against the West, probably by 1953, and Winston Churchill, head of a new Conservative Government, ordered a complete reappraisal of all Britain's defence capabilities. As far as Bomber Command was concerned, the position was serious; the medium bomber force was still mainly equipped with the obsolescent Avro Lincoln, with a small number of B-29 Washingtons and English Electric Canberras beginning to trickle through to the squadrons, and it would be at least another four years before the first of the V-bombers, the Valiant, could be brought into service.

As a stop-gap measure, two companies, Bristol and Vickers-Armstrongs, were invited to submit proposals for an unmanned flying-bomb design in April 1951. The specification (UB.109T) required a weapon that could be launched from a ramp and carry a 5,000-pound warhead at 450 knots and 45,000 feet over a range of 400 miles, just enough to enable it to hit targets in East Germany from sites in the United Kingdom.

The design submitted by Bristol, the Type 182 Blue Rapier, was built entirely of plastic apart from the steel wing spar, and was intended for cheap mass production.

VICKERS VALIANT B Mk.II.

VICKERS VALIANT B Mk.II.

It had a span of 20 feet 10 inches and a length of 33 feet 10 inches, and all-up weight was 9,500 pounds. It had a swept wing and a small delta tailplane mounted on a stubby fin. Launching was to be achieved by means of a steam catapult, the missile cruising to its target under the power of a turbojet mounted under the fuselage. Estimated maximum speed was 600 mph, and Bristol estimated that each round would cost only £600. Tentative Ministry of Supply plans called for a production run of 20,000 rounds, and the weapon was intended to be barrage-launched. Two prototypes were ordered under the designation Bristol 182R; these were to be made of aluminium, equipped with Armstrong Siddeley Viper turbojets, and also fitted with undercarriages taken from de Havilland Venom fighters.

The Vickers design to UB.109T was known as Red Rapier and was built in light alloy, having three Rolls-Royce Soar expendable turbojets mounted on fuselage outriggers. Like Bristol, Vickers commenced construction of a prototype, but both companies abandoned the project when UB.109T was cancelled in 1953. From now on, the emphasis would be on getting the manned V-bombers into service as quickly as possible, and equipping them with a stand-off missile to enhance their survival chances; this missile would become operational, in due course, as Blue Steel.

In 1954, the Ministry of Supply issued another specification, R.156T, which was drawn up around Operational Requirement 330. This called for a very long range reconnaissance aircraft, with a speed of at least Mach 2.5, an operational ceiling of 60,000 feet and a minimum range of 5,000 nautical miles.

Crammed with the latest electronic surveillance equipment, the resulting aircraft would be capable of operating beyond the performance envelope of the latest Russian fighters or surface-to-air missiles. Its design presented the British aircraft industry with a formidable and unprecedented challenge. (The Americans set about solving the high-level, long-range reconnaissance problem in a different way, and came up with the Lockheed U-2. The first prototype was airborne in August 1955 — at which time the British Ministry of Supply was still studying the first submissions to specification R.156T).

Three manufacturers — Vickers, Handley Page and A. V. Roe — submitted designs. Vickers opted for a single-seat aircraft, a canard delta with four Rolls-Royce RB.121 turbojets under the wing and two more in pods under the forward fuselage, while Handley Page also went for the canard delta configuration in their proposal, the HP.100. The Handley Page aircraft, however, had a crew of three and twelve RB.121 engines, boxed in groups of six under the wing. The HP.100 design was subjected to extensive wind tunnel tests and a full-scale mock-up was built, but it and the Vickers project were both dropped in favour of the Avro submission.

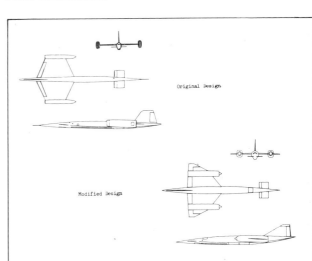

Designation: Avro Type 730.
Role: Prototype Reconnaissance Bomber.
Engines: Eight Armstrong Siddeley P.176 turbojets.
Span: 65 ft. 7 in.
Length: 159 ft.
Weight: 158,000 lb. (Normal Loaded).
Crew: 3.
Service ceiling: 66,000 ft.
Range: 4,740 nautical miles.
Max Speed: Mach 2.7.
Weapons: One megaton-range stand-off bomb.

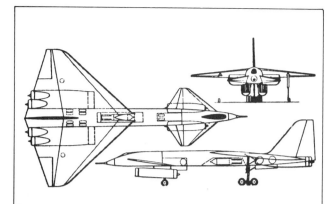

Designation: Vickers 'OR.330'.

Role: Projected Strategic Reconnaissance Bomber.

Engines: Six Rolls-Royce RB.121 turbojets.

Span: 60 ft. $9\frac{1}{2}$ in.

Length: 101 ft. 6 in.

Weight: Empty 78,205 lb. - Loaded 175,000 lb.

Crew: 1.

Service ceiling: 70,000 ft.

Range: 5,010 miles.

Max Speed: 1,650 mph (Mach 2.5) over the target.

Weapons: One 5,000 lb nuclear store.

All performance figures estimated.

This was the Avro 730, detailed drawings of which were submitted to the MoS in May 1955. A prototype contract was awarded a few weeks later.

The Avro 730 was a canard design with unswept flying surfaces, employing stainless steel brazed-honeycomb sandwich construction. It was to be powered by four Armstrong Siddeley P.159 turbojets, mounted in pairs close to each wingtip. The principal reconnaissance system built into the design was a sideways-looking X-Band radar known as Red Drover, with a 52-foot antenna running along the fuselage side.

Longitudinal control was effected by an all-moving canard foreplane with trailing edge elevators, the aircraft having conventional ailerons and rudder. Flying control surfaces were actuated by a quadruple electro-hydraulic power unit designed by Boulton Paul and integrated with an electrical 'fly-by-wire' automatic control system designed by Louis Newmark Ltd. The Dowty Company was responsible for the undercarriage, which consisted of a single centre-fuselage main unit with four wheels, a twin-wheel nose unit and outriggers and the engine nacelles. For very high take-off weights, provision was made for four extra wheels on the main undercarriage axles.

The 730's pressure cabin was situated just aft of the canard foreplane and contained a pilot and two navigators, the latter seated side by side and facing aft. All three crew members had lightweight ejection seats. In the prototype aircraft, the pilot was to have been housed under a cockpit canopy slightly offset to starboard, but in the production version he would have been completely buried in the fuselage, seeing out by means of a retractable periscope. During its flight, the 730 was to have been under the control of fully automated systems, leaving the pilot free to perform certain functions that would normally have been the responsibility of a co-pilot.

Avro received an Instruction to Proceed in September 1955 and planned to fly the first of ten prototypes in 1959, followed by the first production aircraft in 1961. In the meantime, the original design had undergone a number of changes. The Air Staff now saw the Avro 730 as a potential successor to the Vulcan and Victor in the strategic bombing role, and OR.330 was amended to give the aircraft a bombing capability. Under a revised specification, RB.156D, a weapons bay was incorporated and provision made for the 730 to carry a 50-foot stand-off bomb with a thermonuclear warhead. The wing platform was also revised and the original P.159 engines replaced by eight Armstrong Siddeley P.176 engines in rectangular nacelles.

Nothing was left to chance in the Avro 730 development programme. For example, the extreme temperatures that would be encountered by the aircraft in operational use were simulated in a heat-test building that was capable of accommodating a full-size airframe, while a complete fuselage was to be tested to destruction. Two flying scale models were to be built, one going to Armstrong Whitworth for aerodynamic trials and the other to Bristol Siddeley for engine development. The pilot's periscope system was complete and ready to be installed in an Avro Ashton trials aircraft.

Then came 1957, and a notorious White Paper on Defence which, at one stroke, cancelled almost every promising and futuristic British military aircraft project in favour of missiles. The Avro 730 was one of the victims, being cancelled in favour of further development of Blue Streak, Britain's intermediate-range ballistic missile — itself destined to be short-lived in the military role. The prototype Avro 730, which might have become the first operational bomber in the world capable of Mach Two Plus, was broken up and its fuselage cut into huge metal bins for depositing waste in Avro's Chadderton factory.

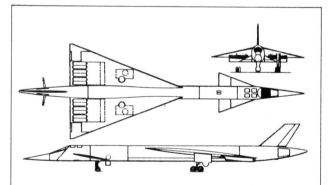

Designation: Handley Page HP.100.

Role: Projected Strategic Reconnaissance Bomber.

Engines: Twelve Rolls-Royce RB.121 turbojets.

Span: 59 ft. 4 in.

Length: 185 ft.

Weight: Not Available.

Crew: 3.

Service ceiling: 70,000 ft.

Range: 6,900 miles.

Max Speed: 1,650 mph (Mach 2.5) over the target.

Weapons: One 5,000 lb. nuclear store or stand-off missile.

All performance figures estimated.

There was, however, a postcript to the sad tale of Britain's supersonic bomber. On 14 April, 1962, a research aircraft called the Bristol 188 took to the air for the first time, powered by two afterburning Gyron Junior turbojets. It had originally been one of the scaled-down Avro 730 research models, differing from the original configuration mainly in having the canard foreplane arrangement replaced by a more conventional 'T' tail. The Bristol 188 was to have been used for high-speed research during prolonged flights at more than Mach 2, but its fuel consumption was extremely high and made sustained hypersonic flight impossible. The research programme was eventually abandoned after the expenditure of some £20 million.

2. Fighter Development, 1945-55: Lost Opportunities

At the end of the Second World War, RAF Fighter Command had one jet fighter, the Gloster Meteor Mk.3, in operational service and another, the twin-boom de Havilland Vampire, scheduled for delivery to some squadrons in 1946. The bulk of the first-line units, however, were still equipped with piston-engined types: the latest marks of the famous Spitfire and the Hawker Tempest, the latter then the fastest and most powerful piston-engined fighter in the world and capable, under some combat conditions, of outflying the early Meteors.

The subsonic Meteor and Vampire would still be Fighter Command's principal equipment in 1950, when American and Soviet fighter squadrons were equipped with the swept-wing, transonic F-86 Sabre and MiG-15. Britain's lead in fighter development, established under conditions of extreme hardship during the war, had been irrevocably lost in less than five years after the last shots were fired. How it came about is still the subject of controversy and, in some areas, of unjust blame.

There had been no lack of forward thinking during the war years. In the autumn of 1943, the Ministry of Aircraft Production had issued Specification E.24/43, astonishing for its day, calling for an aircraft capable of flying at 1,000 mph at 36,000 feet — in other words, a machine advanced enough to make the jump from the subsonic speeds of early jets like the Meteor to a velocity far beyond Mach One, cutting out the transonic phase altogether.

After negotiation with various airframe and engine companies, the Ministry selected Miles Aircraft, which had produced several ingenious experimental prototypes as well as the range of sport and training aircraft for which it had become rightly famous, to work on the design of the supersonic project; the aircraft's gas turbine engine was to be developed by Power Jets Ltd., under the direction of Group Captain (later Air Commodore) Sir Frank Whittle.

Miles received an Instruction to Proceed on 8 October 1943 and started work at the company's Woodley factory under conditions of extreme secrecy; the project had to be as self-sufficient as possible, so Miles set up its own foundry for the production of the necessary metal components and also built a high-speed wind tunnel. To the aircraft itself, the company gave the designation M.52.

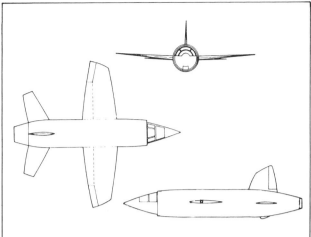

Designation: Miles M.52.
Role: Prototype Supersonic Interceptor.
Engine: One Power Jets W.2/700 + ducted fan.
Span: 26 ft. 10½ in.
Length: 33 ft. 6 in.
Weight: 8,200 lb. (Maximum Loaded).
Crew: 1.
Service ceiling: 50,000 ft. plus.
Range: No data.
Max Speed: 1,000 mph (Mach 1.66) at 38,000 ft.
Weapons (proposed): Two 20-mm cannon.

The design that gradually evolved featured a bullet-like fuselage of circular section, five feet in diameter, constructed of high tensile steel with an alloy covering. The powerplant, a Power Jets W.2/700 of 2,000 lb.s.t., was centrally-mounted and fed by an annular air intake, the cockpit forming a centre cone. The whole cockpit cone, in which the pilot sat semi-reclined, could be detached in an emergency by firing small cordite charges; the pilot would then bale out normally when the capsule reached a lower altitude.

The M.52 was fitted with bi-convex section wings, mounted at mid-point on the fuselage. A full-scale wooden mock-up of this unique high-speed wing design was built and tested on a Miles Falcon light aircraft, L9705, and a model of the tailplane intended for the M.52 was added later on. The Falcon test aircraft flew for the first time on 11 August 1944, and subsequent test flights by Miles test pilot H. V. Kennedy showed that the wing design offered good low speed handling characteristics, which had given some cause for concern, but that landing without flaps on a narrow-track undercarriage — the M.52 had an estimated landing speed of 170 mph — might present difficulties.

As design work went ahead, various refinements were incorporated. It was, for example, decided to modify the W.2/700 engine — which had first been flight tested on the back of a Wellington bomber in 1943 — by fitting an aft fan to increase mass flow, in effect turning the engine into a ducted fan. The addition of rudimentary afterburners in the form of combustion cans situated at the rear of the duct was calculated to produce 1,620 lb of thrust at 36,000 feet and 500 mph, the thrust increasing greatly at supersonic speed. Split flaps were fitted, and an all-moving tailplane. The position of the undercarriage presented some headaches; because of the very thin wing section, the wheels had to be positioned to retract into the fuselage, hence the narrow-track landing problem. An alternative scheme to launch the M.52 from a parent aircraft was proposed, with the flight terminating in a skid landing, but this was dropped.

Detail design work on the M.52 was ninety per cent complete by the beginning of 1946, and the jigs were ready for assembly of the first of three planned prototypes. No snags were envisaged in construction, and it was expected that the first M.52 would fly within six to eight months.

Then, in February 1946, the blow fell. Quite without warning, F. G. Miles received word from the Director General of Scientific Research at the Ministry of Aircraft Production, Sir Ben Lockspeiser, to the effect that all work on the M.52 project was to cease at once. Miles at once went to the Ministry to fight for the project's survival, but to no avail. All Lockspeiser would say was that official policy had changed, there was a need for economy, and — in his personal opinion — aircraft would not fly supersonically for many more years, and perhaps never; an extraordinary statement to make, when one aircraft, the Messerschmitt Me 163 Komet, had already nudged at what was popularly called the Sound Barrier two years earlier.

Secrecy surrounded the cancellation of the M.52, just as it had surrounded its design, and it was not until September 1946 that the British public were made aware that their aircraft industry had been within sight of flying the world's first supersonic aircraft, only to have the chance snatched away. Yet perhaps Sir Ben Lockspeiser had been right in one sense; captured German materials had shown just how little was known about the realms of supersonic flight, and the disasters suffered during the subsequent testing of more conventional transonic aircraft, both in the United Kingdom and elsewhere, seemed to vindicate his opinions at least in part. But he was wrong on one score. Only a year after the M.52's cancellation was made public, Major Charles Yeager, USAF, made history's first supersonic flight in the rocket-powered Bell X-1 research aircraft.

The real reason behind the Ministry decision to cancel the M.52 project, however, was that it had already been decided, early in 1946, to carry out a supersonic research programme with the aid of unmanned models developed by Vickers at Weybridge. The department responsible was headed by Dr. Barnes Wallis, who had achieved reluctant fame through his design of the special mines that destroyed the Mohne and Eder Dams. Between May 1947 and October 1948 eight rocket-powered models were air-launched. Only three were successful, the last achieving a speed of Mach 1.38. In each case of failure (apart from the first attempted launch when the 'parent' Mosquito got out of control in cloud and the model broke away) it was the rocket motor that failed, not the airframe. The irony was that most of the models were based on the design of the M.52; and the double irony was that, in the light of present-day knowledge, the full-scale M.52 would probably have been a success.

Although all the major British aircraft companies had embarked on studies of turbojet-powered aircraft during the war, few reached fruition. The notable exception was the Gloster Meteor, which, although strictly conventional in design, showed a considerable degree of development potential and went on to render invaluable service with many air forces in the day fighter, night fighter and photo-reconnaissance roles.

While they were engaged in development of the Meteor, Glosters also designed and built a small single-jet fighter, the G.42, which became better known by its specification number, E.1/44. Powered by a Rolls-Royce Nene, it had clean lines and featured lateral air intakes, with square-cut wings and a Meteor Mk.4-type three-piece cockpit canopy. The first prototype, SM809, was to have flown in August 1947, but was damaged while in transit by road to Boscombe Down, so the maiden flight was made by the second aircraft, TX145. This was followed by a third prototype, TX148, which had a high-mounted tailplane like that of the Meteor Mk.8. A fourth aircraft, TX150, was allocated for ground testing, and two more fuselages were partially built. The third prototype, TX148, saw lengthy service as a research aircraft at the Royal Aircraft Establishment, Farnborough. A swept-wing version was projected under Specification 23/46, but no work went ahead with this and no production orders were placed.

Meanwhile, in 1946, a Chinese Nationalist Government delegation had arrived in the United Kingdom to investigate the possibility of setting up design and production facilities in this country for the construction of a jet fighter, jet bomber and a turbojet engine. The Chinese team entered into negotiations with Gloster Aircraft, who agreed to assist in the design of the single-seat fighter, and drawing offices were set aside for that purpose at Gloster's Hucclecote factory, on the outskirts of Gloucester. The fighter project was given the designation CXP-1001 and joint work on the design went on for several months, during which time a full-size mock-up and several components were completed. The collapse of the Nationalist regime on mainland China in 1949, however, led to the project being abandoned. In any case, by that time Gloster's main design effort was being channelled towards meeting the requirements of a

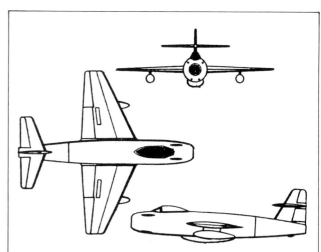

Designation: Gloster CXP-1001.
Role: Prototype Single-seat Fighter.
Engine: One Rolls-Royce Nene turbojet.
Span: 38 ft.
Length: 41 ft. 10 in.
Weight: 13,900 lb. (Normal Loaded).
Crew: 1.
Service ceiling: 40,000 ft.
Range: 1,000 miles with external fuel.
Max Speed: 600 mph.
Weapons: Four 20-mm or two 30-mm cannon.

new all-weather fighter specification, F.4/48; this was to result in the world's first twin-jet delta, the Gloster GA.5, which would ultimately enter RAF service as the Javelin.

Hawker Aircraft, who had taken piston-engined fighter development to the ultimate with their potent Tempest, had investigated several jet-powered projects during the war. In 1940, the company had carried out preliminary design work on a new piston-engined high-speed bomber, the P.1005, and when this was cancelled in 1942 — by which time a mock-up was almost complete — Hawkers studied the possibility of equipping the airframe with two Power Jet gas turbines under the designation P.1011. Another scheme, proposed at about the same time, envisaged a single-seat fighter with one Power Jet engine. Both these schemes came to nothing, but with the advent of more powerful turbojets in 1943 Hawkers were encouraged to go ahead with other projects, mostly designed around the Rolls-Royce B.40 and B.41 engines. The first was the P.1031, a scheme for a B.40-powered night fighter; then came the P.1034, which was the old B.1005 bomber scheme resurrected with two B.41s, the P.1035, which involved the fitting of a B.41 turbojet into a Hawker Fury airframe, the P.1038 and the P.1039, which

were once again variations on the B.1005 jet bomber theme.

The P.1035 project showed more promise than any of the others, and detailed proposals were submitted to the Ministry of Aircraft Production in December 1944, by which time the original design had undergone some changes. The B.41 engine, which was positioned in the fuselage aft of the cockpit and fed by air intakes built into the wing roots, was originally intended to exhaust under the tail, but to minimize thrust loss Hawkers decided to shorten the tail pipe by designing a bifurcated, or split, jet pipe that exhausted on either side of the fuselage just aft of the engine. With this and other modifications the P.1035 was redesignated P.1040, work on which proceeded as a private venture during the winter of 1944-45. We shall return to the fortunes of the P.1040 a little later on.

In 1946, while firms in both the United States and the Soviet Union were putting the finishing touches to designs that would soon equip their combat squadrons with swept-wing, transonic fighters, Britain's Labour government was still firm in its conviction that there would be no major war threat for at least ten years. As a

BOULTON PAUL P.111. Contemporary with the Avro 707 series, the Boulton Paul P.111 was a tailless delta-wing research aircraft powered by a Rolls-Royce Nene engine.

HAWKER P.1052. The P.1052, two of which were built, was a swept-wing version of the Hawker P.1040 with conventional tail surfaces, and carried out deck landing trials in 1952.

direct result, all but two specifications for high-speed single-seat aircraft issued by the Ministry of Supply in 1946 involved experimental machines. The two exceptions were F.43/46 and F.44/46, calling for the development of modern jet fighters to replace the Meteor and Vampire in the day-fighter role and the Mosquito in the night-fighter role. These, however, were to undergo profound changes, and two years were to elapse before the specifications were re-written and, eventually, led to the development of the kind of aircraft the RAF needed.

HAWKER P.1081. The Hawker P.1052 was given swept tail surfaces later in its career and became the P.1081, which was destroyed in an accident.

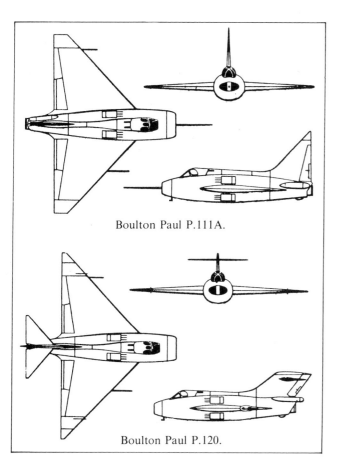

Boulton Paul P.111A.

Boulton Paul P.120.

The first 1946 specification for a high-speed research aircraft was E.27/46, which resulted in the delta-wing Boulton Paul P.111. The prototype, VT935, did not fly until 6 October 1950, powered by a 5,100 lb.s.t. Rolls-Royce Nene turbojet fed via an oval nose intake. The leading edge of the delta wing was swept at 45 degrees. In 1953, the P.111 underwent some modification, four air brakes being fitted on the fuselage aft of the cockpit, and in this form it was redesignated P.111A. During trials, the P.111A reached a maximum speed of 650 mph at sea level and 622 mph at 35,000 feet. The aircraft is today preserved in the College of Aeronautics at Cranfield, Bedfordshire.

On 6 August, 1952, Boulton Paul flew a variant of the basic P.111 design, the P.120, which differed mainly in having a redesigned fin and a high-mounted all-moving tailplane. The P.120 carried out some eleven hours' test flying, showing a performance similar to that of its predecessor, before being destroyed in a crash caused by tail flutter on 29 August 1952.

The second research specification, E.38/46, was met by Hawker Aircraft Ltd, who in October 1945 — as construction of the P.1040 was about to begin — had begun limited design studies of a variant known as the P.1047, which was basically a P.1040 fuselage with a wing swept at an angle of 35 degrees, the whole being powered by a rocket motor instead of a turbojet. The P.1047 was schemed only, but in March 1947, when Hawkers submitted their tender to meet E.38/46, the swept-wing proposal formed the basis of their design. Two months later the company was awarded a contract for the construction of two prototypes, VX272 and VX279, under the designation Hawker P.1052. The two aircraft were built at Hawker's new factory in Richmond Road, Kingston-on-Thames, and VX272 flew for the first time on 19 November 1948. By the summer of 1949 both

prototypes were fully engaged in a high-speed research programme on behalf of the RAE, and their performance showed so much promise that at one point, towards the end of 1948, it was seriously considered placing the P.1052 in quantity production as a replacement for the Gloster Meteor. By that time, however, other fighter designs of far greater potential were on the drawing board, and the idea was dropped.

Nevertheless, the Australian Government had shown considerable interest in the P.1052, and Hawkers felt justified in proceeding with the development of an all-swept variant with a straight-through exhaust. At a meeting with Ministry of Supply representatives on 31 January, 1950, the Company was made fully aware of the RAAF requirement, which was for a fast, cheap-to-produce interceptor armed with four 20-mm cannon that could also double up in the ground attack role with rockets or bombs. The Australians wanted to build the aircraft under licence, and one of the stipulations was that the prototype had to fly within fifteen months.

Conscious of the urgency, Hawkers went ahead and converted the second prototype P.1052, VX279, which they fitted with a 5,000 lb.s.t. Rolls-Royce Nene turbojet exhausting through a jet pipe 'borrowed' from a Vickers-Supermarine Attacker naval jet fighter; it was planned that the production version would be fitted with a 6,250 lb.s.t. Rolls-Royce Tay. The new aircraft, designated P.1081, was taken into the air for the first time on 19 June 1950 by Squadron Leader T. S. ('Wimpy') Wade, Hawker's chief test pilot. Results obtained during flight testing led to some rudder and tailplane modifications, and wing fences were also fitted. The P.1081's performance was fairly spectacular, with a maximum speed of 695 mph at sea level and a climb to 35,000 feet of 9 minutes 12 seconds. The installation of the Tay engine would have improved the rate of climb still further. But it

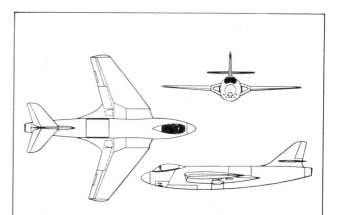

Designation: Hawker P.1081.
Role: Single-seat fighter.
Engine: One 6,250 lb.s.t. Rolls-Royce Tay turbojet.
Span: 33 ft. 6 in.
Length: 44 ft. 3 in.
Weight: 15,000 lb. (Normal Loaded).
Crew: 1.
Service ceiling: 45,000 ft.
Range: 850 miles.
Max Speed: 695 mph at sea level.
Weapons: Four 20-mm cannon plus rockets or bombs.

DE HAVILLAND DH.108. The first turbojet-powered aircraft in the world to exceed Mach 1, the DH 108 was designed to specification E.18/435 for research into swept wing behaviour over a wide speed range.

was not to be: on 3 April, 1951, the sole P.1081 crashed at high speed on the South Downs, killing Squadron Leader Wade. The cause was never fully established, but it seems that the aircraft might have gone out of control in a dive and exceeded its limitations, for witnesses said that they had heard a sonic boom as the P.1081 came down. Whatever the cause, the Australians lost interest, both they and the RAF meeting the immediate requirement for a high-speed fighter with 'offshore' deliveries of F-86 Sabres, and the P.1081 was abandoned. It was a pity, for indications were that the P.1081 would have proved a match for the Russian MiG-15 — which the Gloster Meteor Mk.8 certainly was not, as events in Korea showed — and moreover it had plenty of development potential. Even when more modern fighters eventually replaced it in the interceptor role, the P.1081 could have provided the RAF and RAAF with a formidable fast ground-attack aircraft until the late 1950s. Instead, the ground-attack squadrons of the respective services had to be content with the ageing de Havilland Venom and Vampire.

The makers of the latter aircraft, de Havilland, also made a substantial contribution to early post-war high-speed research, but their design was developed to an earlier specification, E.18/45. The aircraft they evolved, the DH.108, was intended to investigate the aerodynamic characteristics of the swept-wing formula throughout the subsonic speed range. Design work started in October 1945 and three prototypes were ordered by the MoS. The DH.108 airframe consisted of a standard Vampire Mk.1

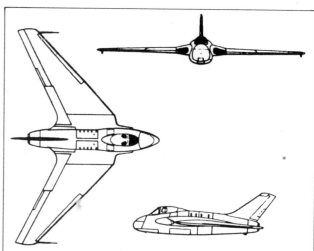

Designation: De Havilland DH. 108.

Role: Aerodynamic research aircraft.

Engine: One 3,000/3,300 lb.s.t. Goblin 2/3 turbojet.

Span: 39 ft.

Length: 24 ft. 6 in.

Weight: 8,960 lb. Loaded.

Crew: 1.

Service Ceiling: 40,000 ft.

Range: 500 miles.

Max Speed: Mach 1.0 at altitude.

Weapons: None.

fuselage married to the new wooden wing, which had a leading edge sweep of 43 degrees and featured split trailing-edge flaps with elevons mounted outboard. The aircraft was fitted with a conventional swept fin and rudder and was powered by a de Havilland Goblin 2 centrifugal-flow turbojet, fed via air intakes at the wing root.

The first DH.108, TG283, was designed for low-speed handling trials and was fitted with various safety devices, including anti-spin parachutes housed in wingtip containers and leading edge slots fitted in the open position. It flew for the first time on 15 May 1946, and during the following four years carried out extensive handling trials in the low-speed range of the flight envelope up to a maximum of 280 mph. The aircraft was destroyed on 1 May 1950, when it went out of control during stalling trials and crashed at Hartley Wintney, Hampshire. The pilot, G. E. C. Genders, was killed.

The second DH.108, TG306, had an increased 45-degree sweepback and was intended to investigate the middle of the subsonic speed range. It was fitted with power controls and automatic leading edge slots, and its engine was a 3,300 lb.s.t. Goblin 3. This aircraft first flew in June 1946 and was demonstrated at that year's SBAC Show, after which it was decided to use it in an attempt on the world air speed record, which then stood at 616 mph and was held by a Meteor Mk.4. Piloted by Geoffrey de Havilland, son of the head of the firm, TG306 made several high-speed trial runs in preparation for the record attempt, but on 27 September 1946 it experienced structural failure at a speed of about Mach 0.9 and crashed into the sea north-east of Gravesend, Kent, killing its pilot.

The third DH.108, VW120, was the high-speed aircraft of the trio and incorporated a number of refinements that included a more streamlined nose and cockpit canopy. On 12 April, 1948, this aircraft established a new 100-km closed-circuit record of 605.23 mph under the power of its Goblin 4 turbojet and with test pilot John Derry at the controls. On 9 September that year, again flown by Derry, VW120 exceeded Mach 1.0 in a steep dive between 40,000 and 30,000 feet, the pilot reporting no problems except for a stiffening of the controls. Despite conflicting claims that arose thereafter, the DH.108 therefore appears to have been the first turbojet-powered aircraft in the world to exceed Mach unity. Unfortunately, this historic machine was totally destroyed in a crash at Birkhill, Buckinghamshire, on 15 February 1950.

The DH.108 programme, although ending tragically, had proved a considerable asset in the development of a de Havilland project for a heavy twin-engined all-weather fighter, the DH.110, which had originated in Naval specification N.40/46. That was issued in June 1946, and two months later was followed by the RAF's all-weather fighter specification, F.44/46. As the two specifications were generally similar, de Havilland decided to offer the RAF a 'de-navalized' version of the DH.110. During the next two years the specifications underwent a number of changes, the RAF requirement being eventually finalized as F.4/49 and the Navy's version as N.14/49, and at the end of 1948 de Havilland received an Instruction to Proceed with the building of two prototypes, one for each Service. Early in 1949, however, the Royal Navy changed its requirements and cancelled its order.

DE HAVILLAND SEA VIXEN.

Despite this, work proceeded with prototype construction, and the first of the two swept-wing, twin-boom DH.110s, — WG236 — flew for the first time on 26 September 1951, powered by two 7,300 lb.s.t. Rolls-Royce Avons. Six months into the flight test programme, on 9 April 1952, this aircraft became the first twin-engined two-seater to exceed Mach 1.0 in a dive. The second DH.110 prototype, WG240, flew on 25 July 1952 and featured modifications that included some strengthening of the wing. Painted a sinister all-black, WG240 was demonstrated by John Derry at that year's Farnborough Air Show on every day except 6 September, when it suddenly went unserviceable. Derry switched to the other 110, WG236, and went into his usual display routine. He was pulling a high-g turn about a mile outside the airfield perimeter when the aircraft broke up without warning as a result of the structural failure of the starboard outer wing section. The results were catastrophic; John Derry and his observer were killed and debris plunged into the crowd, causing many casualties.

The second prototype DH.110 was grounded as a result of this tragic accident, and in 1953 the RAF decided to fill its all-weather fighter requirement with the Gloster Javelin. Yet in many respects, the DH.110 was the better design; it was certainly more manoeuvrable, its handling qualities comparing closely with those of many smaller single-seat fighters, and it was very stable in a high-g turn right down to the stall, which the Javelin was not. Nevertheless, de Havilland resumed testing with the second DH.110 after further structural modifications, with a renewed naval requirement in mind, and in September 1953 it carried out carrier trials aboard HMS *Albion*. A production order for a developed naval version followed, and this ultimately entered Fleet Air Arm service as the Sea Vixen.

Returning to the 1946 requirement for high-speed research aircraft, it was an experimental version of the Royal Navy's first jet aircraft, the Vickers-Supermarine Attacker, that was employed to meet Specification E.41/46. This was the Type 510, which in essence was an Attacker fuselage with swept flying surfaces, and the prototype, VV106, was the progenitor of a line of fast jets that was to culminate in the Supermarine Swift, the first swept-wing fighter to enter service with the RAF. The Type 510, which first flew on 29 December 1948, powered by a Rolls-Royce Nene turbojet, was followed by the Type 535, which was identical except for a longer nose and a tricycle undercarriage; this made its first flight on 23 August 1950 and was in turn developed into the Type 541, which in fact became the Swift prototype.

At one point, the Ministry of Supply seriously considered ordering the Type 535 into production as an insurance against the failure of the more advanced Swift and Hunter, and in November 1950 Vickers-Supermarine were awarded a contract for 100 operational examples, to be fulfilled in the event of the failure of the Type 541. The first prototype 541 (WJ960) flew on 1 August 1951, some months after the Swift had been ordered into super-priority production — a haste occasioned by the Korean crisis.

The Swift F.Mk.1 entered service with No.56 Squadron, RAF Fighter Command, in February 1954, five months before the other super-priority day fighter, the Hawker Hunter F.1, went into service with No.43 Squadron. Both aircraft had been designed in accordance

DH.110. The DH.110 all-weather fighter was eventually developed into the Royal Navy's Sea Vixen.

with Air Ministry Specification F.3/48, which had replaced the earlier F.43/46, and the P.1067 Hunter was the direct lineal descendant of the earlier P.1040/1052 prototypes. In squadron service, the Hunter, although it had its fair share of teething troubles, proved by far the better of the two designs and went on in its various marks to become a first-rate combat aircraft, although in fairness it should be stressed that the Swift's shortcomings were not the fault of the superb Vickers-Supermarine design team. The problem lay in the fact that the Swift had been rushed into service as a panic measure when the Korean War hammered home the lesson that the RAF's current equipment was completely outclassed by that of the Russians, and it had simply not been possible to iron out all the snags. Both the Swift F.1 and F.2 were found to be quite unsuitable for their primary role of air interception, being prone to tightening in turns and suffering frequent high-altitude flameouts as a result of shock waves entering the air intakes when the cannon were fired. By February 1955 the Air Ministry had concluded that the Swift could not be relied upon to carry out its primary role and its time as a day fighter was at an end, the type being replaced by the Hawker Hunter in Fighter Command. Later, two squadrons of Swift FR.5s were used in the low-level fighter-reconnaissance role with 2nd Tactical Air Force, RAF Germany.

Meanwhile, as both Vickers-Supermarine and Hawkers were preparing for series production of the Swift and Hunter in 1951, their respective design teams were turning their attention to transonic successor aircraft — machines that would be capable of operating in level flight over the speed range of Mach 1.0 to Mach 1.5. Every other nation with modern combat aircraft technology was doing the same; in the United States, France and the Soviet Union, North American, Marcel Dassault and Mikoyan and Guryevitch were respectively developing the F-100 Super Sabre, Super Mystere B.2 and MiG-19, successors to the F-86 Sabre, Mystere IV and MiG-17, all of which were in the Hunter/Swift class.

Hawker Aircraft's proposal for a transonic fighter involved a straightforward development of the P.1067 Hunter, with a lengthened fuselage to accommodate an afterburning Rolls-Royce Avon RA.14 turbojet and married to a new thin wing, swept 52 degrees at the leading edge. The project was given the designation P.1083, and detailed design work began in November 1951. This led, on 26 February 1952, to an Instruction to Proceed with the construction of a prototype, which was allocated the serial WN470 and expected to fly before the end of 1953. In April 1952, with Hawkers already at work modifying the airframe of the fourth prototype P.1067 and building the new wing, a tentative production schedule was worked out between Company representatives and members of the Air Staff and Ministry of Supply.

By October 1952, the starboard section of the P.1083 wing had been completed, and the Avon RA.14 engine successfully mated with a mock-up of the rear fuselage. It was now estimated that the first prototype would be ready to fly in July 1953, and plans were made to power production machines with the uprated Rolls-Royce Avon RA.19 engine of 12,500 lb.s.t.; this involved some

VICKERS SUPERMARINE 535.

redesign of the rear fuselage to accommodate the RA.19's bigger jet pipe. Other design changes in the production P.1083 included extra fuel tankage and a slab-type tailplane. The estimated flight profile included an endurance of one and a quarter hours, allowing for climb to 50,000 feet and ten minutes' combat at that altitude, a maximum speed of 820 mph at sea level and 690 mph at 55,000 feet.

By June 1953, the P.1083 prototype, WN470, was eighty per cent complete, and Hawkers were confident that it would be ready in time to take part in that year's Farnborough Air Show. Then the blow fell. Quite out of the blue, Hawkers were informed that work on the P.1083 was to cease forthwith. A rival design, the Supermarine 545, was considered by the Air Staff to have better development potential. The Air Staff also felt, belatedly, that the afterburning RA.19 engine was not the right choice. Hawker's protests fell on deaf ears; on 13 July 1953, the P.1083 project was officially cancelled.

Just as the P.1083 had been based on the Hunter, the Vickers-Supermarine 545 design was based on that of the Swift, although the 545 bore far less resemblance to its precursor than did the P.1083. It was, in fact, a complete redesign with an area-ruled fuselage and a thin crescent-type wing that featured a leading edge sweep ranging from 50 degrees at the wing root through 40 degrees at mid-point to 30 degrees at the outer section. The selected powerplant was a Rolls-Royce Avon RA.14R turbojet developing 14,500 lb.s.t. with full reheat.

While work proceeded on the prototype 545, XA181,

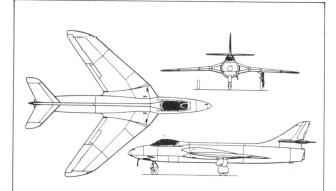

Designation: Hawker P.1083.

Role: Prototype Interceptor.

Engine: One Rolls-Royce Avon RA. 19R of 12,500 lbs. s.t. with reheat.

Span: 34 ft. 4 in.

Length: 45 ft. 10½ in.

Weight: (Normal Loaded) 20,000 lb.

Crew: 1.

Service ceiling: 59,500 ft.

Range: 800 miles.

Max Speed: 820 mph at sea level.

Weapons: Four 30-mm Aden cannon.

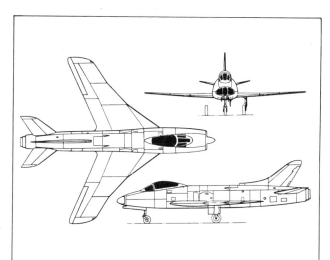

Designation: Vickers-Supermarine Type 545.

Role: Prototype Interceptor.

Engine: One 9,500 lb.s.t. (14,500 lb with reheat) Rolls-Royce Avon RA.14 turbojet.

Span: 39 ft.

Length: 47 ft.

Weight: (Normal Loaded) 20,147 lb.

Crew: 1.

Service ceiling: 59,000 ft.

Range: 750 miles.

Max Speed: 750 mph at sea level.

Weapons: Four 30-mm Aden cannon.

in 1954, Vickers-Supermarine also offered the RAF a follow-on design powered by an RB.106 turbojet. This variant had a lengthened fuselage and a chin-type air intake, like that of the F-86D Sabre. The aircraft would have been capable of an estimated maximum speed of Mach 1.68. In 1955, however, following the abysmal failure of the Swift fighter, all development work on the Type 545 was halted and the prototype cancelled. The failure of the Swift was not the only reason; by this time, the Air Staff had decided to put all its eggs in one supersonic basket, by turning a manned supersonic research aircraft, the English Electric P.1, into a complete weapons system. In its new form, it flew in April 1957 as the P.1B; and as the Lightning, it finally entered RAF service in the summer of 1960.

The RAF therefore succeeded in bridging the gap from subsonic to truly supersonic at one go, cutting out the transonic 'middle man' altogether. It was a formidable achievement, but the consequences for Britain's aviation industry were little short of disastrous, particularly from the export point of view. Apart from Britain, no fewer than sixteen other countries went on to use various marks of the Hawker Hunter; but when some of them, particularly those within NATO, came to look for a transonic successor, Britain had nothing to offer them. It was the United States which stepped in with alacrity to fill the gap, capturing what had until then been traditional British markets, and creating a situation from which Britain's military aircraft export order books have not recovered to this day.

Yet, as we shall see in a later chapter, worse was to come.

HAWKER HUNTER. The Hawker Hunter, seen here in Swiss Air Force markings, was an outstanding aircraft by any standards. A supersonic version, the P.1083, was cancelled – and consequently several overseas customers turned to the USA to fill their supersonic aircraft requirement.

3. Naval Aircraft Development, 1945-55: The Years of Stagnation.

Britain's Fleet Air Arm, which had fought its way gallantly through the early years of the second World War with a variety of obsolescent equipment, ended that conflict with carrier aircraft which compared favourably with any the Americans had. The reason was simple: most of them *were* American, supplied under Lease-Lend — and, in the early weeks of peace, a great many of them were literally shovelled over the side of Royal Navy carriers around the world, because if the Navy had kept them, the British Government would have had to pay for them.

Unlike the United States Navy, however, which had invited tenders for a carrier-borne jet fighter design in 1944, the British Admiralty saw little future in jet aircraft operation. A few deck-landing trials with a Vampire and a Meteor in 1945 had convinced the admirals that jet types had too high a landing speed for safe carrier operations, and so when the Fleet Air Arm's combat squadrons re-equipped in the late 1940s, it was once again with piston-engined types such as the Hawker Fury and later marks of the Fairey Firefly.

Nevertheless, one or two forward-thinking members of the Naval Staff continued to push hard for the development of carrier-borne jets, and so the idea was not allowed to stagnate entirely. The notion of a swept-wing carrier jet fighter was considered to be almost foolhardy, but a straight-wing conventional jet design was treated with much less suspicion. Since both the Meteor and Vampire were deemed to be unsuitable for various reasons, the Admiralty turned to a completely new design — the Vickers-Supermarine E.10/44, which had originally been proposed as a land-based fighter for the RAF. The RAF, however, had decided to adopt the Meteor and Vampire, both of which had a better performance, and so Supermarine offered a navalized version to the Admiralty, who wrote Specification E.1/45

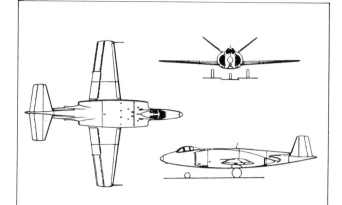

Designation: Vickers-Supermarine Type 508.
Role: Prototype Naval Fighter.
Engines: Two 6,500 lb.s.t. Rolls-Royce Avon RA.3 turbojets.
Span: 40 ft.
Length: 46 ft. 9 in.
Weight: Loaded 18,000 lb.
Crew: 1.
Service ceiling: 45,000 ft.
Range: 800 miles.
Max Speed: 590 mph at sea level.
Weapons: (Proposed): Four 30-mm Aden cannon.

around it. The prototype first flew in its navalized form on 17 June 1947, and, as the Vickers-Supermarine Attacker, the aircraft went into production for the Royal Navy. It did not, however, enter squadron service until August 1951, by which time the Navy's piston-engined Sea Furies and Fireflies were battling against Russian MiG-15s over Korea under every possible disadvantage.

The Admiralty's phobia about operating jets from carriers was expressed in a curious requirement, originating at the end of 1945, for a shipboard fighter

VICKERS SUPERMARINE TYPE 508. The Type 508 was powered by two Rolls-Royce Avon RA.3 turbojets and featured a 'butterfly' tail unit.

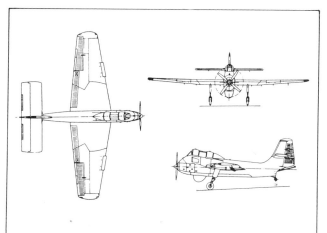

Designation: Short Seamew AS.1.

Role: Anti-submarine warfare aircraft.

Engine: One 1,590 e.s.h.p. Mamba AS.Ma.6 turboprop.

Span: 55 ft.

Length: 41 ft.

Weight: Empty 9,795 lb. - Loaded 15,000 lb.

Crew: 2.

Service ceiling: 24,500 ft.

Range: 750 miles.

Max Speed: 235 mph.

Weapons: Four anti-submarine bombs or RPs.

without an undercarriage. This would have been catapult-launched in the normal way, but would have skid-landed on a flexible flight deck. Supermarine worked up a project around the requirement and submitted it to the Admiralty in 1946 under the designation Type 505; it was a straight-wing design with a V-type 'butterfly' tail, and power was provided by two Rolls-Royce Avons. At the same time, Supermarine also offered the RAF a land-based version with a conventional tricycle undercarriage, increased fuel tankage and two 30-mm cannon. Six prototypes of the Type 505 were ordered in the summer of 1946, but then the requirement for an undercarriage-less fighter was cancelled and Supermarine were ordered to proceed with the development of a more conventional variant with greater endurance and better performance.

Supermarine accordingly took the basic Type 505 design and scaled it up slightly, giving it an armament of four cannon and cramming in more fuel space. Three prototypes of the new aircraft, designated Supermarine Type 508, were ordered in September 1947 and the first of these, VX133, flew for the first time at Boscombe Down on 31 August 1951. VX133 carried out a series of deck landing trials aboard HMS *Eagle* in May 1952. Meanwhile, the second prototype, VX136, had undergone various internal modifications, and although it remained externally similar to the Type 508 it was re-designated Type 529. VX136 first flew on 29 August 1952 and immediately embarked on trials alongside its sister aircraft.

SHORT S.B.6 SEAMEW. The Short S.B.6 Seamew was designed as a light anti-submarine aircraft. It had a fixed undercarriage. Powered by an Armstrong Siddeley Mamba turboprop.

BLACKBURN YB-1. Designed to specification GR.17/45, the Blackburn YB-1 was an unsuccessful competitor to the Fairey Gannet. The original version, the YA-5, was to have been powered by a Napier coupled turboprop, but this was replaced by the Armstrong-Siddeley Double Mamba.

In June 1949, Supermarine had submitted a swept-wing version of the basic Type 508 design to the Air Staff for consideration as a twin-engined fighter under the designation Type 525. The RAF did not take up the offer, but by this time the Navy had at last woken up to the potential of a swept-wing carrier fighter, and Supermarine received a contract to convert the third prototype 508, VX138, to 525 standard. In this form, if flew for the first time on 27 April 1954, and two further prototypes had meantime been ordered under the designation Type 544. The latter aircraft embodied several refinements, such as a blown flap system, which were first tested on the Type 525. VX138 was destroyed in a crash in July 1955, but the production version of the Type 544 went on to enter service with the Royal Navy in 1958. At long last, the Fleet Air Arm, in the form of the Supermarine Scimitar F.1, had its swept-wing strike fighter. The aircraft it replaced, and which had been the mainstay of the Royal Navy's jet attack squadrons during the mid-1950s, was the Hawker Sea Hawk. Its prototype, VP401, had first flown on 2 September 1947 and had met all the requirements of Naval Staff Specification N.7/46. It was, in fact, none other than a revamped and navalised version of the aircraft developed by the Hawker Company as a private venture in the winter of 1944-45, an aircraft the RAF had not wanted: the Hawker P.1040.

In other areas of carrier aircraft requirement, the Navy seemed to know what it wanted with far greater precision, sometimes with unfortunate consequences. A classic example was specification M.123, issued by the Naval

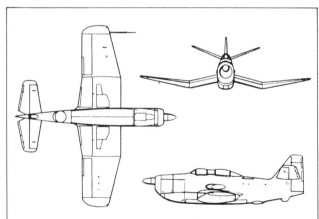

Designation: Blackburn YA.5/YB.1.

Role: Anti-submarine search and strike.

Engine: One Armstrong Siddeley Double Mamba ASMD.1 developing 2,640 s.h.p. plus 810 lb residual thrust (2,950 e.h.p.).

Span: 44 ft. 2 in.

Length: 42 ft. 5 in.

Weight: Loaded 22,000 lb.

Crew: 3.

Service ceiling: 24,000 ft.

Range: 900 miles.

Max Speed: 270 mph at sea level.

Weapons: Torpedoes, mines, depth charges etc up to 2,500 lb.

BLACKBURN YB-1.

Staff in 1951 and calling for a simple, robust anti-submarine aircraft capable of operating from small aircraft carriers in the most adverse of weather conditions. Short Brothers submitted a design, the SB.6, and three prototypes were ordered under the official name of Seamew. The first of these, XA209, flew on 23 August 1953, having been built in the record time of fifteen months, but it was severely damaged on landing. Nevertheless, it was repaired in time for the Farnborough Air Show a few weeks later. XA209 was fitted with an Armstrong Siddeley Mamba AS.Ma.3 turboprop; the second prototype, XA213, had a more powerful Mamba AS.Ma.6. This aircraft carried out successful deck trials in July and December 1955 aboard HMS *Bulwark,* by which time it had been announced that the Seamew AS.1 would go into production for the Royal Navy and a land-based variant, the Seamew MR.2, would be built for RAF Coastal Command. Early in 1956, however, the RAF order was cancelled, and Seamew production cut back to 24 aircraft for the Royal Navy. An export sales drive in Europe produced no enthusiasm for the type, which had some vicious tendencies that Shorts had proved unable to eliminate, and in the end the Seamew programme was cancelled after 21 aircraft had been built. All were placed in storage and eventually broken up. All in all, the Seamew was a sorry example of an aircraft in which handling qualities had inevitably been sacrificed to achieve economy.

The Naval Staff had certainly known what it required when it issued one of its first post-war specifications, GR.17/45. This called for an aircraft combining, for the first time, the roles of search and strike — and an aircraft, moreover, that was capable of carrying a formidable war load of mines, depth charges, bombs and torpedoes internally. Blackburn Aircraft and Fairey Aviation, both with considerable experience (but not always parallel success) in the design of naval torpedo-bombers, each tendered proposals to meet GR.17/45, and the designs they involved were astonishingly similar in configuration.

Blackburn's proposal was the YA.5, a two-seater that was originally intended to be powered by a Napier Coupled Naiad N.Na.C.1 turboprop. Development of this engine was discontinued, however, so Blackburn switched to the best alternative, the Armstrong Siddeley Double Mamba, which had also been selected by Fairey Aviation. The Double Mamba, in fact, had been designed as the result of a suggestion by Fairey that two Mamba engines, suitably coupled, would be ideal for an anti-submarine aircraft, giving single-engined handling qualities together with twin-engined performance and reliability. Cruise range could be extended by shutting down one of the coupled engines, since each unit could be controlled separately, and the arrangement produced none of the asymmetric problems that bedevilled more conventional twin-engined machines.

The abandonment of the Napier Naiad programme caused some delay in the YA.5 test schedule, but in the meantime two prototypes were built and fitted with Rolls-Royce Griffon piston engines so that aerodynamic testing could go ahead. The first of these, the Blackburn YA.7 (WB781) made its first flight on 20 September, 1949, and made its first deck landing on HMS *Illustrious* on 8 February 1950. It was followed by the YA.8, WB788, which made its maiden flight on 3 May 1950 and its first carrier landing on 19 June. Meanwhile, the YA.5 had at last received its Double Mamba engine; it had also been modified to take a third crew station, following a revision of the specification, and featured redesigned outer wing panels with leading edge sweep, a configuration first tested on the YA.8. With these alterations, the YA.5 was redesignated YB.1, and the sole prototype, WB797, first flew on 19 July 1950. Generally, however, the Fairey design was the better of the two, and it was ordered into production for the Royal Navy as the Gannet.

The other competitor in the GR.17/45 stakes was the Short SB.3, which was a modified version of the twin-engined Short Sturgeon target tug. The SB.3 was, in fact, proposed to meet a revised specification, M.6/49, which called for an anti-submarine search and radar patrol aircraft. Shorts took a production Sturgeon, and completely altered the basic airframe, redesigning the front fuselage to accommodate two radar operators in a cabin in front of and below the pilot's cockpit, giving the aircraft a curious looking 'chin'. the prototype SB.3, WF632, was powered by two Armstrong Siddeley Mamba turbines driving four-bladed propellers and flew for the first time on 12 August 1950. Flight testing, however, revealed some serious stability problems, and the SB.3 was never assessed operationally. In the long run, the radar search requirement was met by the Gannet Mk.3.

Chapter Three
Soviet Union: the Race for Parity, 1945-55

1. Strategic Bomber Development

The end of the war in Europe saw the Soviet Union seriously deficient in strategic bombers; only one type, the Petlyakov Pe-8, was in service in any numbers. Production of the Pe-8, a product of the Andrei N. Tupolev design bureau, ended in 1944, and no replacement was planned for it; the Soviet Air Force was essentially a tactical organization, and priority was given to the production of aircraft for the Frontal Aviation (Frontovaia Aviatsiya), which was geared to support the Soviet armies. Even the Soviet Air Force's Long-Range Aviation, which operated the Pe-8 and the twin-engined Tu-2, ceased to exist as an independent force; early in 1944 it was redesignated the 18th Air Army and turned over to tactical duties.

However, as the war drew to a close the Chief Administration of the Soviet Air Force, already mindful of changing political forces that would almost certainly lead to an East-West confrontation of some sort in the early post-war years, had plans in hand for the updating of all combat elements, and these included the formation of a modern strategic bombing force. With the wartime emphasis very much on the development of tactical bombers, assault aircraft and fighters, Soviet designers had had little time to study long-range bomber projects, and it was obvious that even if work on such projects began in 1944 there would still be a dangerous gap before a Soviet long-range bomber could be produced in series. Then, suddenly, a ready-made answer literally fell out of the Russian sky in the shape of a Boeing B-29 Superfortress of the USAAF's 58th Bomb Wing, which force-landed on Russian territory after an attack on a Japanese target in Manchuria. Before the end of 1944, the Russians had acquired three more B-29s in similar fashion.

By copying the B-29 in every detail, the Russians hoped to avoid all the technological problems associated with the development of an aircraft of this kind. The designer chosen for the task was Andrei Tupolev, while the job of copying the B-29's Wright R-3350 engines went to A. M. Shvetsov. The work was not easy; big snags cropped up frequently, particularly in connexion with electronically operated equipment such as the B-29's gun turrets. Despite everything, however, construction of the prototype Russian B-29 — designated Tu-4 — was begun in March 1945, and the first three prototypes were ready for flight testing at the beginning of 1947. The following year these three aircraft were publicly revealed at the big Soviet air display at Tushino, near Moscow — by which time series production of the Tu-4 was well under way, the first examples having already been delivered to squadrons of the Dalnaia Aviatsiya (Long-Range Aviation).

With the Tu-4 in production, the Tupolev design team turned its attention to improving the basic design, the principal object being to increase the bomber's range. Retaining the basic structure of the Tu-4, Tupolev's engineers set about streamlining the fuselage, increasing its length by several feet and redesigning the nose section, replacing the Tu-4's rather bulbous cockpit with a more aerodynamically-refined stepped-up configuration. The area of the tail fin was also increased and the fin made more angular in design. To reduce drag, the nacelles of the ASh-73TK engines were redesigned. The outer wing sections were also redesigned and the span increased slightly, allowing for an increase in fuel tankage of fifteen per cent.

The redesigned aircraft, designated Tu-80, flew early in 1949. Two prototypes were built, and the operational version, while carrying a similar payload to that of the Tu-4, was to have had a defensive armament of ten 23-mm cannon or ten 12.7-mm machine-guns in remotely controlled barbettes. By this time, however, the Soviet Air Force had begun to think in terms of an aircraft that would compare with the Convair B-36, which was beginning to enter service with the squadrons of Strategic Air Command, and the Tu-80 was not ordered into production. Another Tu-4 derivative, the DVB-202, designed by Vladimir Myasishchev, suffered the same fate.

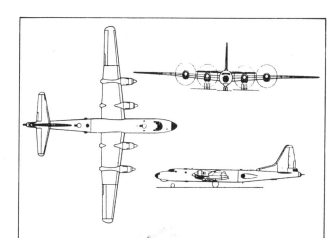

Designation: Tupolev Tu-80.

Role: Long-range heavy bomber.

Engine: Four Ash-73TK radials.

Span: 143 ft. 4 in.

Length: 113 ft. 2 in.

Weight: Loaded 112,000 lb.

Crew: 11.

Service ceiling: 38,000 ft.

Range: 3,500 miles.

Max Speed: 375 mph at 15,000 ft.

Weapons: Ten 23-mm cannon or ten 12.7-mm MGs in remotely-controlled turrets; 12,000 lbs. of bombs.

TUPOLEV TU-80. The Tupolev Tu-80 was a redesigned version of the well-tried TU-4 (B-29 copy). Two prototypes were built.

In mid-1949, in response to the new specification, Tupolev embarked on the design of the biggest aircraft so far constructed in the Soviet Union; it was also the last Russian military type designed to be powered by piston engines. At this time, several engine design bureaux in the USSR were working on powerful jet and turboprop engines that would power the next generation of Soviet combat aircraft, but it would be some time before these became operational, and in the meantime — with relations between East and West deteriorating steadily, particularly as a result of the Russian blockade of Berlin — the race to achieve parity with the United States assumed a high degree of urgency. This was especially true in the strategic bombing field; in 1949 the Soviet Union exploded her first nuclear device and Russian scientists were working hard to produce an operational atomic bomb. Even a small stockpile of fission weapons would mean that the American nuclear monopoly had been broken, but such weapons were useless if the means to deliver them did not exist. The B-36 had given Strategic Air Command the capability to deliver nuclear bombs deep into the heart of the Soviet Union; in 1949 the Russians had no comparable bomber. The Tu-4 had the capacity to lift Russia's early, cumbersome atomic weapons, but only over limited ranges; it was not capable of striking at American targets across the Arctic regions.

The new specification called for an intercontinental bomber capable of carrying an 11,500-lb bomb load over a combat radius of 4,375 miles and then returning to base without refuelling. Tupolev's answer was to produce, basically, a scaled-up version of the Tu-80 powered with new 4,000-hp piston engines. In this way, Tupolev succeeded not only in retaining the proven aerodynamic and technical qualities of the Tu-80 and its predecessor, the Tu-4, but also saved time: only two years elapsed between the start of the intercontinental bomber programme and the first flight of a prototype. By way of comparison, it took the Americans five years to produce the B-36, although the latter was somewhat more revolutionary in concept.

The new bomber, designated Tu-85, began flight testing at the beginning of 1951, powered by four Dobrinin VD-4K engines producing 4,300 hp on take-off. The structure was light, employing a number of

TUPOLEV TU-85. The Tu-85 was Russia's first real attempt to produce an intercontinental bomber. It had a very good performance, but was not ordered into production.

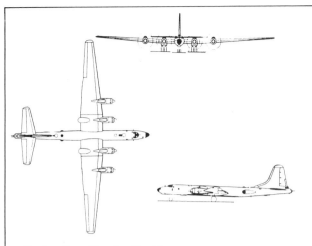

Designation: Tupolev Tu-85.

Role: Long-range heavy bomber.

Engines: Four VD-4K radials of 4,300 hp.

Span: 184 ft. 9 in.

Length: 129 ft. 7 in.

Weight: Loaded 239,680 lb.

Crew: 16.

Service ceiling: 42,900 ft.

Range: 7,500 miles.

Max speed: 351 mph at 15,000 ft.

Weapons: Ten 23-mm cannon; up to 44,000 lbs. of bombs.

special alloys (although for some reason magnesium, which was used in the structure of the B-36, was not incorporated) and the long, slender semi-monocoque fuselage was split into five compartments, three of which were pressurized and housed the 16-man crew. Defensive armament was the same as the Tu-4's, comprising four remotely-controlled turrets each with a pair of 23-mm cannon. The roomy weapons bay could accommodate up to 44,000lb of bombs. With an 11,000-lb bomb load, the Tu-85 had a range of 7,500 miles at 340 mph and 33,000 feet; normal range was 5,530 miles. Maximum speed over the target was 406 mph.

Despite this performance, the Tu-85 was not ordered into production. Times were changing fast; in February 1951, before the Tu-85 began its test flight programme, the US Air Force had decided to order the mighty B-52 Stratofortress, and it was clear that the day of the piston-engined bomber was over. The Russians therefore decided to abandon further development of the Tu-85 in favour of turbojet-powered strategic bombers, although they carefully fostered the impression that it was in service by showing the prototype, escorted by jet fighters, at Aviation Day flypasts.

The production of a strategic jet bomber was entrusted to Tupolev and also to the Myasishchev design bureau; the latter's efforts were to culminate in the four-engined Mya-4, which first appeared at Tushino in 1954 and received the NATO code-name Bison. Although never an outstanding success in the long-range strategic bombing role for which it was designed, the Bison was nevertheless the Soviet Union's first four-engined jet bomber, and was roughly comparable with early versions of the B-52 Stratofortress.

Tupolev's strategic jet bomber design was much more successful. Designated Tu-88, it flew for the first time in 1952 and entered service three years later as the Tu-16,

receiving the NATO code-name Badger. Owing much — in fuselage design at least — to the Tu-80, the Tu-16 was destined to become the most important bomber type on the inventories of the Soviet Air Force and Naval Air Arm for over a decade, about 2,000 examples being produced.

Tupolev also adopted the Tu-80's basic fuselage structure in the design of a new turboprop-powered strategic bomber, the Tu-95. To bring the project to fruition as quickly as possible, the Tupolev team married swept flying surfaces to what was basically a Tu-85 fuselage. Development of the Tu-95 and the Mya-4 proceeded in parallel, and it was intended that both types should be ready in time to take part in the Tushino flypast of May 1954. However, some delay was experienced with the Tu-95's engines, and in the event only the Myasishchev design was test-flown in time. Flight tests of the Tu-95 began in the summer of 1954, and seven pre-series aircraft made an appearance at Tushino on 3 July 1955. By this time the importance of the turbojet-powered bomber was growing, for the performance of the Mya-4 had fallen far short of expectations and as a result production orders were cut back drastically. Even though the Tu-95's engines were still causing problems, it was realised that the Tupolev design would form the mainstay of the Dalnaia Aviatsiya's strategic air divisions for at least the next decade; an ironic turn of events, for in the beginning emphasis had been placed on the production of the Mya-4 in the mistaken belief that the turboprop-powered Tu-95 would be limited to 0.76M.

The Tu-95 entered service in the second half of 1956, and was still serving in the reconnaissance and tanker roles thirty years later. During those years, the strategic nuclear delivery role was gradually assumed by intercontinental missiles, and the Soviet designers once again turned their attention away from long-range bomber development. However, as this book is being written in 1984 the wheel is turning full circle, with the manned bomber assuming new importance; and it is once again the bureau founded by Andrei Tupolev which is at the forefront.

2. Tactical Bombers and Assault Aircraft

At the end of the Second World War, and for some years afterwards, the mainstay of the Soviet Frontal Aviation's tactical bomber squadrons was the twin-engined Tupolev Tu-2, and designing a jet-powered replacement for this aircraft was accorded high priority with the leading Soviet design bureaux. Tupolev's answer, without expending too much time and effort on tactical bomber design — he was fully occupied with strategic bombers from 1944 onwards — was to modify the existing Tu-2 design and power it with two imported Rolls-Royce Derwent turbojets, slung in underwing nacelles. The resulting aircraft, designated Tu-12 (and also known by the manufacturer's designation of Tu-77) was flown for the first time on 27 July 1947 by test pilot A. D. Perelyot. The Tu-12 carried a crew of four and reached a maximum speed of 489 mph; a small pre-series batch was produced, and used to provide a nucleus of Soviet crews with multi-jet experience.

The Tu-12 also served to evaluate the Rolls-Royce Derwent under operational conditions. The Derwent was one of two British turbojets delivered in some quantity to

TUPOLEV TU-12. The Tupolev TU-12 (Tu-77) was used to provide a nucleus of Soviet aircrew with multi-jet experience, but was never employed in the tactical bombing role for which it was designed.

the Soviet Union in 1947 — the other being the Nene — and effectively solved one of the biggest dilemmas that had confronted the Soviet designers in the post-war years. During the war, the Russian aircraft industry — although it had investigated rocket power in a small way — had paid scant attention to jet propulsion, and although the acquisition of large numbers of German turbojets at the war's end formed a basis for further development the German engines were generally underpowered. German aerodynamic knowledge was gradually being incorporated into new Russian designs, but these were of little use without the right kind of powerplant — and by the middle of 1946 it was glaringly

Designation: Ilyushin Il-22.

Role: Medium-range jet bomber.

Engines: Four Rolls-Royce Derwent turbojets.

Span: 76 ft.

Length: 69 ft. 6 in.

Weight: Empty 20,272 lb.

Crew: 5.

Service ceiling: 36,600 ft.

Range: 1,160 miles.

Max speed: 446 mph at 16,000 ft.

Weapons: Four 23-mm cannon; up to 6,600 lbs of bombs.

obvious that, despite all the German expertise, Russian engine technology was lagging a long way behind that of the West.

The supply of British turbojets to the Soviet Union by Britain's post-war Socialist Government, naive though it may appear with hindsight, was not out of character in the climate of the times, and neither engine was then on the secret list. The Russians asked for the engines and got them, and within weeks were turning out their own accurate copies. The British engines arrived just in time to power the first Soviet bomber designed for jet propulsion from the outset: the Ilyushin Il-22.

Originally intended to be powered by four Junkers Jumo 004 turbojets in underwing pods, the Il-22 was in fact fitted with four Derwents before its maiden flight on 24 July 1947 in the hands of test pilot brothers Vladimir and Konstantin Kokkinaki. The sole example caused a sensation in Western circles when it appeared over Tushino soon afterwards, but its career was short-lived, the aircraft being retired after a two-month test programme. The Il-22 had a crew of five and carried a defensive armament of four 23-mm cannon, two in a dorsal turret and two in the tail. It could carry a payload of 6,600lb and reached a top speed of 446 mph. Service ceiling was 36,420 feet and maximum range 1,160 miles. In overall configuration the Il-22 bore a strong resemblance to the wartime German Heinkel He 323 jet bomber project, and there was speculation that this aircraft had in fact been completed and flown by Ilyushin; the Il-22, however, was a completely original design, and was much larger than the Heinkel project.

The Il-22 had been designed to a specification that required a medium-range jet bomber capable of carrying an internal bomb load of 6,600 lb, and three other jet aircraft were also designed around it: the Tupolev Tu-14, Ilyushin Il-28 and the Sukhoi Su-10. The latter aircraft, although conventional in airframe design, had an unconventional engine arrangement in that its four TR-1A (Derwent) turbojets were superimposed one above the other on a thin wing; this method was also adopted by Short Brothers in their design of the SA.4 Sperrin, and had the advantage of leaving the wing aerodynamically clean. The Su-10 was designed to carry a crew of four and a bomb load of up to 8,800 lb, rocket-assisted take-off

ILYUSHIN IL-22. The Ilyushin Il-22 medium-range bomber prototype had a short career, being retired after only two months of test flying.

equipment being used in an overload condition. Defensive armament was four 20-mm cannon, two in a dorsal turret and two in the tail; estimated maximum speed was 584 mph at sea level, combat radius was 560 miles and maximum range 1,243 miles. The prototype Su-10 was almost complete by the beginning of 1948, when it was abandoned in favour of the more promising Il-28, which had already flown, and it was used as an instructional airframe.

Tupolev's design to meet the medium-range bomber requirement, the Tu-72, was a straightforward aircraft using conventional aerodynamics and was designed to be powered by two Rolls-Royce Nenes. Before building of the prototype began, it was decided to incorporate a third turbojet — a Derwent — in the rear fuselage as an added safety measure in case one of the two main engines failed; memories of the frequent failures of the German turbojets were still fresh in the designer's minds. Following this and other modifications the aircraft was re-designated Tu-73, and the prototype was flown for the first time by A. D. Perelyot on 27 July 1947. A second prototype was designated Tu-78, and this joined the test programme in 1948. With the initial test phase successfully completed, plans were made for the series production of the aircraft. By this time, however, flight testing of the Ilyushin Il-28, a smaller, lighter aircraft powered by two RD-45 (Nene) turbojets, had shown it to be the better of the two designs in every aspect except range, and the Il-28 was consequently selected to equip the light bomber squadrons of the Frontovaia Aviatsiya. Known to NATO as the Beagle, it performed its task admirably for many years and was exported in substantial numbers.

The Tupolev design continued to be developed for service with the Soviet Naval Air Arm, and the prototype of the production version, the Tu-81, flew in 1949. This was powered by the latest Soviet version of the Nene, the Klimov VK-1, which was reliable enough to allow the designers to dispense with the tail-mounted turbojet. As the Tu-14 (NATO: Bosun) the jet bomber entered service in the attack role with the Naval Air Arm, and also served in the photo reconnaissance and electronic intelligence roles.

In June 1949 Tupolev also produced a swept-wing variant of the basic Tu-14 design, the Tu-82. Only one prototype was built, powered by two VK-1 turbojets, and although it was not a success it was the first swept-wing Russian jet bomber to fly. Piloted by A. D. Perelyot, the Tu-82 reached a speed of 543 mph and had a 1,700-mile range. Aerodynamically, the aircraft left a great deal to be desired, but a good deal of experimental flying was undertaken with it and Tupolev envisaged a production variant, the Tu-86, powered by two Mikulin AM-2 engines. This, however, reached the design stage only.

With the Il-28 firmly established in Soviet Air Force service, meanwhile, the Ilyushin design bureau lost no time in starting work on a potential successor.

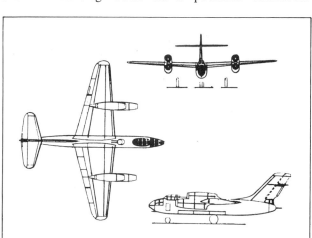

Designation: Sukhoi Su-10.

Role: Medium-range jet bomber.

Engines: Four TR-1A (Derwent) turbojets.

Span: 67 ft. 11 in.

Length: 64 ft. 6 in.

Weight: Loaded 47,349 lb.

Crew: 4.

Service ceiling: 42,900 ft.

Range: 1,243 miles.

Max speed: 584 mph at sea level.

Weapons: four 20-mm cannon; up to 8,800 lbs. of bombs.

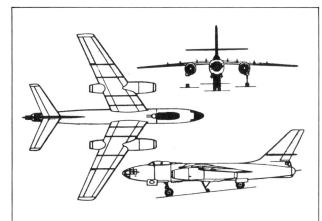

Designation: Ilyushin Il-30.
Role: Light jet bomber.
Engines: Two TR-3 turbojets.
Span: 54 ft. 5½ in.
Length: 59 ft. 4 in.
Weights: No details.
Crew: 4.
Service ceiling: 42,650 ft.
Range: 2,175 miles.
Max speed: 621 mph at sea level.
Weapons: Two 23-mm cannon; up to 6,600 lbs. of bombs.

Designation: Ilyushin Il-46.
Role: Medium-range jet bomber.
Engines: Two 11,020 lb.s.t. Lyulka AL-5 turbojets.
Span: 99 ft.
Length: 89 ft.
Weight: Loaded 94,000 lb.
Crew: 3.
Service ceiling: 40,350 ft.
Range: 3,076 miles.
Max speed: 576 mph at 9,500 ft.
Weapons: Four 23-mm cannon; up to 13,228 lbs. of bombs.

Designated Il-30, this flew in 1951 and was the first Russian bomber to reach a speed of 621 mph (1,000 km/h) in level flight.

An elegant and aerodynamically clean aircraft, the Il-30 was basically an Il-28 with swept flying surfaces, and was reminiscent in both size and concept of American's Douglas A-3 Skywarrior and B-66. The Il-30, which had a 35-degree leading edge sweep and carried a crew of four, was the first Soviet aircraft to feature a novel undercarriage arrangement that was later to be used on several operational Soviet types: twin-wheel main undercarriage units, mounted in tandem in the fuselage, and the twin-wheel outrigger units retracting into the engine nacelles. The Il-30 was powered by two underslung TR-3 turbojets, and defensive armament comprised twin 23-mm cannon in barbettes above and below the forward fuselage, with two more 23-mm cannon in the tail. The aircraft could carry a maximum bomb load of 6,600 lb, range was 2,175 miles and operational ceiling 42,650 feet. A promising concept, despite the fact that it experienced some stability problems, the Il-30 was nevertheless not selected for series production.

Ilyushin's next design was the Il-46, another Il-28 derivative. The Il-46, which was essentially a scaled-up Il-28, began life as a contender in the Soviet Air Force

ILYUSHIN IL-30. The Il-30 tactical bomber was designed as a swept-wing successor to the Il-28, and was roughly the equivalent of the Douglas B-66.

ILYUSHIN IL-46. Ilyushin's next design after the Il-30 was the Il-46, which began life as a contender in the Soviet Air Force requirement for a Tu-4 replacement. In the event, the contest was won by the Tu-16.

requirement for a Tu-4 replacement. The prototype was flown for the first time on 15 August 1952 by V. K. Kokkinaki and was powered by two Lyulka AL-5 turbojets which gave it a maximum speed of 576 mph at 9,840 feet. Normal bomb load on a long-range mission was 6,600 lb, but this could be increased to 13,228 lb over shorter ranges. The bomber carried a crew of three and defensive armament comprised two fixed 23-mm cannon in the nose and two 23-mm cannon in the tail. Maximum range was 3,076 miles and operational ceiling 40,350 feet. In the event, Tupolev's Tu-16 Badger won the contest, being of more advanced design than the Il-46 and possessing a better performance; the Il-46 was offered as a tactical bomber, but this idea was dropped and the aircraft never went into production.

The last of Ilyushin's experimental designs in the decade under review was the Il-54, a three-seat light attack bomber with wings swept at 55 degrees and two underslung Lyulka AL-7 turbojets. The aircraft was built in 1954 and underwent a thorough flight-test programme in the course of the following year, reaching a maximum speed of 714 mph. The aircraft's range was 1,490 miles and operational ceiling 42,650 feet. In 1956, the Il-54 prototype was shown to a Western delegation led by General Nathan F. Twining at Moscow's Kubinka airport; it was immediately allocated the NATO code-name Blowlamp and assumed to be in series production for the Frontovaia Aviatsiya. What the Western delegates failed to realise was that the Il-54's career was

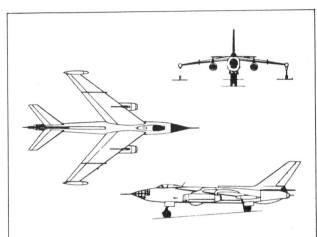

Designation: Ilyushin Il-54 (NATO: Blowlamp).
Role: Light jet bomber.
Engines: Two Lyulka AL-7 turbojets.
Span: 58 ft. 8 in.
Length: 71 ft. 11 in.
Weight: Loaded 64,960 lb.
Crew: 3.
Service ceiling: 42,650 ft.
Range: 1,490 miles.
Max speed: 714 mph at sea level.
Weapons: Three 23-mm cannon; unspecified bomb load.

ILYUSHIN IL-54. The last of Ilyushin's experimental designs before 1955 was the Il-54, which received the NATO code-name of Blowlamp. For some time, it was assumed by Western observers to have entered Soviet Air Force service.

ILYUSHIN IL-20. The ugly Il-20 was Ilyushin's last piston-engined shturmovik design. One prototype only was built and no further development was undertaken.

over and that it was already a museum piece.

During the Second World War, one of the most important aspects of Soviet combat aircraft design — and one that had given the Russians a decided tactical advantage during the armoured battles from 1943 onwards — was the concept of the 'Shturmovik', or heavily-armoured assault aircraft.

The Shturmovik in most widespread use during the war was Ilyushin's Il-2, and this was followed into service by the Il-10. A derivative of the latter, produced in 1945,

was the Il-16, which was fitted with an AM-43 twelve-cylinder liquid-cooled engine, but the type experienced aerodynamic stability problems and by the time these were rectified the Il-16 was already obsolescent. Fifty-three aircraft were built before production was abandoned.

The Ilyushin team nevertheless continued their studies of piston-engined shturmovik designs, and in 1948 they produced the Il-20, which was probably the ugliest aircraft ever to emerge from this famous design bureau.

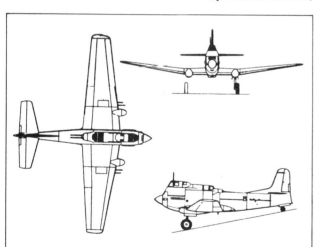

Designation: Ilyushin Il-20.
Role: Assault aircraft.
Engine: One 2,700 hp AM-47F.
Span: 44 ft. 3 in.
Length: 38 ft.
Weights: Not known.
Crew: 2.
Service ceiling: 25,426 ft.
Range: 1,044 miles.
Max speed: 320 mph.
Weapons: Four fixed NS-23 cannon; up to 2,205 lbs. of rocket projectiles and bombs.

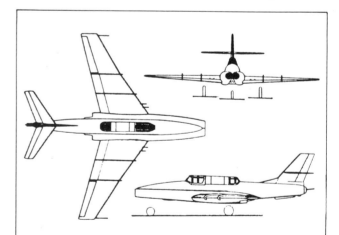

Designation: Ilyushin Il-40.
Role: Assault aircraft.
Engines: Two 5,952 lb.s.t. AM-5F turbojets.
Span: No data available.
Length: No data available.
Weights: No data available.
Crew: 2.
Service ceiling: 38,060 ft.
Range: 620 miles.
Max speed: 600 mph at sea level.
Weapons: Four 37-mm and two 23-mm cannon; bomb load not known.

Unofficially named Gorbach (hunchback), the Il-20 was powered by an AM-47F twelve-cylinder liquid-cooled engine and the pilot's cockpit was perched on top of this to give the best possible all-round visibility. The gunner sat behind the pilot, a step lower down, with a pair of 23-mm NS-23 cannon in a remotely-controlled barbette. Offensive armament of the Il-20 consisted of four fixed 23-mm cannon mounted in the wings outboard of the main undercarriage, and up to 2,205 lb of rockets and bombs. During flight testing, the Il-20 reached a maximum speed of 320 mph; range was 1,044 miles and operational ceiling 25,426 feet. However, only one prototype was built and no further development was undertaken.

Ilyushin's last venture into shturmovik design, before the concept was finally abandoned — at least insofar as a specialized aircraft was concerned — was the twin-jet Il-40, which flew in 1953. The Il-40 was powered by two AM-5F turbojets mounted side-by-side in the centre fuselage and exhausting aft of the wing trailing edge. The engines were fed via individual circular nose intakes, an arrangement that gave the aircraft a curious pig-like snout. The thick-section wing was low-mounted, with a 35-degree leading edge sweep, and carried four 37-mm cannon. Defensive armament comprised twin 23-mm cannon in a remotely-controlled tail barbette; these were operated by a rear gunner seated behind the pilot in a long, armoured cockpit compartment. The Il-40 was very heavily armoured, with a resulting weight increase that reduced its performance below acceptable levels; manoeuvrability also left much to be desired, and the aircraft would have been hard pressed to survive in a hostile fighter environment. Several prototypes were built and evaluated in 1953-54, and the best performance figures included a top speed at sea level of 600 mph and a range of 620 miles. So the last of Russia's shturmoviks lapsed into oblivion, its role eclipsed by a new generation of strike fighters, developed in the main from the jet interceptors which, in the early 1950s were enabling the Soviet Air Force to confront its potential NATO adversaries on an equal — and sometimes more favourable — footing.

3. Fighter Development

With the acquisition of the first captured German turbojets at the end of 1944, various Soviet design bureaux were ordered to begin a crash programme aimed at producing operational fighters designed around these engines. The bureaux involved were Mikoyan and Guryevich (Mig), Lavochkin, Sukhoi and Yakovlev, and by the time initial design studies were nearing completion copies of the German engines were already in production, the BMW 003 as the RD-20 and the Jumo 004 as the RD-10.

Each design bureau tackled the problem in its individual fashion, all from a starting point in February 1945. While Mikoyan and Guryevich set about designing a fighter around a pair of BMW 003A engines, Sukhoi adopted a design with twin underslung engines reminiscent of the Messerschmitt 262; Lavochkin came up with an aircraft built around a Jumo 004 engine mounted in a fuselage pod, while Yakovlev opted for an adaptation of their existing and well-proven Yak-3 fighter.

The MiG design was the I-300, the 'I' standing for Istrebitel, or interceptor. Although the aircraft was powered by two engines, mounted side-by-side in the centre fuselage, it was by no means heavy, the loaded weight being in the region of 11,000 lb. The I-300 featured the first tricycle undercarriage installed on a Russian-built aircraft, the narrow-track mainwheels retracting outwards into the wings. Three I-300 prototypes were built, the first of which flew on 24 April 1946 with test pilot Alexei Grinchik at the controls, and during subsequent testing the maximum speed was gradually pushed up to 566 mph. Severe vibration was experienced in the higher speed range, and it took a considerable time before the cause was pinpointed: the jet efflux, exhausting under the tail, was buffeting the fireproof sheathing of the rear fuselage undersurface and setting up resonance throughout the airframe.

A month after the I-300's first flight, Grinchik was carrying out a high-speed, low-level run in the first prototype when the aircraft suddenly developed an uncontrollable pitch and dived into the ground, killing its pilot. Grinchik's place was taken by Mark Gallai who, together with Grigori Shianov, continued the flight test programme with the other two aircraft. Both pilots experienced a high workload, for the I-300 was a difficult and often unpleasant aircraft to fly — many of the problems resulting from the haste with which the prototypes had been completed. On one occasion, Gallai almost came to grief when, during a high-speed run at 0.8M, the nose of the aircraft pitched down violently; the pilot reduced power and managed to restore full control, but after landing it was found that both the tailplane and elevator had become distorted. In all probability, Gallai had experienced the phenomenon that had killed his colleague Grinchik. On another occasion, Gallai was carrying out a high-speed run at 2,000 feet when the I-300 virtually went out of control; fortunately the nose went

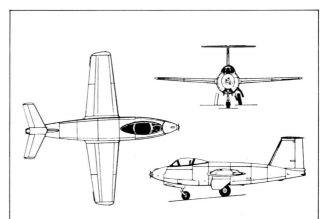

Designation: MiG I-270 (ZH).
Role: Target defence interceptor.
Engine: One RD-2M-3V bi-fuel liquid rocket motor.
Span: No data available.
Length: No data available.
Weight: Loaded 9,228 lb.
Crew: 1.
Service ceiling: 49,215 ft.
Range: No data available (endurance 9 mins. 3 secs.).
Max speed: 620 mph.
Weapons (proposed): Two 23-mm NR-23 cannon.

YAKOVLEV YAK-19. Yakovlev's Yak-19 was the first of that bureau's jet designs after the Yak-15 and served as the prototype of a more refined version, the Yak-25.

up instead of down and the aircraft gained several thousand feet of altitude, vibrating badly, with the pilot practically helpless in the cockpit. Gallai reduced power and restored partial control, looking back to check the tail; to his dismay he saw that the port tailplane was no longer there, and the starboard tailplane was badly distorted. To make matters worse, fuel from a ruptured tank was seeping into the cockpit and there was a severe fire risk. Gallai would have been quite justified in baling out, but he was a test pilot of the highest calibre. Cutting both engines, he managed to bring the aircraft back for a dead-stick landing.

Despite its vicissitudes, the I-300, with a redesigned nose to accommodate one 37-mm and two 23-mm cannon, was ordered into production for the Soviet Air

Force as the MiG-9, and was the first Russian jet type to reach squadron service, the first deliveries being made in December 1946. Although technically far from reliable, it provided Russian fighter pilots with valuable experience in jet operation.

The MiG-9's contemporary, the Yakovlev Yak-15, entered service with the Soviet Air Force early in 1947 and does not really merit treatment here, for it proved to be a successful aircraft. The prototype did not differ greatly from production machines, and the Yak-15 was produced in far greater quantities than the MiG-9. Although, like the MiG-9, the Yak-15 was an interim fighter that bridged the gap until the advent of more modern types, it was more manoeuvrable than the Vampire or the F-80 Shooting Star and became the first

YAKOVLEV YAK-30. *The Yak-30 was built to the same specification as the MiG-15, but during comparative trials the Mikoyan fighter emerged as the better design all round.*

jet fighter to be exported to the Soviet Union's satellite countries. It was followed into service by the Yak-17, a more modern variant with an uprated RD-10A turbojet, a tricycle undercarriage and redesigned vertical tail surfaces.

While striving to bring the MiG-9 and Yak-15 to production standard, Mikoyan and Yakovlev were also studying other fighter projects which, in the event, were not adopted. In 1946, Mikoyan built and tested a rocket-powered target defence interceptor, the I-270 (ZH), which was based on the design of the wartime Messerschmitt Me 263A rocket fighter project. Whereas the Me 263A had been a swept-wing design, however, the I-270 employed an upswept wing of thin section and slightly swept horizontal tail surfaces, mounted T-fashion on top of the vertical surfaces. The Russian aircraft was powered by an RD-2M-3V bi-fuel rocket motor, which was a slightly modified version of the Walter HWK 509C; it was equipped with main and cruising chambers, the former giving a maximum endurance of 4 minutes 15 seconds and the latter 9 minutes 3 seconds. Under test, the I-270 reached an altitude of 32,810 feet in 2.37 minutes, and 49,215 feet in 3.03 minutes. Maximum speed was 620 mph, and the proposed armament was two 23-mm cannon. However, other warplane designs offered greater flexibility and turbojet engines greater reliability than the rocket motors of the day, and the project was abandoned.

In the late 1940s Yakovlev built the prototypes of three single-seat fighter designs, none of which came to fruition. The first, in 1947, was the Yak-19, a simple and uncomplicated aircraft with unswept flying surfaces and powered by an RD-500 (Derwent) turbojet. The Yak-19, in fact, served as the prototype of a more refined design, the Yak-25; this had a similar powerplant, but was fitted with swept tail surfaces and wingtip drop tanks. The Yak-25 was intended to fulfil the same tactical role as the Republic F-84 Thunderjet, but it had extremely disappointing performance figures and was consequently abandoned, its designation being allocated to a later —

and vastly more successful — fighter type, the Yak-25 Flashlight.

The other Yakovlev jet fighter design of the 1940s was the Yak-30, a swept-wing fighter built to the same specification as the MiG-15 — and by which it was eclipsed. Powered by an RD-45 turbojet, the Yak-30 flew in 1948; maximum speed was 640 mph, service ceiling 49,500 feet and range 900 miles. The Yak-30 underwent comparative trials with the MiG-15, from which the Mikoyan fighter emerged as the better aircraft on all counts.

In the original race to produce a jet fighter in 1945-6, Mikoyan had been ordered to design an aircraft around two Junkers Jumo 004A turbojets; the result, as we have seen, was the MiG-9, the first jet fighter to enter Russian service. Another designer with the same brief was Pavel Sukhoi, whose SU-2 ground-attack aircraft had filled a vital gap during the war until the service debut of the Il-2 but whose subsequent designs, although often advanced and sometimes aerodynamically better than others which achieved production status, had laboured under a series of misfortunes — often caused by the lack of suitable engines — and had consequently never met with the success they deserved. Nevertheless, Sukhoi was one of Russia's most experienced aeronautical engineers, and it was logical that his expertise should be put to good use in the jet fighter development programme.

Sukhoi approached the design of his first jet fighter, the Su-9, with a good deal of caution, preferring to adopt a similar configuration to that of the Messerschmitt Me 262 — although the aircraft that emerged was by no means a copy of the German fighter. The Su-9's engines were placed in underwing nacelles and the aircraft had an Me 262-style cockpit, but there the resemblance ended. The flying surfaces were less angular and the wings were unswept, while the fuselage was deeper and slimmer than the 262's. The only aspect — apart from the engines — which might be said to have been copied from the Me 262 was the tricycle undercarriage, and even here there were distinct differences.

SUKHOI SU-9. The Sukhoi Su-9 had the same configuration as the Messerschmitt Me 262, but was by no means a copy of the German fighter. Although a much better aircraft than the MiG-9, it was not adopted.

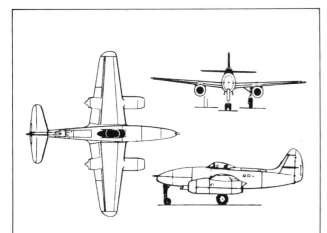

Designation: Sukhoi Su-9.
Role: Jet interceptor.
Engines: Two RD-10 turbojets.
Span: 36 ft 11 in.
Length: 34 ft 7 in.
Weight loaded: 13,395 lb.
Crew: 1.
Service ceiling: 41,174 ft.
Range: 708 miles.
Max speed: 526 mph at sea level.
Weapons: Three 23-mm cannon.

compensated for this, and it also carried more ammunition. In view of the MiG-9's appalling safety record, there seemed no reason why the Sukhoi aircraft should not have been selected in preference.

But there was a reason, and it was an extraordinary one. It appears that other Soviet designers, eager to have their own aircraft accepted, 'ganged up' on Sukhoi at a conference in 1946 and persuaded Josef Stalin that any machine that resembled the Messerschmitt 262 would be unacceptable because the German fighter had proved dangerous to fly. Stalin was by no means an aviation expert, but he had seen photographs of the Me 262 — and possibly a captured example as well — and to his mind the Su-9 was sufficiently like it to be seen in an

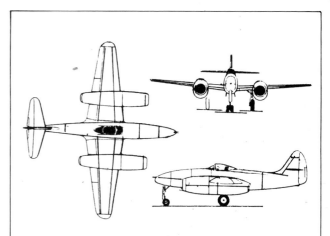

Designation: Sukhoi Su-11.
Role: Jet interceptor.
Engines: Two TR-1 turbojets.
Span: 38 ft. 11 in.
Length: 34 ft. 7 in.
Weight: Loaded 14,060 lb.
Crew: 1.
Service ceiling: 39,600 ft.
Range: 1,250 miles.
Max speed: 531 mph at sea level.
Weapons: Three 23-mm cannon; 1,000 lbs. of bombs.

Like the MiG-9, the Su-9 was armed with one 37-mm and two 23-mm cannon, and for short take-off a pair of solid-fuel rockets could be attached under the fuselage. The Su-9 was generally a more refined design than the MiG aircraft; among other items, it featured a compressed-air ejection seat, modelled on German equipment, and a braking parachute. The aircraft flew for the first time in 1946, some months after the MiG-9, and the performance figures for the two aircraft were not dissimilar. The Su-9's maximum speed at sea level was 526 mph, rising to 559 mph at 16,400 feet, service ceiling was 41,174 feet and range 708 miles at 408 mph. Although the Su-9 was slightly inferior to the MiG-9 at high altitude, therefore, its range performance adequately unfavourable light. In all probability, Stalin's concern was not so much for safety but for a desire to show the world that the Soviet regime was capable of producing modern aircraft without being accused of copying those of its former enemy. So, after one brief appearance at the Tushino air display on 3 August, 1947, development of the Su-9 was abandoned.

So was a further development, the Su-11, which was powered by two RD-500 Derwents and flew late in 1947. This aircraft featured a pressurized cockpit and was intended for the close-support role, provision being made for a 1,000 lb bomb load.

Following this disappointment, Sukhoi now pinned his hopes on the development of two advanced jet fighter projects, the Su-15 and Su-17. By 1948, the Russians — again relying heavily on German technology — had developed an AI radar known as Izumrud (Emerald) which was intended to equip a new generation of all-weather fighter aircraft. Sukhoi's response to the specification was the Su-15, which was also known as the Samolyot P. Powered by two RD-45 (Nene) turbojets, the aircraft had a mid-mounted wing with a leading-edge sweep of 37 degrees, the twin engines being mounted one above the other in a deep centre fuselage and exhausting below the fuselage aft of the wing trailing edge. The AI scanner was housed in a small radome situated above the nose air intake, and armament was two 37-mm cannon mounted one on either side of the nose. With a loaded weight of 23,000 lb the Su-15 was a very heavy aircraft; nevertheless, its designers estimated that it would have a maximum speed of 641 mph, a service ceiling of 45,930 feet, and the ability to reach 32,800 feet in 6½ minutes. These figures were never proven, because the Su-15 disintegrated following severe vibration on an early high-speed run, the pilot ejecting, and no further prototypes were built.

Work continued in 1949 on the Su-17 supersonic fighter project, which was to have been powered by a Mikulin TR-3 axial-flow turbojet and had wings swept at 50 degrees. Estimated performance figures included speeds of 1.08M at 36,090 feet and 1.02M at sea level, with a service ceiling of 50,850 feet. A novel feature of the Su-17 was that the fuselage nose, including the cockpit, was intended to be blasted clear of the rest of the airframe by

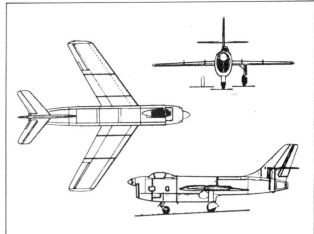

Designation: Sukhoi Su-15.
Role: Jet interceptor.
Engines: Two RD-45 (Rolls-Royce Nene) turbojets.
Span: 42 ft. 6 in.
Length: 50 ft. 11 in.
Weight: Loaded 23,000 lb.
Crew: 1.
Service ceiling: 45,930 ft.
Range: 755 miles (est.).
Max speed: 641 mph (est.).
Weapons: Two 37-mm cannon.

explosive charges in an emergency and stabilised by a drogue, the pilot subsequently ejecting in normal fashion. By this time, however, Sukhoi had fallen out of favour with the Ministry for Aeronautical Development and Production, and in 1949, on orders from Moscow, his factory was closed down. All work on the Su-17, the airframe of which was partly complete, was brought to a halt and the aircraft broken up for scrap. Despite these misfortunes, Pavel Sukhoi was to bounce back into the limelight of Soviet aircraft design, as we shall see later.

The first venture into the jet fighter field by the other leading Soviet designer, Semyon A. Lavochkin, was the La-150, which was powered by a single RD-10 (Jumo-

SUKHOI SU-15. The twin-engined Sukhoi Su-15, also known as the Samolyot-P, was fitted with Izumrud (Emerald) AI radar. The sole prototype was destroyed during flight testing.

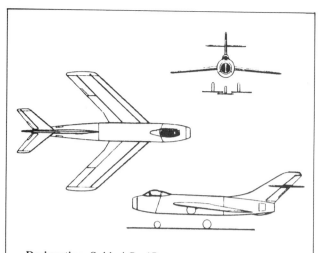

Designation: Sukhoi Su-17.
Role: Jet interceptor.
Engine: One TR-3 turbojet.
Span: 32 ft. 9 in.
Length: 50 ft. 3 in.
Weight: Loaded 1,553 lb.
Crew: 1.
Service ceiling: 50,850 ft. (est.).
Range: 675 miles (est.).
Max speed: 1.02M at sea level (est.).
Weapons: Two 37-mm cannon.

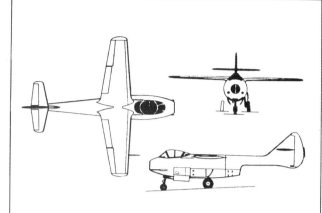

Designation: Lavochkin La-150.
Role: Jet interceptor.
Engine: One RD-10 (Jumo 004A) turbojet.
Span: 27 ft. 9 in.
Length: 31 ft.
Weight: Loaded 7,477 lb.
Crew: 1.
Service ceiling: 41,000 ft.
Range: 315 miles.
Max speed: 500 mph at 16,400 ft.
Weapons: Two 23-mm NS cannon.

004A) turbojet. The aircraft, which was flown for the first time in September 1946 by test pilot A. A. Popov, featured a 'pod and boom' design, with unswept shoulder-mounted wings and the tricycle undercarriage mounted in the lower fuselage. Armament comprised two 23-mm NS cannon, one on either side of the nose. Two prototypes were built, and these reached a maximum speed of 500 mph at 16,400 feet; service ceiling was 41,000 feet. Three more aircraft were completed and fitted with uprated RD-10F engines, being re-designated La-150M, but the flight characteristics of the Lavochkin design left much to be desired and further development was abandoned in April 1947 — which did not prevent the Russians from displaying one of the aircraft at Tushino in

August to foster the impression that it was in production for the Soviet Air Force.

In the meantime, Lavochkin had also begun work on three more fighter prototypes, the La-152, La-154 and La-156, all of which featured a configuration that was closer in style to that of Yakovlev's successful Yak-15. The fuselage undercarriage arrangement was retained, but the wing was mounted at mid-point and the cockpit was positioned well aft, over the trailing edge. However, although the handling characteristics of these three aircraft were somewhat better than those of the La-150, performance was actually poorer, and they were used only for experimental flying.

By the middle of 1947, Russian designers were

LAVOCHKIN LA-156. The La-156, developed from the La-150, featured a configuration similar to that of Yakovlev's successful Yak-15.

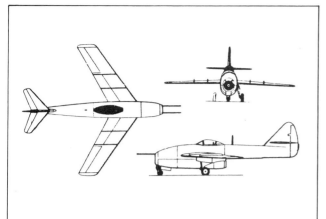

Designation: Lavochkin La-160.
Role: Jet Interceptor.
Engine: One RD-10A turbojet.
Span: 29 ft. 6 in.
Length: 33 ft.
Weight: Loaded 13,398 lb.
Crew: 1.
Service ceiling: 36,300 ft.
Range: 315 miles.
Max speed: 652 mph at 18,700 ft.
Weapons: Two 37-mm NS cannon.

the La-174TK, the 'TK' denoting Tonkoe Krylo, or Thin Wing. Apart from the wing design, the main difference between this aircraft and the La-152, La-154 and La-156 was that it was powered by an RD-500 (Derwent) engine and carried an armament of three NS-23 cannon. The La-174TK flew early in 1948, and during trials reached speeds of 603 mph at sea level and 599 mph at 9,840 feet.

The La-174TK was, in fact, something of an anachronism, and contributed nothing to Soviet aeronautical knowledge except to underline the fact that the straight, thin wing offered no advantages over the swept planform. Before the La-174TK even flew, Lavochkin was already studying two infinitely more advanced jet fighter designs, produced to the same

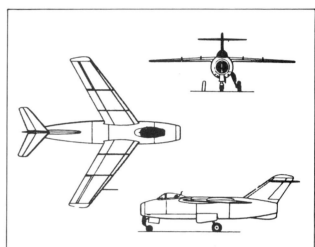

Designation: Lavochkin La-168.
Role: Jet interceptor.
Engine: One NII-1 (RD-500) turbojet.
Span: 31 ft. 3 in.
Length: 34 ft. 9 in.
Weight: Loaded 14,560 lb.
Crew: 1.
Service ceiling: 48,000 ft.
Range: 796 miles.
Max speed: 670 mph at 16,400 ft.
Weapons: Two 37-mm NS cannon.

overcoming an early aversion to the use of sweepback (an aversion that was shared by their British and French counterparts), and Lavochkin decided to fit the basic La-152 fuselage with swept flying surfaces. The result was the La-160, which had a wing swept at the optimum 35 degrees and an armament of two NS-37 cannon. The aircraft flew for the first time in 1947 and was claimed to be the first post-war swept-wing jet fighter, but in fact it was used purely for aerodynamic research and never went into production. During flight trials, it reached a speed of 652 mph at 18,700 feet and yielded a great deal of information that was subsequently applied to the design of more advanced swept-wing jets.

The last of Lavochkin's straight-wing jet designs was

LAVOCHKIN LA-174TK. The La-174TK was fitted with a new thin wing. During flight trials, it reached a speed of 603 mph at sea level.

LAVOCHKIN LA-168. The La-168 was Lavochkin's first really successful jet design. The second prototype, fitted with a Rolls-Royce Derwent, was re-designated La-174.

specification as the highly successful MiG-15. The first of these was the La-168, which was intended to be powered by an RD-10 turbojet, but when the Lavochkin team discovered that the MiG design, which weighed about the same as their own, was to be fitted with a much more powerful Nene engine derivative they realised that the La-168's chances of success were very slender indeed by comparison. Lavochkin therefore set about building a second prototype, similar in configuration to the La-168 but powered by the production version of the RD-500 Derwent. Somewhat confusingly, this aircraft was given the designation La-174.

Meanwhile, the La-168 was completed with an NII-1 engine, which was the pre-production version of the RD-

Designation: Lavochkin La-190.
Role: Jet interceptor.
Engine: One Lyulka AL-5 turbojet.
Span: 32 ft. 7 in.
Length: 53 ft. 11 in.
Weight: loaded: 20,700 lb.
Crew: 1.
Service ceiling: 51,180 ft.
Range: 715 miles.
Max speed: 750 mph at 16,400 ft.
Weapons: Two 37-mm NS cannon.

500. There had been some delay in the completion of this aircraft, because Lavochkin wished to assess results from test flying the La-160 before committing himself fully to the swept-wing formula, and this was to have an adverse effect, for by the time the La-168 flew in the summer of 1948 the MiG-15 had already been under test for six months and, despite the crash of the first prototype, was working its way through the State Acceptance Trials with remarkably few major snags.

The prototype of Lavochkin's La-174 flew shortly after the La-168 and, as the La-15, went on to enter Soviet Air Force service in 1949. However, its performance proved inadequate for the interceptor role and only a few ground-attack units were equipped with it, the MiG-15 becoming the standard Soviet interceptor of the late 1940s. Nevertheless, the La-15 continued in service until the late 1950s, mainly as a combat trainer, and a developed version, the La-176, was evolved from it to meet a specification for a transonic fighter. The La-176 first flew in December 1948, powered by an RD-45F turbojet, and on 26 December, flown by Colonel I. V. Fedorov, it became the first Soviet aircraft to exceed Mach 1.0 in a dive from 32,810 feet to 19,685 feet. Flight testing continued and the La-176 was re-engined with the more powerful Klimov VK-1 engine, but it was another Mikoyan design — the MiG-17 — that eventually met the Soviet Air Force requirement for a second generation swept-wing jet fighter.

The success of the MiG-17 also eliminated a Yakolev design, the Yak-50, just as the MiG-15 had eliminated its predecessor, the Yak-30. Powered by a Klimov VK-1A turbojet, the Yak-50 flew in 1950 and reached a maximum speed of 718 mph during its trials; its service ceiling was 54,700 feet. Generally, the Yak-50's performance was higher than the MiG-17's, but the handling qualities of the Mikoyan aircraft were far better and so the MiG-17 was selected for production.

It was a Mikoyan aircraft, too — the MiG-19 — that was selected for production as the Soviet Air Force's first supersonic fighter, eliminating other designs submitted by rival bureaux. Among these was the Lavochkin La-190, which was powered by a Lyulka AL-5 turbojet and featured the world's first zer-track undercarriage, the twin-wheel main unit being positioned directly under the

MIKOYAN I-320. Mikoyan's I-320 (R) all-weather fighter design was based on the MiG-15. However, its flight characteristics were poor and it was abandoned.

centre fuselage. The aircraft was fitted with a conventional nosewheel and wingtip outriggers. The wing was swept at 55 degrees, and a delta tailplane was mounted at slightly above fin mid-point. The La-190 first flew in February 1951, and during trials reached a top speed of 750 mph at 16,400 feet; its service ceiling was 51,180 feet and range 715 miles. The fighter carried an armament of two 37-mm NS cannon. Flight trials showed the La-190 to be heavy and underpowered, and further development was abandoned.

One of the Soviet Air Force's main preoccupations, in 1950, was to bring a true all-weather fighter into service. A specification written around this requirement had been issued two years earlier, and the leading Soviet design bureaux had responded to it; Sukhoi, as we have already seen, produced the Su-15, which broke up in mid-air. The main problem encountered by the designers was that existing powerplants were inadequate to compensate for the weight increase that went with the installation of bulky AI radar equipment and the requirement that the proposed fighter had to be a twin-engined machine.

The main contenders were Mikoyan, Lavochkin and Yakovlev. Mikoyan's design, the single-seat I-320 (R), was powered by two VK-1 turbojets and first flew in 1949; it was based on the MiG-15, but the engine installation resulted in a bulky, ungainly aircraft with poor handling characteristics and even worse visibility for the pilot, whose forward view was badly obscured by a long nose and radome. Lavochkin's design, the La-200A, was a better proposition from several points of view, but

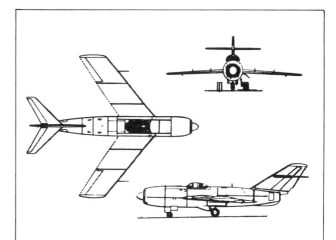

Designation: Lavochkin La-200A
Role: All-weather interceptor.
Engines: Two Klimov VK-1 turbojets.
Span: 42 ft. 7 in.
Length: 54 ft. 9 in.
Weight: Loaded 22,873 lb.
Crew: 2.
Service ceiling: 59,700 ft.
Range: 1,250 miles.
Max speed: 660 mph at 16,400 ft.
Weapons: Three 37-mm NS cannon.

LAVOCHKIN LA-200B. The La-200B was designed to the same requirement as the Yak-25 Flashlight, to which it proved inferior. With its massive radome, it was one of the ugliest fighter aircraft ever built.

suffered from the same engine arrangement as the I-320(R). In both cases, the VK-1 engines were fed via a common nose air intake, but the engines were installed in tandem, the first exhausting under the fuselage and the second from the tail, and this necessitated some complex ducting that resulted in an inordinately large fuselage. A central air intake cone housed the La-200A's Izumrud radar and the fighter was a two-seater, the pilot and radar observer seated side by side. The La-200A had a fuselage-mounted undercarriage and carried an armament of three 37-mm cannon, which contributed to the high all-up weight of 22,873 lb. Like the I-320(R), the La-200 flew in 1949, and during trials reached a maximum speed of 660 mph at 16,400 feet; service ceiling was 59,700 feet. Neither aircraft underwent extensive operational trials, because in 1950 a developed version of the Izumrud AI radar was successfully installed in a two-seat MiG-15 variant known as the SP-5; both MiG-15s and MiG-17s were subsequently equipped with AI.

These variants, however, did not meet an urgent requirement for an all-weather fighter fitted with a long-range search radar, and a specification for such an aircraft was issued in November 1951. Lavochkin set about modifying their La-200A to carry a new radar scanner in a lengthened fuselage nose, and the result was the La-200B, one of the ugliest fighter aircraft ever flown. The massive radome ruled out a single nose air intake, so the engines were fed by three ducts, one on either side of the nose and one underneath it. Bulky auxiliary fuel tanks were fitted under the wings, and to compensate for the extra weight — the aircraft now weighed 24,750 lbs loaded — the undercarriage was strengthened. The La-200B, however, was greatly inferior to the other main contender, the Yakovlev Yak-25 Flashlight; this aircraft first flew in 1952 and was ordered into full production for the Soviet Air Force, entering service with a development unit in 1955 and becoming fully operational the following year.

In comparison with Western combat types that were making their appearance in the early 1950s, Soviet designs appeared crude, lacking the elegance and refinement that were the hallmarks of a successful aircraft. But Soviet designers were learning quickly, and before the end of the decade the Soviet Air Force would have at its disposal some of the most effective military aircraft in the world. In 1955, after a slow and uncertain entry into the jet age, the Russian design bureaux were poised to make a great leap forward.

Chapter Four

France: A Phoenix from the Ashes, 1945-55

At the end of the war in Europe, France's aircraft industry — which, in 1939, had begun to produce superlative new combat aircraft which were the equals of any in the world, but in numbers too few and too late to stem the German Blitzkrieg — lay in ruins, its factories destroyed or dismantled, its designers scattered far and wide. In seeking to establish a leading role in post-war aviation, therefore, France was faced with a mammoth twofold task. The first priority was an industrial one, to rebuild the factories and reassemble the design bureaux; the second was of a purely technical nature, involving the design and production of new combat types to meet the demands of the Armée de l'Air in the jet age.

The second priority was much harder to achieve than the first. Although some French designers had made studies of jet aircraft projects in secret during the occupation, they lagged far behind the Germans and the Allies in the field, from the viewpoint of both airframe and engine design, and at the war's end, even with the knowledge that turbojet-powered aircraft were the only answer to meeting future high-performance requirements, some designers persisted in launching new piston-engined projects that resulted only in a waste of time and dissipation of resources.

One of the main problems that confronted the French designers was the acquisition of suitable turbojet engines. Indigenous studies had been carried out in France since 1939 by various companies, including the Société Rateau, which had designed a primitive turbojet called the SRA-1, and the Société de Construction et d'Equipements Mécaniques pour l'Aviation, whose design was designated TGA-1. The initials stood for Turbo Groupe d'Aviation, which name was enterprisingly altered to read Turbo Group d'Autorail to fool the Occupation authorities. Both these studies, however, were carried out in complete ignorance of parallel work that was going on in Britain and Germany, and nothing ever came of them.

A third company, Turbomeca, also embarked on a programme of jet engine design in the closing months of the war, and exhibited a model of a prototype engine at the 1946 Salon d'Aeronautique. The engine was to have developed an estimated seven tons of thrust and was to have been about 15 feet long, with a diameter of 4½ feet; it was to have been installed in a fighter project, the NC 260, but this never progressed beyond the design stage. Nevertheless, Turbomeca's embryo engine launched the company on a long and successful career.

It was clear, in 1946, that French turbojet design was not going to provide an immediate answer to the problem. However, two other options remained open, the first of which was to develop existing German turbojets. The engine selected was the BMW 109-003, an axial-flow turbojet that stemmed from original design work carried out at Spandau by the Bramo Company in 1938. A prototype engine was tested in 1940, by which time Bramo had been taken over by BMW, and two of the

first production batch were used to power the Messerschmitt Me 262V-1. Series-production 109-003-A2s also powered the Heinkel He 162 and Arado Ar 234. In early post-war France, development work on the 109-003 was undertaken by a team led by Dr. H. Oestrich and composed of technical personnel who had worked at the Atelier Technique Aeronautique Rickenbach, a BMW plant installed near Lake Constance during the war. The factory's initials gave the new engine its name: Atar.

Production Atar 101s, however, would not be available before 1948, and so the French engineers had to exercise the second option, which was to build British turbojets under licence. In 1946, therefore, Hispano-Suiza signed a contract with Rolls-Royce for the licence production of the Nene 101 and 102 engines, and it was the latter which in the event, was to power France's first generation of jet combat aircraft.

Yet it would be some time before the first Nenes came off the French production line, and in the meantime French designers were forced to make do with German Junkers Jumo 109-004 turbojets to power their early experimental machines. By this time, French engineers and aircrew had acquired a limited amount of jet experience with the aid of three Me 262s, which had been assembled by SNCASA and delivered to the Flight Test

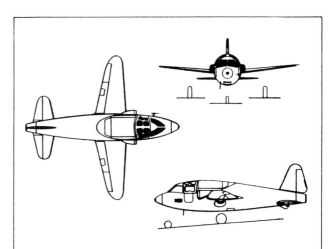

Designation: Sud-Ouest SO. 6000 Triton.
Role: Turbojet-powered research aircraft.
Engine: One 4,850 lb.s.t. Rolls-Royce Nene turbojet.
Span: 32 ft. 8 in.
Length: 34 ft. 4 in.
Weight: Loaded 10,032 lb.
Crew: 1.
Service ceiling: 39,360 ft.
Range: 350 miles.
Max Speed: 593 mph at sea level.
Weapons: None.

AEROCENTRE NC 1080. The Aerocentre NC 1080, which first flew on 29 July 1949, was another unsuccessful French naval strike fighter. Like the NC 1071, its powerplant was the Rolls-Royce Nene engine. (Musée de l'Air).

Centre at Bretigny; the first one had flown on 16 June 1945, and subsequent test flying had revealed all too harshly the shortcomings of the Jumo 004 engines on which the French design bureaux were now forced to rely.

It was a Jumo 004 that powered France's first experimental jet aircraft, the SO.6000 Triton, which flew for the first time on 11 November 1946 with test pilot Daniel Rastel at the controls, and also the Arsenal VG-70, which flew on 23 June 1948. Other experimental jets were powered by Rolls-Royce Derwent engines, purchased directly from the UK; these were the SO M-2, a flying scale model of a larger project, and the twin-jet Nord 1.601, which had originally been intended to have a pair of Rateau SRA-1s. When Rolls-Royce Nenes became available, they were earmarked to power a trio of naval fighters — the Aerocentre NC 1080, Arsenal VG-90 and Nord 2200 — as well as a twin-jet naval strike aircraft, the NC 1071. Nenes were also to have powered several land-based types: the SO 6020 Espadon fighter, the twin-jet SE 2400 attack aircraft, and the SO 4000 and NC 270 twin-jet bombers. In the event, only one early Nene-powered French design ever achieved series production; this was the Dassault MD 450 Ouragan, the first French jet fighter to be ordered in quantity.

Of all the early French designs, with the exception of the Ouragan, the most promising was undoubtedly the NC 270, which — had it reached fruition — would have been the contemporary of the English Electric Canberra, the B-45 Tornado and the Ilyushin Il-28. The NC 270 was

AEROCENTRE NC 1080. (Musée de l'Air).

designed by a government department, 'Guerre et Transport' — roughly the equivalent of Britain's Ministry of Supply — under the direction of M. Robin, and the aircraft that gradually emerged on the drawing board was very elegant indeed, with a circular-section fuselage, slightly swept wings and tail surfaces with the tailplane mounted on top of the rudder, and the two Nene engine nacelles mounted flush with the fuselage sides at the wing roots. The aircraft was to carry two crew, a pilot and navigator, the latter also being responsible for the operation of a TV-controlled tail turret of German origin and armed with four 15-mm cannon. A five-ton bomb load was to be carried.

The flight characteristics of the NC 270, the prototype of which slowly took shape in the factory of the SNCAC at Billancourt, were to be tested with the help of two flying scale models: the NC 271-01, which was a glider, and the NC 271-02, which was to be powered by a liquid-fuel rocket motor. The NC 271-01, first revealed publicly at the 1946 Salon, was of mixed wood-and-metal construction and was a quarter-scale model of the prototype bomber. It was a single-seater, and in an emergency the entire nose section could be jettisoned with the pilot inside. To test the separation system, several test flights were made with a mock-up of the nose section suspended under a Handley Page Halifax.

The NC 271-01 glider version took to the air for the first time in November 1948, mounted on the back of an SE-161 Languedoc (F-BCUT), and made eleven more captive flights in the next three months. Its first free flight was made on 28 January 1949, with Claude Dellys at the controls; it lasted for seven minutes, the little aircraft reaching a maximum gliding speed of 140 mph.

Meanwhile, at Billancourt, the second NC 271 had been built. Its rocket motor, a Walter HWK 109-509A, was taken from a Messerschmitt Me 163 Komet, and was to have boosted the NC 271-02 to an estimated maximum speed of 560 mph, slightly more than would have been achieved by the full-size bomber. The latter, meanwhile, was nearing completion; the fuselage was intact, with wings and engines mounted and tail fin in place, while the outer wing sections and tailplane were also complete and awaiting final assembly. The first flight was scheduled for September 1949, after the rocket-powered model had completed its test programme.

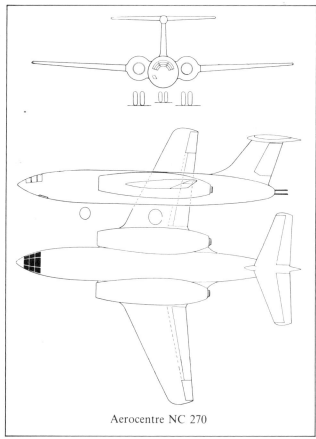

Aerocentre NC 270

The NC 271-02, complete with rocket motor, was taken to Orleans-Bricy in May 1949, where the plan was to mount it on the back of a Heinkel He 274 bomber and launch it at an altitude of 33,000 feet. While preparations for this flight were under way, however, SNCAC went into liquidation, with the result that both the NC 271 models were scrapped. So was the full-size NC 270, which was then 85 per cent complete.

The other jet light bomber design, the SNCA du Sud-Ouest SO.4000, was powered by two Rolls-Royce/Hispano-Suiza Nene 102 engines, mounted side by side in the centre fuselage. This aircraft, too, was preceded by two scale models, the SO M-1 and M-2. The first of these, a glider, was registered F-WFDJ and was aerodynamically tested on a rig mounted on the back of the He 274; it was subsequently transferred to Languedoc F-BCUT at Orleans-Bricy and made its first gliding flight on 26 September 1949 from a height of 16,400 feet. Before that, however, the SO M-2 (F-WFDK) had also flown on 13 April 1949, powered by a Rolls-Royce Derwent turbojet. Both scale models were piloted by Jacques Guignard, Sud-Ouest's chief test pilot, and in May 1950 he reached a speed of 621 mph while flying the M-2.

The SO.4000 bomber prototype was rolled out on 5 March, 1950. Registered F-WBBL, it was generally similar in configuration to the scale models. The two crew members were seated in tandem in a small pressurized cockpit in the extreme forward fuselage, which was of large oval section. The low aspect ratio wing was swept 31 degrees at quarter-chord and was mounted in high-mid position at mid-point on the fuselage, above the weapons bay, and it was planned that production aircraft should also carry an armament of two remotely-controlled cannon, mounted in wingtip barbettes. The undercarriage was complex, having four mainwheels, each with independent levered-suspension legs, and a tall single nosewheel member. The undercarriage, in fact, proved to be too fragile, because it collapsed during taxying trials on 23 April 1950, causing extensive damage.

Repaired and with a strengthened undercarriage, F-WBBL flew for the first time on 15 March, 1951, with Daniel Rastel at the controls. The aircraft proved to be seriously underpowered and unstable, and it never flew again. Sud-Aviation subsequently turned its attention to meeting a French Air Staff specification, issued in July 1951 and calling for an aircraft capable of fulfilling three separate tasks: all-weather interception, close support and medium-and high-level bombing. This was to emerge as the SO.4050 Vautour, which first flew in October 1952 powered by Atar 101B turbojets.

It was Sud-Ouest, too, who were responsible for the design and manufacture of France's first post-war jet fighter, the SO.6020 Espadon (Swordfish). Its designer was Lucien Servanty, and the first prototype, the SO

NC 271-01. The NC 271-01 glider scale model of the proposed NC 270 bomber mounted on its Languedoc parent aircraft.

(Musée de l'Air).

SUD-AVIATION (SUD-OUEST) SO-4000. *First flown on 16 March 1951, the SO.4000 was France's first jet bomber design. A two-seater aircraft, it was powered by two 5,000 lbs. thrust Hispano-Suiza Nene 102 turbojets mounted side-by-side in the fuselage.*

6020-01, (F-WFDI) flew for the first time on 12 November 1948, powered by a Rolls-Royce Nene 102 turbojet fed through a ventral air intake under the rear fuselage. This intake arrangement caused many problems, and the second prototype, the SO.6020-02 (F-WFDV), which flew on 15 September 1949, featured flush air intakes under the wing trailing edges. This aircraft was the first to carry a full armament of six 20-mm cannon. A third prototype, the SO.6020-03, (F-WFRG) flew on 28 December 1949 and was fitted with a long ventral air intake, a fairing at the rear of which housed a SEPR 251 liquid-fuel rocket motor; it was redesignated SO.6025 shortly afterwards. The fourth prototype, the SO.6021 (F-WFKZ), flew on 3 September 1950 and featured a lighter structure, servo controls and an increased wing area. In 1952, the SO.6020-01 first prototype was retrospectively fitted with a ventral air intake and a Turbomeca Marboré turbojet was also installed at each wingtip, while -02 was fitted with a SEPR 251 rocket motor, fed via wingtip fuel tanks. In its new guise it was redesignated SO.6026, and on 15 December 1953 it reached Mach 1.0 in level flight over Istres. By this time, however, Dassault's Ouragan and Mystère II fighters, powered by the Atar 101, were coming off the production line, and further development of the Espadon was abandoned.

The other early Nene-powered land-based design, the Sud-Est SE.2400 attack aircraft, developed into the SE.2410 Grognard ('Grumbler', a name bestowed upon the soldiers of Napoleon's Old Guard). The prototype, the SE.2410 Grognard I, first flew on 30 April 1950, powered by two Hispano-Suiza Nene 101s mounted one above the other in the rear fuselage and with wings swept at an angle of 47 degrees. The aircraft reached a maximum speed of 645 mph at 4,920 feet. The second prototype, the SE.2415 Grognard II, flew on 14 February 1951 and was a two-seater with a sweepback of 32 degrees. This aircraft attained a maximum speed of 596 mph, but trouble was experienced with tail flutter and then the aircraft was damaged in a belly landing as a result of a false fire warning in the air. While trials with the two prototypes progressed, albeit at a much slower rate than had been anticipated, Sud-Est's designers were working on the details of the production version, which was designated SE.2418 and which was to have been powered by the Rolls-Royce Tay turbojets. The finalised aircraft had an estimated maximum speed of 675 mph at sea level, and armament was to have comprised two 30-mm DEFA cannon and a combination of rockets and bombs. Sud-Ouest's promising Vautour design, however, was adopted to meet the Armée de l'Air's ground attack requirements, and further development of the Grognard was abandoned.

Of the Nene-powered shipboard prototypes, the first to fly was Aerocentre's NC.1071 twin-jet attack aircraft, on 12 October 1948. The pilot was F. Lasne, with M.

SUD-AVIATION (SUD-OUEST) SO-6025 ESPADON. *France's first jet fighter design, the SO Espadon (Swordfish) flew for the first time on 12 November 1948, powered by a 5,000 lbs. thrust Nene 2 turbojet.*

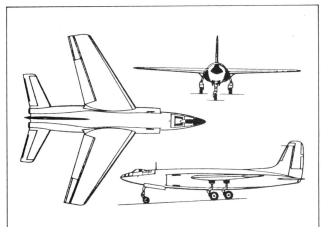

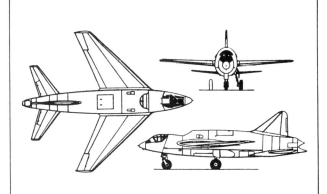

Designation: Sud-Ouest SO.4000.
Role: Light bomber.
Engines: Two 4,983 lb.s.t. Nene 102 turbojets.
Span: 58 ft. 6 in.
Length: 64 ft. 9 in.
Weight: Loaded 48,510 lb.
Crew: 2.
Service ceiling: 42,000 ft. (est.).
Range: 1,200 miles (est.).
Max speed: 528 mph at 29,530 ft. (est.).
Weapons: Two 20-mm cannon in wingtip barbettes (proposed); up to 4,000 lbs of bombs.

Designation: Sud-Est SE.2410 Grognard I.
Role: Ground attack aircraft.
Engines: Two 4,850 lb.s.t. Hispano-Suiza Nene 101 turbojets.
Span: 44 ft. 6½ in.
Length: 50 ft. 6 in.
Weight: Loaded 31,967 lb.
Crew: 1.
Service ceiling: 38,000 ft.
Range: 530 miles.
Max speed: 645 mph at 4,920 ft.
Weapons: Two 30-mm DEFA cannon; various combinations of bombs and RPs.

Blanchard as flight engineer. A sole prototype was produced, and development came to an end when Aerocentre went into voluntary liquidation in the summer of 1949. The company's factory at Bourges was absorbed into the Nord (SNCAN) group, and this company was made responsible for the further development of another Aerocentre design, the NC.1080 single-engined naval fighter, which test pilot Lasne took into the air for the first time on 29 July 1949. The prototype, however, was totally destroyed in a flying accident on 7 April 1950.

Nord's own shipboard fighter design, the Nord 2200,

SUD-AVIATION SE-2410 GROGNARD. Designed as a single-seat ground attack by the SNCA du Sud-Est, the Grognard (Grumbler) prototype flew on 30 April 1950, powered by two 4,850 lbs. thrust Hispano-Suiza Nene 101 turbojets mounted one above the other in the fuselage.

NC 1071. The NC 1071 was a twin-jet naval strike aircraft prototype. Power was provided by Rolls-Royce Nene engines and the aircraft was France's first twin-jet design. First flight was on 12 October 1948. (Musée de l'Air).

made its maiden flight on 19 December 1949. Somewhat resembling the Dassault Mystère II in outline, it was not fitted with folding wings or armament, but incorporated catapult attachment points and arrester gear. As a result of initial flight trials, a servo control system was installed, an AI radar fitted and the vertical tail surfaces enlarged. Testing of the sole prototype continued into 1952, but no production order was placed.

The third post-war naval jet fighter design, the Arsenal VG-90, was a direct development of the VG-70 research aircraft. After the end of the war, the Arsenal de l'Aeronautique had been preoccupied with the development of a piston-engined fighter, the VB-10, which was powered by two Hispano-Suiza 12Z engines mounted in tandem; the prototype flew at Lyon-Bron on 7 July 1945 and, after being taken on charge by the Flight Test Centre at Bretigny in May 1946, it made 144 test flights before 25 March 1948, after which it was dismantled and scrapped. Two more prototypes were built, together with two pre-production aircraft, but an initial order for 200 aircraft, placed in 1945, was reduced to 50 photo-reconnaissance aircraft in the following year

NC 1071. (Musée de l'Air).

NC 1071. (Musée de l'Air).

ARSENAL VG-70. The Arsenal VG-70, one of France's early experimental jet aircraft, was powered by a Junkers Jumo 004 turbojet. (Musée de l'Air).

and this order, too, was cancelled in 1948.

The cancellation of the VB-10, although predictable in view of jet aircraft development, was a severe blow to Arsenal, and the company's hopes were now pinned on the VG-90. The first prototype, the VG-90.01 (F-WFOE) flew on 27 September 1949, but was destroyed in an accident on 25 May the following year, killing its pilot. The second prototype, the VG-90.02, flew in June 1951, incorporating several modifications that included a taller fin. A protracted test programme continued at Melun-Villaroche, but on 21 January 1952 prototype 02 was also destroyed, the pilot being Claude Dellys. These two prototypes, following the pattern of the VG-70, had been of wooden construction, but the third, 03, used metal and was designed to take the Atar 101F turbojet. This aircraft, however, never flew, and its fuselage was used to carry out various aerodynamic tests in the supersonic wind tunnel at Modane-Avrieux. No production order for the VG-90 was ever placed, and the Aeronavale's requirement for a shipboard fighter was eventually filled by the de Havilland Sea Venom, which was built under licence as the Aquilon by SNCASE, and later by the Dassault Etendard IV.

It was Marcel Dassault who won the race to give the Armée de l'Air a series of interceptors that would bring France to technical parity with any other nation in the world during the early 1950s. The Ouragan was designed, built and flown in fourteen months, and thereafter it was a relatively simple step to produce a follow-on aircraft based on the Ouragan's design, but with fully swept flying surfaces. This emerged as the Mystère I, which first flew on 23 February 1951 powered by a Nene 104B, and it was followed by two further prototypes designated Mystère IIA, powered by Tay 250 turbojets. Three pre-production machines were also Tay-powered, but the remainder were fitted with the Atar 101; this engine also powered the production aircraft, which entered Armée de l'Air service as the Mystère IIC.

A two-seat all-weather version, the Mystère III, was flown on 18 July 1953 and featured lateral air intakes to make room in the nose for AI radar equipment, but only

one prototype was built and was later used for ejection seat trials.

Development of a more advanced interceptor, the Mystère IV, proceeded in parallel with that of the II, and structural troubles with the latter led to it being overtaken on the production line by the Mystère IVA, 325 of which were ordered in April 1953 under the US Offshore Procurement Programme. Variants of the basic type were the Mystère IVB, which had a redesigned rear fuselage to accommodate a Rolls-Royce Avon RA-7R engine with reheat, and which subsequently served as a test bed with a SEPR rocket motor mounted under the rear fuselage as part of the Mirage development programme; and the Mystère IVN, a two-seat version with a nose radome for night and all-weather interception. Between them, Ouragan and Mystère laid the foundations for a continuing export success story, being built under licence in India and acquired by Israel. In the mid-1950s, the lesson that French combat aircraft were becoming world-beaters was further underlined with the first flight, on 2 March 1955, of the Super Mystère B.1, powered by an Avon RA.7R; on the day after, it became the first production aircraft of European design to exceed Mach 1.0 in level flight at 40,000 feet.

More surprises, illustrating the advanced thinking of Dassault's design team, were on the way. In 1952, to meet a Ministry requirement for a lightweight, high-altitude, rocket-assisted interceptor capable of using grass strips, Dassault had begun the design of a small single-seat Delta designated MD-550. Renamed Mirage I, it flew for the first time on 25 June 1955, powered by two Bristol Siddeley Viper turbojets. In May 1956 the Mirage I reached Mach 1.15 in a shallow dive, and on 17 December 1956, with the additional boost of a SEPR 66 rocket motor, it attained Mach 1.3 in level flight.

The Mirage I, which was too small and lacked sufficient power to be an effective interceptor in its own right, was regarded by Dassault as the development aircraft for the Mirage II, which was to be powered by two Turboméca Gabizo turbojets fitted with reheat. Before the Mirage I had begun its transonic trials

ARSENAL VG-70. (Musée de l'Air).

however, Dassault had already decided to abandon the Mirage II in favour of a larger and more powerful variant, powered by an afterburning SNECMA Atar 101G-2 turbojet. This aircraft eventually flew in prototype form on 17 November 1956, as the Mirage III-001.

The Mirage I, progenitor of one of the world's most successful lines of combat aircraft, was in direct competition with two government-backed projects, the Nord 1500 Griffon and the SO.9000 Trident.

Like Dassault, Nord Aviation based its design on a delta-wing configuration, following the pattern of an earlier high-speed research prototype, the Nord 1402 Gerfaut 1. This machine, which made its first flight on 15 January 1954, was the first high-powered jet delta-wing aircraft to fly in France, and on 3 August 1954 it became the first aircraft to exceed Mach 1.0 in level flight without the use of an afterburner or rocket power. The diminutive aircraft had a wing span of only 21 feet, and was powered by a SNECMA Atar 101D3 turbojet. A second prototype, the Gerfaut 1B, had larger wings; it exceeded the speed of sound in level flight for the first time on 11 February 1955. An uprated version, the Gerfaut II, flew on 17 April 1956 and subsequently made many supersonic test flights The Gerfaut II's rate of climb was quite startling; it was able to reach 49,200 feet in 3 minutes 56 seconds, from a standing start.

The Nord 1500 Griffon was essentially a research aircraft too, although it had definite interceptor

Designation: Arsenal VG-70.
Role: Research aircraft.
Engine: One 1,890 lb.s.t. Junkers Jumo 004B-2.
Span: 29 ft. 10 in.
Length: 31 ft. 9 in.
Weight: Loaded 7,480 lb.
Crew: 1.
Service ceiling: 35,000 ft.
Range: 370 miles.
Max speed: 559 mph at 22,965 ft.
Weapons: None.

ARSENAL VG-70. (Musée de l'Air).

ARSENAL VG-90. The Arsenal VG-90 was developed from the VG-70 to meet a requirement for a turbojet-powered strike fighter for the French Navy. The first prototype was destroyed in an accident. No production order was ever placed, and the requirement was met by the de Havilland Sea Venom (Aquilon). (Musée de l'Air).

potential. From the outset, it was designed to test an airframe design capable of being equipped with a combination turbojet-ramjet propulsion unit. The prototype 1500-01 Griffon I made its first flight on 20 September, 1955, powered only by a SNECMA Atar 101F turbojet with afterburner; after the completion of the first phase of testing, the airframe was modified to take a propulsion unit consisting of an Atar 101E engine and a Nord ramjet. Under this new guise, the aircraft was redesignated the 1500-02 Griffon II. It flew for the first time on 23 January 1957, and on 17 May it exceeded Mach 1.0 in level flight with its ramjet ignited although the full power of the combination propulsion unit was not used. As far as it is known, this was the first time that a piloted ramjet-powered aircraft exceeded the speed of sound. No combat aircraft was developed from the Griffon, which went on flying into the 1960s under a U.S. research contract.

Sud-Ouest's design, the SO.9000 Trident, was based on a combination of turbojet and rocket power. Design studies began as early as 1949, and building of the first prototype, the SO.9000-01 Trident I, began at Courbevoie in October 1951. At a time when swept or delta wing planforms were considered mandatory for supersonic flight, the Trident's designer, Lucien Servanty, took the bold step of selecting a short, thin, unswept wing spanning less than thirty feet, mounted on

ARSENAL VG-90. (Musée de l'Air).

a bullet-like fuselage and having a Turboméca Marboré II turbojet attached to each wingtip.

The prototype Trident I flew for the first time on 2 March 1953 at Melun-Villaroche, under the power of its wingtip-mounted Marborés, and appeared publicly at Le Bourget in July that year, where it failed to make much of an impression alongside more exotic swept-wing types. Meanwhile, a second prototype, the SO.9000-02, was also nearing completion, and this machine made its maiden

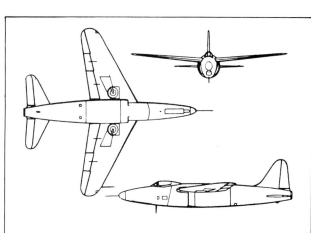

Designation: Arsenal VG-90.
Role: Shipboard fighter.
Engine: One 4,800 lb.s.t. Rolls-Royce Nene.
Span: 41 ft.
Length: 44 ft. 1 in.
Weight: Loaded 17,800 lb.
Crew: 1.
Service ceiling: 38,000 ft.
Range: 580 miles.
Max speed: 596 mph at 19,680 ft.
Weapons: Three 20-mm cannon; up to 2,200 lbs. of bombs.

DASSAULT MD-550 MIRAGE I. First flown on 25 June 1955, the Mirage I was designed in response to a French Air Force requirement for a lightweight interceptor. It was powered by two Armstrong Siddeley Viper turbojets and later fitted with a SEPR 66 rocket motor.

flight on 30 August 1953; it was also its last, because it crashed and was a total write-off. Development continued with -01, and on 4 September 1954 this aircraft flew for the first time with a SEPR-481 triple-chamber rocket motor installed. The addition of the rocket engine meant that the Trident's Marboré turbojets were not powerful enough to get the machine airborne when it was carrying a full load of rocket fuel, so they were replaced by two Dassault MD30 (Viper ASV.5) engines. In this configuration, the Trident flew on 17 May 1955.

In the meantime, Dassault had been building the prototype of a more advanced version which was to be the forerunner of a fully-operational variant. Designated SO.9050 Trident II, this machine made its first flight under turbojet power only at Melun-Villaroche on 17 July 1955. After that, it was taken to the Centre d'Essais en Vol (Flight Test Centre), for rocket-powered trials, and the first of these was carried out on 21 December 1955. Test pilot Charles Goujon, who was to lose his life in the Trident in 1957, described the flight, which was

SUD-AVIATION (SUD-OUEST) SO-9000 TRIDENT. The SO-9000 Trident was an experimental short-range interceptor, the prototype of which flew on 2 March 1953. A second prototype also flew but crashed soon afterwards. The Trident's engines were two wingtip mounted Marbore IIs, but these were later replaced by MD.30s (Armstrong Siddeley Viper A.S.V.5s).

made by Commandant Marias. The flight plan called for the Trident to take off with rocket assistance; it was then to climb to 20,000 feet, where the rocket motor was to be re-lit. The aircraft was then to make a full-power climb until its rocket fuel was exhausted.

Following its initial climb, the Trident levelled off at 20,000 feet and Marias' voice came over the R/T.

"Contact, Chamber One."

'A burst of black smoke behind the aircraft. Then the flame. The immense flame that seems to run in pursuit of the Trident and climb with it in the assault on the sky. Marias' experience now enabled him to gauge the most favourable angle of climb.

' "OK, Commandant?" Pierrot (in ground control) murmurs into the microphone.

' "26,000, 28,000, 30,000 feet...Mach .78, .80, .82..." 'Gilles looks at his chrono. Only a few seconds more before burn-out. Pierrot counts, then calls "cut-off" on receiving word from Marias. From the ground, we can see the cloud that signals the extinction of the rocket motor. Commandant Marias, chief test pilot of the Flight Test Centre at Brétigny, has just broken almost every climb record . . .'

A second Trident II prototype, the SO.9050-002, was destroyed on its first flight that same month, but Charles Goujon went on to fly -001 to a speed of Mach 1.7, (1,122 mph) at that time the highest attained by any piloted aircraft in Europe. In January 1956 an order for six pre-production machines was placed by the French Air Ministry, and the first of these flew on 3 May 1957.

Then came tragedy; on 21 May, 1957, Trident -001 was destroyed during a test flight when its highly volatile rocket fuels, furaline and nitric acid, became accidentally mixed and caused an explosion. The pilot, Charles Goujon, was killed. Further development of the Trident was halted shortly afterwards.

Another contender in the race to produce a French supersonic interceptor was the Sud-Est SE.212 Durandal, although it emerged somewhat later than the others and was eclipsed by the more promising Mirage III. A single-seat delta-wing lightweight fighter, it was powered by a SNECMA Atar G-3 and a SEPR 65 rocket motor, the latter being installed in a detachable fairing under the fuselage, complete with fuel tanks and pumps. It was a clever arrangement, enabling the propellant tanks to be recharged away from the aircraft and therefore simplifying the handling of the volatile fuel. As an alternative, an extra kerosene tank could be fitted in place of the rocket pack to augment the internal fuel tankage. The Durandal prototype, designed to carry a Matra 510 AAM under the rocket pack, flew for the first time on 20 April 1956 powered only by the Atar turbojet, and during subsequent test flights the machine attained Mach 1.6 at altitude in level flight. It could also be rolled at Mach 1.2, without its AAM. A second Durandal prototype was built, and a projected developed version, the Durandal IV, was on the drawing-board, but the programme was cancelled.

After the development of modern interceptors to assure the defence of the homeland, the main preoccupation of the French Air Ministry in the early 1950s was to re-equip the Armée de l'Air's tactical fighter-bomber squadrons, which were then using a mixture of elderly types that included the A-26 Invader, P-47 Thunderbolt and a solitary jet type, the Mistral, which was a licence-built version of the de Havilland Vampire. The requirement was for a jet fighter-bomber capable of operating from unprepared strips, for by 1951 the French, together with other contemporary air forces, were well aware of the difficulties experienced by the USAF's fighter-bomber squadrons in Korea. What was needed was an aircraft that could move up with advancing ground forces and be totally independent of runways.

Sud-Est's Polish-born designer, W.J. Jakimiuk, turned

SUD-AVIATION DURANDAL. An experimental interceptor, intended to carry a single AAM, the Durandal flew for the first time on 20 April 1956, powered by an Atar 101G turbojet and a SEPR rocket motor.

SUD-AVIATION SE-5000 BAROUDEUR. Like the wartime Messerschmitt Me 163 rocket fighter, the SE Baroudeur (Franco-Arabic: Warrior) was designed to be launched from a trolley and land on skids. The first of two prototypes flew on 1 August 1953, powered by a 5,280 lbs. thrust Atar 101B turbojet.

to a German concept to find the answer to the problem. During the war, the German Messerschmitt 163B Komet rocket interceptor, and the Arado Ar 234 bomber in its early days, had both been launched from take-off trolleys and then used retractable skids for landing. Jakimiuk decided to use the same principle in his design, but with a difference: his aircraft would actually be able to taxi on its skid right up to the point where it could be hauled on to its trolley, so eliminating a host of ground handling problems.

The advanced, swept-wing jet fighter that gradually took shape on Sud-Est's drawing board was given the designation SE.5000 and named Baroudeur, a nickname that was applied to the tough soldiers of the French Foreign Legion and which may be loosely translated as 'Battler'. Its wings, which spanned 32 feet 10 inches, were swept at 38 degrees, the fin at 55 degrees and the tailplane at 42. The aircraft had a built-in armament of two 30-mm Hispano 603 cannon in the lower nose and was designed to carry a heavy load of offensive underwing stores while operating from fields only 750 yards long.

Powered by an Atar 101B turbojet, the prototype Baroudeur, the SE.5000-01 flew for the first time on 1 August 1953. It was followed, on 12 May 1954, by the second prototype, -02, which differed from its predecessor in having an uprated Atar 101C engine, slightly modified tail surfaces and a 3-degree increase in wing anhedral. On 17 July 1954 this aircraft exceeded Mach 1.0 in a dive, and subsequent test results were sufficiently encouraging for the French Air Ministry to place an order for three pre-production machines under the designation SE.5003 and designed to take the more powerful Atar 101E.

During trials, the Baroudeur demonstrated its ability to operate from uncultivated fields, sand and pebble

beaches and muddy, snow-covered or frozen ground. It was also, under certain conditions, able to take off on its skid alone, without use of the trolley. Normally, it was mounted on the latter by a winch-equipped jeep in an operation that could be undertaken in under two

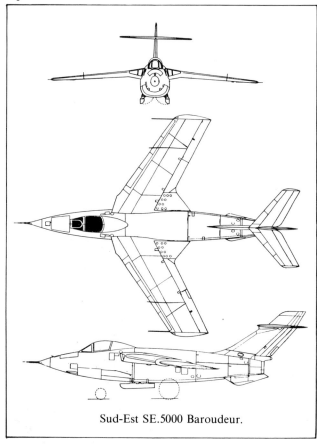

Sud-Est SE.5000 Baroudeur.

minutes. The trolley itself, of welded steel tubing, reproduced the general layout of a nosewheel undercarriage, all its wheels having soft low-pressure tyres to prevent it sinking into soft surfaces. The rear wheels were fitted with brakes which were operated by the pilot while the aircraft was on the trolley, or automatically after the Baroudeur had taken off. The trolley could be fitted with six rockets, two or four being used for take-off depending on the type of terrain, and two for emergency use.

Despite its promise, however, and partly because of a shift in policies resulting from governmental changes, the Baroudeur was never given the production go-ahead. Instead, the Armée de l'Air's tactical jet fighter requirements were met initially by small numbers of F-84 Thunderjets, purchased from the USA, and later by the more advanced F-84F Thunderstreak, which equipped the 4e and 9e Escadres.

Equally as promising, but radically different in concept, was an aircraft that would almost certainly have had a considerable application as a counter-insurgency type in many countries during the troubled years ahead. It was the Potez 75, and, like the Baroudeur, its concept was born out of the lessons emerging from the war in Korea, where events had proven the need for a cheap, rugged and manoeuvrable aircraft for use primarily as an anti-tank weapon. A twin-boom, fixed-undercarriage machine powered by a Potez 8D32 piston engine, its two crew members protected against ground fire by heavy armour plating, the prototype Potez 75 (F-ZWSA) flew on 1 June 1953 and was followed by a second prototype, F-WGVK. In the summer of 1956, following successful trials, the French National Defence Department proposed the purchase of 15 pre-production and 100 production machines for policing duties, primarily in Algeria, but the order was never confirmed. Production aircraft would have had an armament of four fixed 7.5-mm machine-guns, each with 1,200 rounds of ammunition, and up to eight SS.10 air-to-ground wire-guided missiles in underwing racks, the missiles being directed by the observer who sat in the forward cockpit.

As mentioned earlier, the French Aéronavale's requirement for a shipboard jet fighter-bomber was filled by the Aquilon (Sea Venom) and, later, the Etendard; but in the late 1940s two French designers had piston-and turboprop-powered designs to fill the gap. On April 1, 1949, Sud-Ouest flew the prototype of a twin-boom, long-range naval strike fighter designated SO.8000 Narval, powered by an Arsenal 12H-02 engine (a modified Junkers Jumo 213). A second prototype was flown on 30 December 1949 and both aircraft were extensively tested, but the day of the piston-engined combat aircraft was over and the Narval programme was abandoned.

The design proposed by Louis Breguet, on the other hand, showed far more promise. Named Br.960 Vultur, it was equipped with an Armstrong Siddeley Mamba AS.Ma.1 turboprop and a Nene 101 turbojet, a combination designed to give both good endurance and high performance for combat and take-off with full loads. The first prototype flew on 3 August 1951 and was followed by a second on 15 September 1952, this aircraft having a more powerful Mamba AS.Ma.3 turboprop and a Nene 104. In 1954, however, the Aéronavale specification was radically altered with the realisation that a naval strike aircraft would have to be capable of engaging shore-based fighters, which the Vultur was not equipped to do. Breguet consequently abandoned the strike fighter idea and decided to modify the second Vultur to serve as the prototype of a new shipboard anti-submarine aircraft. It flew in this form on 26 March 1955 with the designation Br.965, and was followed by three prototypes of the new anti-submarine aircraft: the Breguet Br.1050 Alizé, which went into operational service with the Aéronavale and was also exported to India.

BREGUET 960 VULTUR.

LEDUC 021. The extraordinary Leduc 021 was designed to be a research vehicle for a proposed ramjet-powered interceptor. A more refined prototype, the Leduc 022, was also built and flown; it could climb to 82,000 feet in four minutes, and had an estimated maximum speed of 2.4M. Endurance was a limiting factor, however, and the programme was cancelled. (Musée de l'Air).

No survey of French aerospace research and development during the early 1950s would be complete without mention of one of the most radical aircraft designed anywhere during that decade of experiment: the Leduc 022 ramjet-powered prototype interceptor. René Leduc's experiments with ramjet-powered aircraft dated back to 1937 and a small research ramjet designated Leduc 101 eventually took to the air in November 1946, mounted on the back of a Bloch 161 transport, and made its first gliding flight on 21 October 1947. On 21 April 1949, after a series of gliding trials, it flew for the first time with ramjet lit, and on 31 May that year it reached a speed of 562 mph at 25,000 feet. Subsequent testing was not trouble-free; on 27 November 1951 it was badly damaged in a crash-landing, its pilot being badly injured, and on 25 July 1952, after repair, it struck its Languedoc launch aircraft on release and had to make a belly-landing.

Meanwhile, on 2 May 1951, a second research ramjet, the Leduc 016, had made its first flight, tethered to the back of its parent aircraft. The first free flight, with two small turbojets mounted under the wings, was made on 15 January 1952, but the undercarriage collapsed on touchdown and the aircraft was damaged. The same thing happened again on 9 May. Several more flights were made before 1954, when the machine was allocated to the Musée de l'Air.

Meanwhile, Leduc had been building a larger and more powerful ramjet research vehicle, the Leduc 021. Air tests began on 16 May 1953, with the aircraft mounted above a Languedoc, and several gliding trials were made before the first powered flight on 7 August 1953. Subsequent flight trials were carried out throughout the flight envelope up to a limiting Mach number of 0.85, and among other spectacular performance figures the 021 showed an initial climb rate of 39,370 feet per minute and a ceiling of 65,600 feet. A second Leduc 021 was built, and this flew under its own power for the first time on 1 March 1954. The 021's pilot was housed semi-reclined in a bullet-like nose fairing that protruded from the main engine tube; it could be jettisoned in an emergency, a parachute system being located immediately aft of the pilot. Aft of the cabin, the central body contained the Turboméca Artouste I turbine which drove the fuel pumps and generators, together with fuel tanks, batteries and radio. Aft of this central core were 21 burners arranged in seven banks through which fuel was sprayed; each bank could be lit separately, depending on the amount of power required.

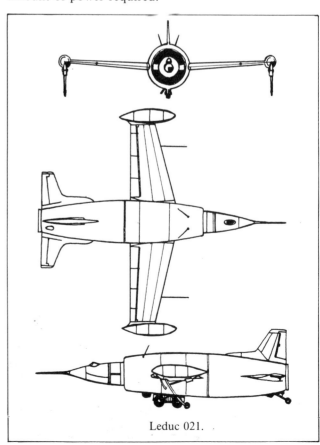

Leduc 021.

DASSAULT MIRAGE IIIA. How the French got it right: the Dassault Mirage IIIA, progenitor of the famous combat aircaft series. It owed its existence to the requirement for a NATO lightweight fighter.

DASSAULT MIRAGE III & F1. . . . And how the French went on getting it right: The Mirage III and one of its developments, the Mirage F.1, two of a family line that captured a host of overseas markets.

LEDUC 021. (Musée de l'Air).

The Leduc 021 was designed to be the research vehicle for an operational interceptor, and as the next step towards this end a more advanced prototype, the Leduc 022, was designed and built. The 022 was larger than its predecessors and had swept flying surfaces; it was equipped with an Atar 101D-3 turbojet, installed inside the ramjet duct, that enabled the aircraft to take off under its own power and accelerate to the point where the ramjet could take over. The aircraft flew for the first time on 26 December 1956 and quickly showed enormous performance potential, including an ability to climb to 82,000 feet in four minutes. With flight testing of 022-01 well under way, construction of a second prototype was started. However, the 022's limiting factor was endurance; at an estimated maximum combat speed of Mach 2.4, the aircraft could carry sufficient fuel for only ten minutes' flying.

Besides, French Air Ministry requirements were now turning more towards the ideal of a multi-role combat aircraft, a policy dictated by wildly escalating costs as much as by operational considerations. The era of the pure interceptor was at an end.

Chapter Five
Great Britain, 1955-60: The Lost Opportunities

In 1953 — at a time when American research aircraft were already attaining speeds of up to Mach 2.5 and altitudes of over 80,000 feet — Great Britain still had no aircraft that was capable of exceeding Mach 1.0 in level flight or of reaching altitudes in excess of 50,000 feet. It would be the summer of 1954 before the English Electric P.1, precursor of the Lightning, touched these values. The development potential of the P.1 was soon to become apparent; what was by no means apparent, when the prototype flew in August 1954, was that its developed version would become the *only* operational combat aircraft of all-British design ever to reach a speed of Mach 2.0.

By 1951, it was already clear to British aircraft designers that a dangerous fighter performance gap was looming on the horizon. The Korean war was proving beyond all doubt that Soviet aviation technology was catching up with that of the West, and in some cases outstripping it; this, together with indications that the Russians were giving high priority to advanced jet bomber development, led to a complete re-appraisal of the RAF's fighter requirements.

The Air Staff envisaged that by 1960, the Russians would be in a position to threaten the West with two principal types of manned bomber: one a long-range aircraft cruising at up to 0.9M and the other a supersonic medium-range type capable of an over-the-target speed of up to 2.0M. Both types, it was believed, would be capable of operating at altitudes in excess of 60,000 feet.

The RAF requirement for an aircraft to deal with this threat — an interceptor with an initial rate of climb of 50,000 feet per minute and a maximum speed of over 2.0M — crystallized in O.R. 301, issued in 1951. It presented a formidable challenge, and designers who rose to meet it naturally turned to the one power plant that had already proven itself in the target defence role under operational conditions: the rocket motor.

The combination of Germany's wartime Messerschmitt Me 163B airframe and Walter HWK509A-2 bi-fuel rocket motor — dangerous and unstable though it had been — had served to demonstrate the potential of the rocket-powered target defence interceptor, and in the years after the war the Ministry of Supply had authorized a limited research programme to investigate the possible use of rocket motors in future RAF fighters. In 1946, Armstrong Siddeley and de Havilland had begun work on two such motors, the Snarler and the Sprite, using different propellants. The 2,000 lb thrust Snarler used a combination of methyl alcohol, water and liquid oxygen, while the 5,000 lb thrust Sprite used high-test hydrogen peroxide. In addition to powering a new generation of fast-climbing fighters, it was also envisaged that the rocket motors would provide auxiliary take-off power at overload weights for the new jet bombers that were then on the drawing-board.

In 1950 the Snarler was installed in the tail of the prototype Hawker P.1040, which was then re-designated P.1072 and the first powered flight trial was made on 20 November that year. De Havilland's Sprite was test-flown under a Comet in April 1951. Tests with the Snarler produced a considerable performance increase, especially with regard to rate of climb, but some technical problems were encountered and the project was dropped. Armstrong Siddeley, however, went on to develop the Screamer, the first British variable-thrust rocket, while experience gained with the Sprite led de Havilland to start work on their own second-generation rocket motor, the Spectre.

On 21 February 1952, following preliminary design studies, specification F.124T was written around O.R. 103 and issued to several leading British aircraft companies. The specification called for a small rocket-powered interceptor armed with a battery of air-to-air missiles and able to take-off in a very short distance; like the Messerschmitt 163, it would glide back to earth after combat. Short, Blackburn, Bristol and Avro all submitted tenders; the Avro design, involving a small tailless delta, was potentially the most promising.

At this point another company, Saunders-Roe, entered the running. Saro, although pre-occupied with the SRA/1 jet fighter flying-boat and the mighty ten-engined Princess, had also carried out extensive research into high-speed, high-altitude flight, and had made some studies of a rocket aircraft capable of reaching an altitude of over 80,000 feet. For some reason the company had not been invited to tender to F.124T — in fact, the specification had not even been issued to it. A protest was made, and in March 1952 a somewhat embarrassed Ministry of Supply invited Saro to submit their design together with the other firms. In just over a month, Saunders-Roe turned in a detailed design project involving a single-seat fighter powered by an 8,000 lb thrust rocket motor giving it an estimated climb rate of 52,000 feet per minute at 50,000 feet and a maximum speed of 2.44M at 60,000 feet. Unlike the other companies, Saro also proposed equipping the fighter with a small turbojet engine that would enable it to recover to an airfield instead of having to make a glide landing somewhere out in the country.

The Air Ministry liked the idea, and all the companies involved in F.124T were asked to incorporate a similar arrangement in their designs. The amendment came as something of a relief, for the performances of both the Screamer and Spectre rocket motors were falling short of expectations and a mixed power plant seemed a possible solution to the problem.

Originally, Saunders-Roe had planned to equip their design with their own rocket motor and an Armstrong Siddeley Viper turbojet, which had been developed to power the Jindivik target drone. As design studies progressed, however, it was realised that further

SAUNDERS-ROE SR.53. First flown on 16 May 1957, the SR.53 experimental interceptor employed the mixed-power concept, using an Armstrong-Siddeley Viper turbojet and a DH Spectre rocket motor.

development of Saro's own rocket motor would prove too expensive, and so the Spectre was adopted instead. A scheme to incorporate a jettisonable cockpit was also dropped, and a conventional Martin-Baker ejection seat proposed to replace it. The resulting design had an all-up weight of 15,000 pounds and was given the designation SR.53.

In October 1952, Saunders-Roe received an Instruction to Proceed with three SR.53 prototypes (XD145, XD151 and XD153). Apart from the provision of a turbojet engine, the finalised aircraft differed considerably from the original concept, having slotted flaps and ailerons instead of combined flaps and ailerons, a tailplane mounted on top of the fin and a straight-through jet exhaust instead of a bifurcated one. The turbojet, which was set high in the fuselage to make room for the rocket motor, was fed via twin intakes set immediately aft of the cockpit. Projected armament was still fifty rocket projectiles in a retractable pack, but in December 1952 this was changed to an armament of de Havilland Blue Jay AAMs mounted under the wings. The amended specification, issued at this time, was F.138D. At a later date the Blue Jays — renamed Firestreaks — were mounted on the wingtips.

The SR.53 design underwent further changes in the spring of 1953. Aerodynamic research by the Royal Aircraft Establishment indicated that the wing needed greater anhedral, and as a result modifications had to be made to wing, fuselage centre-section and undercarriage. It was the end of April before design work was sufficiently complete to be presented to the Ministry of Supply, but after that things moved quickly; within a week, Saunders-Roe had received a formal contract for the production of the three prototype aircraft.

In parallel with the SR.53, the Ministry of Supply had also given A. V. Roe and Company an Instruction to Proceed with their own design to OR.301, the Avro 720, which went ahead under Specification F.137D. The Type 720 was to be fitted with a Viper turbojet plus an Armstrong Siddeley Screamer rocket motor, the latter burning liquid oxygen and kerosene.

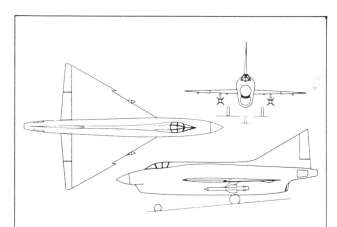

Designation: Avro Type 720.
Role: Interceptor.
Engines: One Armstrong Siddeley Viper turbojet; one AS Screamer rocket motor.
Span: 27 ft 3½ in.
Length: 48 ft 6 in.
Weight: Loaded 15,000 lb.
Crew: 1.
Service ceiling: 60,000 ft +.
Range: 350 miles approx.
Max speed: 2.0M.
Weapons: Two DH Blue Jay (Firestreak) AAMs.

Aerodynamic experience with the Avro 707 family of research deltas and the Vulcan bomber, which was then flying in prototype form, had convinced Avro that the tailless delta provided the optimum aerodynamic efficiency, offering minimum drag, a low wing loading and the desired handling characteristics over the aircraft's whole speed range up to about 2.0M. To keep drag as low as possible, the smallest possible envelope was designed around the fuel and oxidant tanks, and extensive use was made of honeycomb sandwich structure. The central cylindrical portion of the fuselage was almost entirely occupied by the liquid oxygen tank and the forward fuel tank, a small semi-cylindrical portion being hollowed out at the base to provide accommodation for the Viper turbojet. The latter's air intake was situated under the forward fuselage and the exhaust duct under the rear fuselage, which housed the rear fuel tank and carried the mountings for the Screamer rocket motor, the vertical fin and the air brake reaction points. The nosewheel retracted aft, with the intake ducts for the Viper passing on each side of the well, and the main units retracted forward, turning through 90 degrees to lie flat in the wing. Proposed armament for the Avro 720, like the SR.53, was two Blue Jay AAMs mounted on launching pylons outboard of the main undercarriage members.

It was not long before both the Avro and Saunders-Roe design teams realised that the combination of Viper turbojet and rocket motor would not match what was required of the proposed combat aircraft. What was needed was a bigger, more powerful jet engine, one that would sustain the aircraft in high Mach cruise; the rocket motor would be used for the climb and combat manoeuvres. This, together with extra fuel tankage to meet an extended range requirement and the inclusion of AI radar equipment, would mean a larger and more complex aircraft. Early in 1954, following discussions with the Ministry of Supply, both companies therefore began design studies of bigger, more powerful variants of their original concepts.

Saunders-Roe went ahead as rapidly as possible with work on their SR.53, although it was soon apparent that the aircraft would be nowhere near ready to meet the target date for the first flight, optimistically set for July 1954 (the aircraft, in fact, would not fly until May 1957). At the same time, a new High Speed Development Section was set up to begin work on the design of the more advanced version, which was designated P.177. The aircraft started life as a straightforward development of the SR.53, but as the weeks went by its configuration underwent a series of changes, mainly to meet a requirement that called for its use by both the RAF and the Royal Navy. After investigating several turbojet alternatives, Saunders-Roe eventually settled for the 8,000 lb.s.t. de Havilland PS.38, which was later to be named the Gyron Junior. In May 1955 the company received a design contract from the MoS, and this was followed in September by an Instruction to Proceed.

Avro, meanwhile, had submitted their design for a revamped Type 720 in October 1954, stressing that if a 4,850 lb.s.t. Bristol Orpheus turbojet were used as an interim engine, the aircraft could be flying by the end of 1955. The company also proposed a naval version, the Type 728, with increased wing area and a lengthened undercarriage. Rocket power for both variants was to be provided by the Spectre, and developed aircraft were to be fitted with the Gyron Junior turbojet. Like the P.177,

the developed 720/728 was to carry advanced AI equipment. Work on the original Avro 720, which was now intended to be a test-bed for the more potent variant, was proceeding at a much faster rate than development of the rival SR.53, and by the end of 1955 the prototype — XD696 — was virtually complete. The full-scale test specimen programme included a complete static test structure which was built before the prototype so that, in the event of any failure of the honeycomb structure under test, the prototype could be suitably modified. In the event the structure stood up to static tests very well.

Then came the blow: the Ministry of Supply suddenly cancelled the Avro 720 project on the grounds that the cost of supporting two similar projects was too high and that the proposed rocket fuel combination of liquid oxygen and kerosene would prove dangerous to store under operational conditions, primarily on aircraft carriers. High-test peroxide was easier to handle, and better safety measures had been evolved for its use.

As a further economy measure, the Ministry also cancelled one of the SR.53 prototypes, XD153. Work on the other two proceeded, and in the summer of 1955 the United States allocated one and a half million dollars towards the project on the basis of an agreement under which US funds were released to support projects of high military value to NATO. Plans were made to test the first prototype at Hurn; a storage building for the HTP fuel was built, together with other necessary installations, and a Meteor F.8, allocated by the MoS, was flown in to test specialised items of radio equipment.

However, Hurn was never used in the SR.53 test programme. The first prototype, XD145, was taken to the A&AEE Boscombe Down in June 1956 for assembly and all subsequent test flying was undertaken from that establishment. Ground running of the installed Spectre rocket motor began on 16 January 1957, followed by similar ground testing of the Viper turobjet on 16 April. Taxying trials got under way on 9 May, and on 16 May, 1957, XD145 took to the air for the first time in the hands of Squadron Leader John Booth, DFC, Saunders-Roe's chief test pilot. In September the SR.53 was demonstrated publicly at the 1957 SBAC Show, Farnborough; no-one who saw it, including the writer, will ever forget the breath-taking climb that took it from the runway to the clouds almost faster than the eye could follow, a tiny dart streaking upwards at the end of a long black pencil-mark of smoke as Booth cut in the Spectre rocket. What the crowds did not realise was that the SR.53 had, at the time, accumulated only four hours' flying time before it went on display. John Booth said afterwards:

"Normally a minimum of ten hours is required before an aircraft appears at Farnborough, but the conditions were waived in view of the special circumstances connected with the 53's performance. Actually I flew her on ten sorties (about twenty minutes each) before Farnborough: the last was the delivery flight!"

On 8 December 1957 the second SR.53 XD151, also joined the test programme. This machine was fitted with a revised HTP tank system and made eleven flights before being totally destroyed on 18 March 1958. The crash, in which John Booth was killed, was never satisfactorily explained, and it brought an end to the SR.53 test programme. XD145 was grounded while the MoS Accident Investigation Department tried to establish what had gone wrong, and it never flew again. It

SAUNDERS-ROE SR.53.

eventually went to the Rocket Research Establishment at Westcott, and from there in 1969 to the museum at RAF Henlow. In all, the two prototypes had completed 42 sorties.

Despite this setback, the future for the bigger operational version, the P.177, seemed promising. The Air Staff viewed the project with enthusiasm, foreseeing a potent interceptor force comprising squadrons of Lightnings and P.177s, to be fully operational in the early 1960s, while the Naval Staff was also keeping a close interest in P.177 development. The requirements of both Services were detailed in two operational requirements, OR.337 for the RAF and NA.47 for the Navy; Saunders-Roe went to great lengths to integrate everything in a single design, which was covered by MoS Specification F.177D.

By the end of 1955, work had already begun at Cowes on the development of jigs and tools for the production of an initial batch of twenty-seven P.177s for the RAF and RN. Sub-contractors were selected for the design and development of various airframe components and parts of the fuel system, and two Service officers, Commander P. S. Wilson, RN and Wing Commander P. C. Cleaver, RAF, were appointed to liaise with Saunders-Roe throughout the development phase up to the prototype's first flight. The schedule called for the completion of five P.177s, without weapons or AI, by January 1958.

Early in 1957 the P.177 programme was gathering momentum. De Havilland was now heavily involved, having acquired a one-third share holding in Saunders-Roe, and Armstrong Whitworth had been selected to build the 177's wing. What was even more promising was the interest being shown towards the project by the German Defence Ministry, which in 1956 had begun to look for a supersonic interceptor to replace its F-86 Sabres. West Germany's air defence problems were more critical in many respects than the United Kingdom's; because of the reduced warning time of an air threat from the East, reaction times needed to be much shorter. What the Luftwaffe needed was an aircraft that could get off the ground and climb to its interception height in seconds, rather than minutes, and in this respect the P.177 seemed the ideal formula.

In the summer of 1956, discussions had started between members of the German Defence Staff and a Saunders-Roe team headed by the Director, Robert Perfect, and M. J. Brennan, the Chief Designer. In November, the British Government agreed to the opening of negotiations with the Federal Republic of Germany with a view to securing an order for the 177; at this stage, the Germans were indicating that they might want about 200 examples. The Germans sent a technical team to Cowes in January 1957 to assess the project at close quarters while Bonn and London worked out financial details.

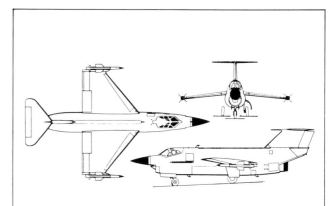

Designation: Saunders-Roe P.177.

Role: Interceptor.

Engines: One 8,000 lb.s.t. Gyron Junior turbojet; one 8,000 lb Spectre 5A rocket motor.

Span: 30 ft.

Length: 50 ft.

Weight: Loaded 18,000 lb.

Crew: 1.

Service ceiling: 60,000 ft +.

Range: 400 miles.

Max speed: 2.35M.

Weapons: Two Red Top AAMs.

LOCKHEED F-104 STARFIGHTER. The Lockheed F-104 Starfighter, which became the standard interceptor with several European air forces in the 1960s. Some of them might have used the Saunders-Roe P.177 instead had the British project not have been abruptly cancelled . . .

Then, in April 1957, the whole P.177 project was rocked to its foundations with the publication of the Duncan Sandys notorious White Paper on Defence, which stated that the English Electric P.1B would be the last manned fighter to enter RAF service and that henceforth all efforts would be concentrated on perfecting guided missiles for defence. As a result, the Air Staff immediately cancelled OR.337, which left the entire

ENGLISH ELECTRIC LIGHTING. The 1957 Defence White Paper left the English Electric Lighting – seen here in Saudi Arabian markings – as the RAF's last all-British interceptor and the only British aircraft to have flown at Mach 2.

project resting on the intentions of the Naval Staff and the Germans.

Then, in August, the Navy's requirement was cancelled too. Even so, the P.177 project might have been rescued; Aubrey Jones, the Minister of Supply, authorized the continued development of the first batch of five aircraft in anticipation of a German order, even though Duncan Sandys wanted to see the P.177 programme scrapped in its entirety. Even at this critical stage, the P.177 was undergoing design changes; at the last moment the aircraft was re-designed around the Rolls-Royce RB.133 engine instead of the Gyron Junior and its wing section was made thinner.

The German Defence Ministry, too, was becoming increasingly frustrated by the British Government's lack of interest in the project. Moreover, the Luftwaffe's requirement had been modified: what was now required was a medium and low-level interceptor. Towards the end of 1957, the Federal German Government informed London that it was no longer interested in the P.177; the Luftwaffe turned instead to the United States, and the F-104 Starfighter.

The P.177 project was dead, and in Saunders-Roe the sense of numbed shock was in no way diminished by all the prior indications that the axe would fall. The epitaph for one of the most promising and advanced combat aircraft ever to take shape on the drawing boards of a British aircraft designer came in the form of a statement from the Ministry of Supply in January 1958: "This aircraft commands general recognition as an excellent and unique design in its class. Unfortunately, it no longer fits into the broad pattern of the United Kingdom defence programme."

Duncan Sandys' preoccupation with guided weapons at the expense of manned combat aircraft was to cost Britain's military aircraft industry dearly, although in fairness it must be said that Sandys was not wholly at fault in formulating a disastrously wrong air defence policy; plenty of others in high places agreed with him at the time, and few strong voices were raised against him. The fault in the cancellation of a whole range of promising aircraft projects lay as much with the failure of the industry to present a concerted front against what was clearly an erroneous measure, and with the failure of various Government departments not only to liaise with one another effectively, but also to make decisions that might still have secured foreign orders which, in the event, were quickly lost to the United States. It is too easy, with hindsight, to find a single scapegoat for the vacillations of the late 1950s.

As we have seen, the Saunders-Roe P.177 was to have formed part of a mixed interceptor force together with the Lightning, and these two aircraft were to have been the mainstay of Fighter Command until the mid-1960s. After that, according to Air Staff thinking, Britain's air defences would standardize on a supersonic all-weather interceptor with long range and a missile armament. Early thoughts turned towards an advanced version of the Gloster Javelin, which in the mid-1950s was in super-priority production for the RAF's all-weather fighter squadrons; the new aircraft, designated P.376, would have a thin wing and be powered by two 16,000 lb.s.t. Olympus engines giving it a speed in excess of 1.77M at 45,000 feet. A large aircraft, with a span of over 60 feet and a length of 72 feet, the thin-wing Javelin was to be armed with 30-mm cannon and the massive Vickers Red Dean AAM. Eighteen examples of the P.376 were ordered under Specification F.153D in January 1955, but eighteen months later both the thin-wing Javelin and the Red Dean missile were cancelled.

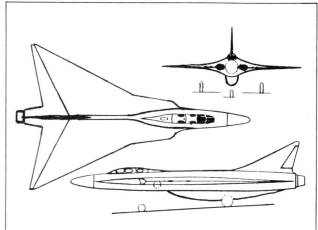

Designation: Hawker P.1092.
Role: All-weather interceptor.
Engine: One Rolls-Royce Avon with reheat.
Span: 35 ft.
Length: 55 ft.
Weight: Loaded No data.
Crew: 2.
Service ceiling: 55,000 ft.
Range: 550 miles.
Max speed: 1.5M at 36,000 ft.
Weapons: Two Red Top AAMs.

SHORT SB.5.

The Air Staff had decided to take an enormous leap forward and go for an all-weather fighter that would be capable of reaching a speed of Mach 2 at 60,000 feet. The new Operational Requirement, OR.329, called for an ability to reach that altitude within six minutes of take-off. A Specification, F.155T, was written around the OR and issued in February 1955.

Among the companies rising to meet the demands of F.155T was Hawker Aircraft, who already had considerable experience in the design of an advanced all-weather fighter. In the early 1950s, at a time when the DH.110 and the Javelin were undergoing comparative trials and experiencing many teething troubles, the Hawker team had evolved a two-seat design, the P.1092, which featured a slender delta wing. Hawkers claimed that with an afterburning Avon engine this aircraft would have achieved a speed of about 1.5M and, using AI equipment then under development, could have been in RAF service by 1957. This project came to nothing, but when F.155T was issued Hawker responded with a new and much larger design, the two-seat P.1103, which was to have been powered by a Gyron engine.

The other principal contender in the F.155T stakes was Fairey Aviation. This company, noted for its long association with naval aircraft, had entered the high-speed research field in 1947, when it built a series of small delta-wing models designed to be launched from mobile ramps. Tests with these rocket-powered designs continued at Woomera in Australia until 1953, when the Ministry of Supply lost interest in the vertical-launch concept.

In 1947, however, Fairey had received a Specification, E.10/47, for a manned delta wing aircraft to investigate the full range of flight characteristics of a ramp-launched machine which could eventually be developed into a high-speed interceptor suitable for use from small ships or aircraft carriers. The result was the FD.1, which flew for the first time at Boscombe Down on 12 March 1951. The original plan was that the FD.1 would be fitted with large booster rockets for vertical or angled ramp take-off; control at take-off speeds was to be effected by four swivelling jet nozzles in the rear fuselage which could be operated by normal controls. With the waning of MoS interest in the ramp-launch idea, however, the FD.1 was fitted with a conventional tricycle undercarriage. Powered by a Rolls-Royce Derwent turbojet, its estimated performance included a maximum speed of 587 mph at 40,000 feet and the ability to climb to 30,000 feet in four and a half minutes. Before the first flight, however, the aircraft was fitted with a small tailplane mounted on top of the fin, and this imposed an airframe limitation of 345 mph. The FD.1 undertook a great deal of test flying, investigating lateral and longitudinal stability, rolling performance and the effectiveness of braking parachutes. The test programme was terminated in 1953 and this interesting little machine ended its days as a ground target.

Meanwhile, in February 1949, Fairey had been asked

FAIREY FD.1. The Fairey FD.1 was designed to investigate the handling characteristics of a projected delta-wing VTO fighter. Powered by a Rolls-Royce Derwent turbojet, it also had provision for a rocket motor, although this was never fitted.

FAIREY FD.2. The last British aircraft to hold the World Air Speed Record, the Fairey Delta 2 was designed to specification E.R.103, calling for a research aircraft capable of flying at speeds of up to Mach 1.5. Powered by a 9,500 lb thrust Rolls-Royce Avon R.A.14 turbojet, the aircraft flew for the first time on 6 October 1954.

to investigate the design of a single-engined transonic research aircraft, which was covered by Specification ER.103. In December 1949 the Company came up with firm proposals for a highly streamlined delta-wing machine that was, in essence, a supersonic envelope just big enough to house a pilot, engine and fuel. Frontal areas were cut to a minimum and all possible external bulges removed. Maximum clearance between the Rolls-Royce Avon RA.14R engine and the fuselage skin was less than six inches, while the delta wing, spanning 26 feet 10 inches, was as thin as possible, with a thickness/chord ratio of only 4 per cent. Leading edge sweep was 60 degrees.

Fairey received a contract to build two aircraft in October 1950, but considerable delay resulted from the fact that the Company was heavily involved in the production of the Fairey Gannet for the Royal Navy, and detailed design work did not start until the summer of 1952. By this time, Fairey had a new Chief Engineer: he was R. L. Lickley, who had been head of the Department of Aircraft Design at Cranfield. Under his direction, the aircraft — now known as the FD.2, or Delta Two — gradually took shape, and the first drawings were released to the shops in September 1952.

The finalised FD.2 design differed from the original concept only in minor detail. The biggest modification involved the nose section; to improve the pilot's vision during the landing phase, Fairey's design team devised a 'droop snoot' whereby the whole nose section, including the cockpit assembly forward of the front bulkhead, could be hinged downwards at a ten-degree angle. The wing, despite its thinness, was a remarkably solid structure, being a light alloy structure with three main and two subsidiary spars forming a rectangular torsion box. Each wing contained four integral fuel tanks which, together with the fuselage collector tank, provided a total capacity of 322 Imp. Gall. The wing trailing edge carried inboard elevators and outboard ailerons, which were power-operated.

Fairey's chief test pilot was Group Captain Gordon Slade, but it was his deputy, a young ex-Fleet Air Arm officer named Peter Twiss, who took the FD.2 into the air for the first time at Boscombe Down on 6 October 1954. Before the flight, Twiss built up his experience of high speed flight with supersonic dives in Hunters, Swifts and Sabres, and by flight-testing the little FD.1.

Right from the beginning, the FD.2 showed itself to be an aircraft of enormous potential. Twiss made thirteen flights, gradually building up his confidence in the machine, and plans were afoot to begin the real work of high-speed, high-altitude research when, during the fourteenth flight on 17 November, 1954, something went wrong. At 30,000 feet, thirty miles from Boscombe Down, the engine failed as a result of an internal pressure build-up which collapsed the fuselage collector tank. Twiss did some rapid calculations and worked out that he could just about glide home for a dead-stick landing. He scraped across the boundary fence, selecting undercarriage down at the last moment, but only the nosewheel extended. Twiss said later:

"I no longer doubted that we should finish up in one piece, although I believe it looked quite spectacular from the ground. The nosewheel touched first, and we dragged along on this and the tail end, with sparks streaming off the runway. Fortunately, the engine failure had been caused by a fuel stoppage, so there was no fuel near the engine and little fear of fire. Anyway, we gradually lost speed. Eventually the starboard wing dropped and we began careering towards the control tower at about 100 knots. On the grass we slowed quickly and, at about 40 knots, the starboard wing dug in and brought us to a grinding standstill."

Twiss escaped with a severe shaking, and later received the Queen's Commendation for Valuable Service in the Air. The Delta Two, however, had sustained damage that put it out of action for eight months, and the test programme was not resumed until August 1955. In

September the FD.2 prototype, WG774, took part in the SBAC Show at Farnborough, although Peter Twiss kept it throttled well back for security reasons; the Fairey team, almost to their surprise, were beginning to learn that the aircraft was capable of very high speeds, and as yet it had not even used its afterburner. The first supersonic flight was made on 28 October 1955, and further supersonic flights confirmed Fairey's view that the Delta Two was capable of speeds well in excess of 1,000 mph. Urged by Gordon Slade and Peter Twiss, the Company began to think seriously of using the aircraft in an attempt on the world air speed record, which at that time was held by a North American F-100C Super Sabre at 822.26 mph.

The idea was put to the Ministry, whose initial attitude was one of flat disbelief that the FD.2 could fly at anywhere near 1,000 mph. Grudging approval was finally obtained after a lot of hard work on Fairey's part, but the Ministry of Supply made it clear that it did not wish to be associated with the attempt. No finance was forthcoming, and Fairey had to pay for the necessary insurance cover as well as for the services of the team of recording specialists from the RAE, Farnborough.

The attempt on the record was prepared under conditions of stringent secrecy, and on 10 March 1956, Peter Twiss took WG774 to a new average record speed of 1,132 mph (1.731M) at 38,000 feet over a 9.65-mile course off the south coast between Thorney Island and Worthing. It was the first time that the record had been raised above the 1,000 mph mark, and it exceeded the previous American-held record by 37 per cent, the biggest leap so far.

The achievement astounded the rest of the aviation world, and Fairey felt secure in their belief that the Delta Two's design had proven itself to the point where proposals could be put forward for a family of supersonic fighters based on it. Two FD.2s were now flying — the second, WG777, having flown on 15 February 1956 — and between them the two aircraft had made well over 100 flights by the time Peter Twiss captured the air speed record

As a first step towards the development of a supersonic fighter based on the Delta Two, Fairey proposed ER.103/B, a variant with a modified fuselage housing a de Havilland Gyron or a Rolls-Royce RB.122 turbojet with reheat. This was to be followed by ER.103/C, which would be a prototype fighter fitted with AI and armed with Firestreak missiles mounted on the wingtips. It was estimated that the aircraft's performance would include a speed of 2.26M at 55,000 feet and 1.8M at 60,000 feet, with a time to 45,000 feet of 1.9 minutes.

At the same time, Fairey considered various proposals to meet the demanding F.155T Specification for a supersonic all-weather fighter, and came to the conclusion that the weapons system required by the Air Staff was so complex that it would not be fully developed before 1962, at the very earliest. To bridge the gap, the Company proposed a simpler delta-wing fighter that would be capable of meeting any air threat that was likely to develop within that period; it would be powered by an afterburning Gyron, plus two Spectre Junior rocket motors, and would be armed with Firestreak Mk.4 AAMs (later renamed Red Top) mounted at the wingtips. The aircraft would have a maximum level speed with reheat of 2.5M at 59,000 feet. With optimum early warning the fighter would be capable of intercepting a target at 60,000 feet 118.5 nautical miles from base; even

under the worst conditions, it would be able to reach an intercept point 50 nautical miles from base in 9.2 minutes, using reheat and one rocket in the climb and both rockets during the intercept manoeuvre.

Later in 1956, Fairey modified the design somewhat. The overall two-seat delta configuration was retained, but the single Gyron was replaced by two afterburning RB.128 engines and the rockets were deleted. It was also considered changing the armament to a pair of big Red Dean AAMs. As a further carrot, Fairey indicated that the design could be readily adapted to the medium/low-level intercept, strike and reconnaissance roles.

It was all for nothing, On Monday, 1 April 1957, Fairey received a strong indication from the Ministry of Supply that they were favourites in the running for F.155T. The following Thursday, Duncan Sandys announced the immediate cancellation of the whole programme.

Meanwhile, as a result of a ban restricting supersonic flying over the United Kingdom to altitudes of over 30,000 feet, Fairey had asked the French Flight Test Centre at Cazeaux if the FD.2 might be based there for a time to undergo further high-speed trials. WG774 was accordingly flown to Cazeaux on 15 October 1956, and in the course of the following month it made fifty-two flights in a total of eighteen hours' flying. A third of the flying time was supersonic, the aircraft achieving 1.04M down to 3,000 feet. The French looked on with interest, and gave new priority to the development of their family of delta-wing Mirage fighters. (It was afterwards hinted, somewhat spitefully in certain British government circles, that the French had copied the Mirage concept from the FD.2. This was quite untrue, and something of a slur of the technical ability of Marcel Dassault's excellent design team. In fact, the progenitor of the Mirage family, the Dassault MD.550 Mirage I, had already flown in June 1955).

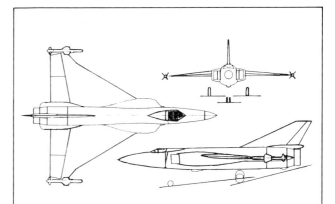

Designation: Fairey F.155T.

Role: All-weather interceptor.

Engines: Two Rolls-Royce RB.128 turbojets with reheat.

Span: 37 ft 7in.

Length: 56 ft 3 in.

Weight: Loaded 30,100 lb.

Crew: 2.

Service ceiling: 60,000 ft +.

Range: 400 miles.

Max speed: 2.5M at 59,000 ft.

Weapons: Two DH Red Top AAMs.

Testing of the FD.2 continued, and in June 1958 one of the aircraft was flown to Norway for further low-level supersonic flight trials intended to provide design information on the behaviour of an axial compressor engine over a wide range of flight conditions. Engine intake design had previously been dependent, to a great extent, on the testing of wind-tunnel models, and the main purpose of the trials was to record the pressure distribution in the engine intakes at various altitudes under subsonic and supersonic flight conditions up to the maximum speed of the aircraft, while taking simultaneous measurements of the stresses in the first-stage compressor blades.

Together, the two FD.2 prototypes made an enormous contribution to high-speed aerodynamic research. After its flying career was over, the second prototype, WG777, went to the RAF Museum at Finningley and later to Hendon; the other, WG774, was almost completely rebuilt and, fitted with a model of the ogival wing planform that was to be used on Concorde, flew again as the BAC 221 in May 1964 — at about the time, ironically, that France's Mirage was beginning to capture markets all over the world.

Returning to 1955, Hawker Aircraft had been pursuing their own answer to the stringent demands of OR.329/F.155T, the Gyron-powered P.1103. The design appeared to have plenty of development potential, and in 1956, at the instigation of the Air Staff, the Hawker design team under Sir Sydney Camm set about designing two variants, the P.1116 and P.1121, which were respectively two-seat and single-seat strike derivatives. In the event Camm's main effort was devoted to the development of the P.1121, which, had it come to fruition, would have emerged as a supersonic multi-role combat aircraft in the same class as the McDonnell F-4 Phantom.

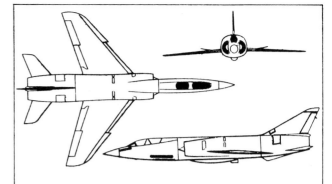

Designation: Hawker P.1129.
Role: Tactical strike and reconnaissance.
Engines: Two Rolls-Royce RB.142 or Bristol Siddeley Olympus 6 turbojets.
Span: 44 ft 7 in.
Length: 72 ft 9 in.
Crew: 2.
Service ceiling: 60,000 ft.
Range: 2,200 miles.
Max speed: 2.30M at 36,000 ft.
Weapons: Conventional or nuclear stores.

Development of the P.1121 went ahead with considerable enthusiasm during 1957, for it was planned to have a prototype flying in the following year. It was a fairly conventional swept-wing design, with a leading edge sweep of 40.6 degrees; power was to be provided by a single de Havilland Gyron of 17,400 lb.s.t. (23,800 lb.s.t. with reheat), although plans were made for the production version to take either the Rolls-Royce Conway or Bristol Olympus. The big engine was fed by an under-fuselage air intake. In the event, the Gyron was found to suffer from critically unbalanced pressure distribution on the intake face, so, after some delay, Hawker opted for the Olympus 21R as an alternative.

Work on the P.1121, financed entirely by Hawker, continued after the 1957 White Paper brought an abrupt end of OR.329. By the summer of 1958 the wing and fuselage assemblies of the prototype were complete, but it was becoming increasingly apparent that the Air Staff were no longer interested in the project and that it would be a waste of company funds to fly the prototype of an aircraft nobody wanted any more. The 1957 axe had left the British aircraft industry with only one long-term project for a manned combat aircraft: OR.339, an operational requirement for a tactical strike and reconnaissance machine, and along with the other leading British manufacturers Hawker was compelled to change course with the prevailing wind. Taking a proposed variant of the basic P.1121 design — the P.1125, which was to have been powered by two RB.133 engines — Camm enlarged it and completed an initial design tender for submission in January 1958. Later in the year, however, with the emergence of the Hawker Siddeley Group, the design was modified to incorporate features from a separate design submitted by Avro.

Work on the Hawker Siddeley OR.339 submission, designated P.1129, continued throughout 1958. Then, towards the end of the year, it was learned that a rival design, submitted by the Vickers/English Electric consortium, had been adjudged the winner.

Its name was TSR-2.

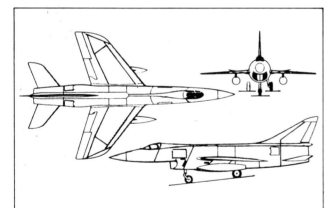

Designation: Hawker P.1121.
Role: Strike and air superiority.
Engine: One 17,270 lb.s.t. Bristol Siddeley Olympus turbojet with reheat.
Span: 37 ft.
Length: 66 ft 6 in.
Weight: Loaded 43,500 lb.
Crew: 1.
Service ceiling: 64,000 ft.
Range: 1,200 miles.
Max speed: 2.25M at 36,000 ft.
Weapons: Various proposed combinations of bombs, RP and cannon.

TSR-2: The Assassination of an Aircraft

In May 1951, when the English Electric Canberra first entered squadron service, it was beyond doubt the world's finest jet light bomber. With some justification, the Air Staff felt that Bomber Command possessed a tactical aircraft capable of delivering a wide variety of weapons to targets in Eastern Europe with a high probability of survival for the best part of a decade.

Only a year later, the picture had change. MiG-15s in large numbers were equipping the fighter squadrons of Russia and her allies, and there was an unvoiced but growing feeling that, if the Canberra had to go to war — especially in daylight — the tragedy of May 1940, when the RAF's Fairey Battle light bombers were shot out of the sky over France by the Luftwaffe's fighters, might be repeated.

In 1952, therefore, the Ministry of Supply issued Specification B.126T, calling for design studies of a bomber capable of carrying a six-ton nuclear store over a combat radius of 1,500 nautical miles at very low level and a high subsonic speed — not less than 0.85M. Several firms submitted proposals, but the requirement was well in advance of existing technological developments and it was shelved. However, the contest remained open for a low-level naval strike aircraft capable of operating from existing aircraft carriers and delivering a kiloton-range nuclear weapon against land or sea targets by the toss-bombing method. This requirement was covered by Specification M.148T, which was written around Naval Air Staff Target NAST.39, and in 1955 the design competition was won by Blackburn Aircraft with their B.103. A development batch of twenty aircraft was ordered in July that year, and the robust B.103 went on to enter service with the Royal Navy as the Buccaneer.

On the face of it, the Buccaneer might have seemed the ideal aircraft to meet the RAF's requirement for a Canberra replacement. In fact, although its airframe was quite adequate for the kind of low-level precision strike work envisaged by the RAF, its systems as they existed at the time were not. Admittedly, there was plenty of room for further development, but the Buccaneer was not fast enough; by 1956, the Air Staff had modified B.126T, which had been resurrected, to include an over-the-target speed at low level of 1.3M and the incorporation of an inertial nav/attack system that would enable the aircraft to deliver conventional weapons with pinpoint accuracy.

A year later, in the wake of the 1957 White Paper, the RAF's requirement was formalised as General Operational Requirement 339. Eight firms were invited to submit tenders by the end of January 1958; the eight did not include the Hawker Siddeley Group, which had already submitted preliminary drawings of the P.1125 project and which was well in the running with its P.1129 variant. The other firms were left in no doubt that they would have to get together and submit joint proposals if they were to seriously contest Hawker Siddeley; GOR.339 was likely to be the only major British military aircraft project for the foreseeable future, and it was too complex to be tackled by the resources of any single company. For the traditional structure of Britain's aircraft industry, GOR.339 spelt the beginning of the end.

English Electric, who had already done a lot of research into a Canberra replacement, had a head start with the design of a two-seat delta-wing project known as the P.17A, which was to be powered by two RB.142

engines. In collaboration with Short Brothers, English Electric's proposal was for a vertical take-off assembly in which the P.17A would be mounted on a Short-designed VTO platform designated P.17D; this was to be powered by forty-four RB.108 fixed lift engines, sixteen RB.108 swivelling lift engines and ten RB.108 engines for forward propulsion. Together, the P.17A/17D combination would weigh somewhere in the region of 150,000 lb. In addition to its primary role of getting the P.17A into the air and so dispensing with vulnerable runways, the P.17D could be used to transport freight and fuel to forward combat areas. The idea was by no means as far-fetched as one might think; Shorts were at that time heavily involved with pioneer VTOL techniques and their prototype SC.1 VTOL aircraft had already flown in conventional flight. Apart from technical considerations, the main drawback to the P.17D was that its development costs were likely to prove prohibitive. In addition to the low-level strike version of the P.17A, English Electric also proposed a long-range interceptor variant, the P.22.

Bristol Aircraft and Vickers-Armstrong also submitted their proposals for OR.339. The Vickers entry, the Type 571, was an advanced twin-engined design incorporating an integrated terrain-following nav/attack system; the aircraft was, in fact, a complete weapons system, and although the Air Staff were coming down heavily in favour of English Electric's P.17A they were sufficiently impressed by the Vickers design to want to incorporate certain features of it in the finalised OR.339 requirement. As a result of this a new operational Requirement, OR.343, was issued in the spring of 1958; it dispensed with the vertical take-off concept, which brought about the end of Short Brothers' participation, and virtually demanded the amalgamation of Vickers and English Electric to bring the required aircraft to fruition. Together with the Bristol Aeroplane Company, they were eventually to form the British Aircraft Corporation in February 1960.

Meanwhile, on 1 January 1959, it was announced that Vickers-Armstrong and English Electric had been awarded the contract to develop a new tactical strike and reconnaissance aircraft, known as TSR-2, to replace the Canberra. Its airframe was to be developed from that of the P.17, and it was to be powered by two afterburning Bristol Siddeley Olympus 22R engines. The choice of powerplant was pushed through in the face of severe criticism from the Vickers and English Electric design teams, who wanted a Rolls-Royce engine, and as events were to prove it was an unfortunate one. Nevertheless, *at the time* the Olympus 22R was the only engine available for immediate development as a massive reheat unit to provide up to 33,000 lb.s.t. with an acceptable specific fuel consumption, with a configuration suitable for twin rear-fuselage installation.

Development work proceeded at Weybridge and Warton, and a Management Board comprising representatives of the RAF, the Ministry of Aviation and BAC was set up to control the entire project and sort out any problems. In fact, the very reverse was to prove true: throughout its development, TSR-2 was to be bedevilled by the Board's decisions and compromises. In effect, it was the first time in the history of British aviation that decisions affecting the design of an aircraft were taken away from the design team involved and placed in the hands of a committee.

While the TSR-2 airframe gradually took shape, various sub-contractors were given the responsibility for developing the necessary systems. The contract for the automatic flight system went to Elliott Automation, who had amassed an enormous amount of experience in developing the inertial navigation for the V-Force's Blue Steel stand-off missile; Ferranti were given the task of developing the TFR and nav/attack system, and EMI the sideways-looking radar, while Marconi were made responsible for avionics such as the ILS. By the spring of 1960, it was apparent that the cost of developing the aircraft's advanced electronic systems was going to greatly exceed the estimated figures; this was the first of a series of cost escalations which were to contribute to the project's eventual downfall. Funds were diverted from other cancelled projects to keep TSR-2 going, but there was little slowing in the overall upward trend.

By the autumn of 1962 the design of TSR-2 had been finalised and BAC were able to provide the Ministry of Aviation with realistic estimated performance figures. These included a cruising speed of 0.9M—1.1M at sea level and 2.05M at altitude. Combat radius with external fuel would be 1,500 nautical miles, or 1,000 nautical miles with a 2,000-lb internal bomb load on internal fuel only. Initial rate of climb at sea level would be 50,000 feet per minute. A variety of flight profiles was envisaged, most involving lo-lo sorties at heights of not more than 200 feet at 0.9M. The aircraft could carry a formidable range of weapons, both in the nuclear and conventional strike roles.

TSR-2's main function, had it entered RAF service, would have been to carry out deep reconnaissance and

TSR-2's precursor: the English Electric P.17A.

Designation: English Electric TSR-2.
Role: Tactical Strike and Reconnaissance.
Engines: Two 19,600 lb.s.t. Olympus 22R turbojets.
Span: 37 ft.
Length: 89 ft.
Weight: Loaded 95,900 lb.
Crew: 2.
Service ceiling: 60,000 ft +.
Range: 2,870 n.m. with external tanks.
Max speed: 2.05M at altitude.
Weapons: Various combinations of conventional and nuclear stores.

TSR-2. TSR-2 XR.219 on the gunnery range at Foulness after the programme was abandoned.

attack missions against targets that required deep penetration of enemy territory, such as large bridges, airfields, missile and radar sites, marshalling yards, communication centres and concentrations of vehicles and armour. As a deep penetration system, TSR-2 was years ahead of its time; it was also the only strike aircraft in the world capable of a true short-field performance, which would have enabled it to operate in areas of the globe where large stretches of concrete did not exist, as well as increasing its own chances of survival in the event of an enemy attack on its bases. The use of an all-moving tailplane, replacing conventional elevator and aileron control, allowed maximum use to be made of full-span blown flaps as a high-lift device for short take-off and landing and permitted the aircraft to operate from semi-prepared or low-grade surfaces only 3,000 feet long. Another feature was TSR-2's long-stroke undercarriage with low-pressure tyres, specifically designed for operation from rough surfaces. The nosewheel strut could be extended during take-off to position the aircraft in take-off attitude and so shorten its run.

The nav/attack system incorporated in the aircraft, the most advanced of its type anywhere, exploited the latest developments in radar-computer/flight control techniques. Briefly, the system comprised a Doppler/inertial dead reckoning navigation system of very high accuracy which was corrected over 100 miles or so by fixes obtained from the sideways-looking radar. A forward-looking radar enabled the aircraft to follow the contours of the terrain either automatically or manually, the pilot having the benefit of a head-up display,

regardless of weather at a pre-selected height above the ground. Data from the navigation and TFR systems was fed by a complex of digital and analogue computers into an automatic pilot which was capable of flying the aircraft to and from a predetermined target, the flight plan being fed into the digital computer on punched tape. Throughout the flight, the ground position of the aircraft was displayed to the crew on a moving map. The particular attack mode required could be pre-selected and carried out automatically, without visual reference to the target.

In the reconnaissance role, TSR-2 was designed to carry a very complete reconnaissance pack in a pannier in the weapon bay. Its equipment included the EMI sideways-looking radar, moving target indication which could blot out all returns from stationary objects to disclose any movement in the area, and linescan, which took a TV-type picture by day or night and could be used to transmit information direct from the aircraft to a ground station in the forward area to provide up-to-the-second intelligence.

Because of the requirement that called for TSR-2 to be capable of supersonic flight at both high and low altitude, much attention was given in design to reducing the aircraft's response to gusts in order to make working conditions tolerable for the crew at very high speed and low altitudes. During the initial design phase of TSR-2, research into low-level turbulence using Canberras over the Libyan desert at speeds of about 0.7M (Operation 'Swifter') had shown that 'bumps' of $\frac{1}{2}$g could be expected, on average, 27 times a minute, which was more

ENGLISH ELECTRIC TSR-2.

BLACKBURN BUCCANEER MK. 2. With the demise of the TSR-2 and the American F-111, the RAF adopted the Buccaneer Mk. 2 as its primary low-level strike aircraft. The Buccaneer did the job remarkably well and could have been in RAF service several years earlier, saving enormous expenditure.

than twice the rate regarded as intolerable for the operating crews. Gust response is a factor of wing loading, and broadly speaking the lower this is, the rougher the ride for a given speed. The optimum solution is variable sweep, but TSR-2's designers opted for a delta planform and a small wing area, a leading-edge sweep of 60 degrees and a very thin section, mounted as high as possible on the fuselage. To minimise the low-speed Dutch Roll characteristic of highly-swept wings, the tip sections were given a sharp anhedral of 23 degrees.

A lot of thought was given to crew comfort and safety in TSR-2's design. The windscreen, for example, which was made of alumino silicate, was designed to stand a 1-lb bird strike at speeds in excess of 1.0M, and the cockpit incorporated a first-class air conditioning system, including refrigeration for high-speed flight. Both crew members had rocket-powered Martin-Baker ejection seats, capable of safe operation through every phase of the flight envelope from the take-off roll!

A contract for nine development TSR-2s had already been placed in October 1960, and this followed by a preliminary order for eleven pre-production aircraft in June 1962. At this stage, it was still hoped to fly the first prototype in the autumn of 1963, with delivery of the first batch of pre-production machines to follow two years later. Research and development costs were estimated at £90 million in 1960, but by the beginning of 1963 this figure had doubled and the whole schedule had slipped by two years. The problem of too many committees, each responsible for its own slice of the development work, still dogged the project, and even the setting up of a Steering Committee in 1963 to co-ordinate matters more closely did not do much to alleviate it.

Moreover, the project was now beset by worrying technical problems, mainly involving the Olympus 22R engine. The fifth Vulcan B.1, XA894, had been allocated to Olympus development work; the engine, fuelled from two tanks in the bomb bay, was mounted in a nacelle beneath the Vulcan's fuselage. First flight with the 22R was made on 23 February 1962, and later in the year XA894 was fitted with the more powerful Olympus 22R-1, featuring a high performance reheat system. All went well until 3 December 1962, when, during a full reheat ground run, the LP shaft of the 22R-1 failed and the engine disintegrated, spewing out metal fragments which ruptured both the bomb bay and main fuel tanks. Such was the force of the break-up that the LP turbine disc was hurled for half a mile in bounds of 150 yards, narrowly missing the Bristol 188 research aircraft. There were no casualties, but the Vulcan was completely burned out. The cause was resonance, which led to the break-up of the LP shaft at a certain RPM, but it was a long time before Bristol Siddeley established what had gone wrong, and in the meantime other Olympus 22R test engines failed, fortunately on the ground. Modifications were made, but these, together with other engine design changes, caused severe problems in marrying the Olympus to the TSR-2 airframe. The LP shaft problem had not been completely cured when the aircraft made its first flight, and failures were still occurring when the engine was run up to high RPM from a cold start — a procedure that was very necessary in a military aircraft, especially one whose whole effectiveness relied on getting airborne in the minimum time.

· By the end of 1963, the writing was already on the wall for TSR-2, although neither the government nor BAC would admit it. Escalating R and D costs had made the project the subject of heated political controversy; the

Labour opposition, influenced by 'advisors' who had a minimal knowledge of military aviation, and even less of the RAF's operational requirements, made political capital out of the funds that were being diverted to keep TSR-2 alive, and left the electorate in no doubt about what they would do to the project if they got into power. But there were sinister forces at work within the Ministry of Defence, too; the Chief of the Defence Staff, Lord Louis Mountbatten, made no secret of the fact that he favoured a land-based version of the Buccaneer to meet the RAF's requirement, while the Ministry's Chief Scientific Advisor, Sir Solly Zuckermann, told everyone concerned that he thought TSR-2 a waste of public money and that better value could be obtained by buying equipment from the United States.

Predictably, in-fighting such as this had an adverse effect on government attempts to promote the TSR-2 overseas. The Australians, in particular, had shown an active interest in the aircraft since 1960, and two years later were favouring the British machine as a Canberra replacement. Yet there was no sales drive aimed at convincing the Australian Government that TSR-2 was the aircraft the RAAF needed, so it was hardly surprising that Australian interest began to wane after Lord Mountbatten, during a tour of South-East Asia, expressed the opinion that mounting costs and complexity would prevent the aircraft ever coming into service. It was not until the end of 1963 that a British Government delegation led by Hugh Fraser, the Secretary of State for Air, went to Australia to mount a sales drive, but by that time it was too late. Soon afterwards, the Australians decided to meet the RAAF requirement by ordering twenty-four General Dynamics F-111As — at a cost that was eventually to outstrip anything they might have spent had they opted for TSR-2.

The prototype TSR-2, XR219, flew from Boscombe Down on 27 September 1964 with Roland Beamont at the controls, after carrying out twelve taxi runs. Some undercarriage problems delayed the next flight until the last day of the year, but after that the test programme picked up rapidly and seven flights were made in January 1965. The aircraft went supersonic for the first time on 21 February, and high-speed low-altitude trials began in March. By this time the second prototype had also joined the flying programme, and work was progressing on a third prototype and twenty pre-production aircraft, five of which were partly complete.

The Labour Government, which had taken office under Prime Minister Harold Wilson shortly after TSR-2's first flight, had kept the project going so that the aircraft could be evaluated against its American rival, the F-111. At that time, Wilson — acting on faulty advice — seriously believed that some £300 million might be saved by buying the American aircraft; his Cabinet thought so too, and the final nail in TSR-2's coffin was hammered home on 6 April 1965, when Chancellor James Callaghan, during his Budget speech, announced that the project was to be cancelled forthwith. The assassination was to be complete; no trace of the project was to survive. Orders were issued for the destruction of the two completed prototypes and those on the assembly line, and of all the jigs and tools used by the manufacturing companies.

It is fair to say that the decision to cancel TSR-2, at its stage of development, was probably the most ill-advised ever made by a British Government involving the aircraft industry. Admittedly, there were still snags to be overcome: but fewer snags than those that afflicted the F-111, for which the Government opted. Soaring costs and technical problems in the F-111 development programme eventually led to the cancellation of the British order, at considerable cost.

The gap was filled, in 1969, by the Buccaneer Mk.2, which Blackburn had wanted the RAF to have ten years earlier, and an admirable job it has done ever since. But it was not until 1982, with the debut of the Tornado, that the strike squadrons of the Royal Air Force at last possessed an aircraft capable of carrying out all the tasks for which the ill-fated TSR-2 had been intended.

Chapter Six
Formulae for Success

At this juncture, it is instructive to take a look at the overall picture of combat aircraft developments since 1945. From the viewpoint of individual countries, certain aspects at once become apparent.

In the United States, the main years of experimentation in jet combat aircraft developments were those from 1945 to 1949. After that, thanks to the F-86, F-84 and F-80 and progressive developments of these aircraft, the Americans started to get things right, and the subsequent history of military aviation in the United Sates is not blemished by the tombstones of aircraft that fell by the wayside.

Developments in the Soviet Union followed roughly the same timescale, once post-war technology had got off the ground with the help of German data and engines supplied by the United Kingdom. The difference was that the Russians produced far more prototypes to meet a single requirement, and that in one respect — bomber development — they lagged far behind the USA. Also, Soviet avionics were in an embryo state, which had an adverse effect on the development of all-weather fighters until the mid-1950s.

France's aircraft industry, recovering with astonishing speed from the effects of the Second World War — despite the damaging effects of successive government policies — was beginning to produce first-class combat aircraft such as the Dassault Ouragan and Mystere IIC within six years of the end of hostilities. The peak of French experimental work came in the early 1950s, when French designers, striving to make the necessary technical breakthrough that would enable them to make good the lost years, concentrated on radical concepts like the Baroudeur and Trident and the ramjet-powered Leduc 022. Bold and ambitious though these were, they were in the nature of red herrings; it was Dassault's strictly conventional Mirage family that ultimately brought France into the front rank of world military aviation.

Great Britain, battered by a succession of economic crises in the years after the war, nevertheless remained at the forefront of advanced aerodynamic research and engine technology until 1950, when work slowed down dramatically. The principal reason for this was twofold; first, economic restraints imposed a heavy burden on the industry, and second, much of the available funding was devoted to the creation of an independent British nuclear deterrent. Even so, as we have seen in an earlier chapter, British designers were still capable of producing aircraft that were more than a match for any others, and there would undoubtedly have been a dramatic upturn in the

Thanks to aircraft such as the Lockheed F-80 Shooting Star, the Americans began to get things right early in the jet era. For example, the F-80 formed the basis for the F-94 Starfire all-weather fighter.

LOCKHEED F-94 STARFIRE.

industry's fortunes if the UK government had made the right decisions in 1956-57 — and had not adopted the disastrous all-eggs-in-one-basket policy that crystallized in TSR-2.

The main problem that beset military aircraft development in Britain in the early days of the jet age, however, was that there was little attempt to centralise effort or pool knowledge. Admittedly, designers made use of the growing research facilities at the Royal Aeronautical Establishment, Farnborough, and its various offshoots, but their work progressed along independent lines, often with a wasteful duplication of effort.

This was certainly not true of the United States, where from 1946 research and development facilities were concentrated at Muroc, a vast dry lake in California. There were in fact two lakebeds at Muroc, and during the Second World War the southern lakebed was used as a USAF training base. The northern lakebed, on the other hand, housed the most secret flying establishment in the United States, and it was here, on 1 October 1942, that the first American jet aircraft — the Bell XP-59A Airacomet — made its maiden flight. It was from Muroc, too, in 1944, that the first US combat jet, the Lockheed XP-80 Shooting Star, took to the air.

During the next two years, Muroc was turned into one vast experimental centre encompassing both lakebeds. From 1946 to 1958, it was to play a major role in the supersonic breakthrough that followed hard on the heels of the turbojet revolution. That breakthrough came on 14 October, 1947, when USAF test pilot Charles E. 'Chuck' Yeager reached a speed of 1.06M in the Bell XS-1 rocket-powered research aircraft at altitude after being air-launched from a B-29 parent aircraft.

The act of centralising aerodynamic research and test flying at Muroc, using aircraft built purely for research by the various American aircraft companies under programmes sponsored by the USAF and US Navy, as well as by the civilian NACA (later NASA), made

possible the evolution of a series of operational combat aircraft which, over the next two decades, were to put the United States a long way in front of any other major aircraft-producing nation. The Bell X-1 series of rocket research aircraft, which pioneered flight beyond Mach One, was followed by the swept-wing Douglas Skyrocket, which was developed under a programme sponsored by the US Navy. In 1953, flown by NACA test pilot A. Scott Crossfield, the Skyrocket became the first aircraft to exceed Mach Two. Then came the Bell X-2, a highly unstable and dangerous aircraft which in 1956 pushed the speed up to 3.196M on its thirteenth and final flight; it subsequently crashed, killing its pilot, Milburn Apt.

The sum total of the research carried out under the various programmes at Muroc in the late 1940s and early 1950s — research that cost the lives of several pilots as they pushed their aircraft into the realms of the unknown — was incorporated in the generation of Mach Two Plus combat aircraft that were to equip the first-line squadrons of the USAF and US Navy by 1960. Perhaps the best example of a research type that led directly to the development of such a combat type was the stiletto-like Douglas X-3, flown for the first time by test pilot Bill Bridgeman on 20 October 1952. The primary purpose of the X-3 was to test the aerodynamics that were to be incorporated in the design of a radical new interceptor conceived by Lockheed in 1951, at a time when the lessons of the Korean War were bringing about profound changes in combat aircraft design on both sides of the Iron Curtain. That aircraft, the F-104 Starfighter, eventually flew in February 1954, only eleven months after a contract had been placed for two XF-104 prototypes — a measure of how much preliminary work had already been done in the air by the X-3 at Muroc.

By this time, Muroc had changed its identity. In December 1949 it was renamed Edwards Air Force Base in memory of Captain Glen W. Edwards, an outstanding test pilot who was killed in the crash of one of Northrop's YB-49A flying wing bombers.

The primary function of Edwards AFB has always been to develop, test and validate new defence systems, and every combat aircraft to enter service with the US forces since 1947 has undergone an exhaustive programme of flight and ground testing at the base. In 1959, the Air Force Flight Center — to give Edwards its proper title — began a new phase of activity with a lengthy period of research into hypersonic flight, research that would come to fruition with the operational use of the Space Shuttle. The first steps were taken with the early flights of the North American X-15, which, air-launched from a B-52 mother ship, eventually reached a speed of 6.72M (4,250 mph) and an altitude of 67 miles in the early 1960s.

Much of this research was directed towards the completion of the X-20A Dyna-Soar project, a manned orbital bomber/reconnaissance spacecraft designed to 'skip' across the outer layer of the atmospheric envelope and glide back to its base. The Dyna-Soar project was cancelled in 1963, but the concept survived, and immediately afterwards the Flight Test Center, in conjunction with NASA, embarked on a programme of development involving low-speed 'lifting bodies', aerodynamic test shapes designed to evaluate the performance and handling qualities of re-entry vehicles at various stages of the flight envelope. Research was concentrated on three principal designs, the Northrop M2-F2/F3 and HL10, and the Martin X-24A/X-24B. Flight testing these aircraft convinced both NASA and the USAF that the future Space Shuttle would be quite capable of making an unpowered gliding descent after re-entry, followed by a precision approach and a conventional landing on an ordinary concrete runway. To prove the point still further, NASA modified a

General Dynamics F-111A variable geometry fighter-bomber and showed that a precise terminal guidance approach to land, even in marginal weather conditions, would be quite feasible for the returning spacecraft.

America's bold and often radical approach to the development of new hardware, whether for use inside the earth's atmosphere or in space, stems mainly from the time of the Korean War, which revealed a pressing need for aircraft designed to carry out specific functions ranging from high-level reconnaissance to tank busting. Even in the mid-1950s, it was no longer acceptable to adapt an existing bomber type, say, to carry out long-range reconnaissance missions high in the stratosphere, and the unsuitability of fast jet fighters for anti-armour operations had been apparent for some time. In the strategic bomber field, Strategic Air Command's preferred mix of ICBMs and manned aircraft like the B-52 meant that bombers would be around for the foreseeable future, but the next generation of manned bombers would have to penetrate to their targets at very low level and would have to be capable of a sustained Mach Two dash whilst in the target area, not merely to frustrate enemy defences but also to avoid the devastating effect of the thermonuclear weapons they carried. In the late 1950s, some of those weapons had a yield of 20 megatons or more.

So, from 1955, the US industry began to evolve a new generation of military aircraft, designed either to perform a specific task or a multiplicity of tasks, and every new design was proven and often refined at Edwards AFB. Airframe and engine technology, as well as the necessary aerodynamic knowledge, were now all in an advanced state; designers no longer had to fumble in the dark for the formulae that would take their creations to extremes

The straight-wing Republic F-84 Thunderjet, of Korean War vintage (seen here harmonizing its 0.5-inch machine-guns) was developed into the swept-back F-84F Thunderstreak, which remained one of NATO's principal strike fighters until the 1960s.

REPUBLIC F-84F THUNDERSTREAK.

One of the most powerful and secret aircraft of all time, the Lockheed SR-71A Blackbird has a speed of 3.5M and a ceiling in excess of 88,000 feet.

of altitude and speed. The aircraft that emerged from the drawing boards of the US companies in the 1950s were technically better equipped than ever before to carry out the specialist tasks they were intended to perform.

From Lockheed came the graceful U-2 strategic reconnaissance aircraft, virtually a powered glider, which for five years roved over the Soviet Union unmolested until one fell victim to a SAM in May 1960. It was followed by another creation of Lockheed's ultra-secret 'Skunk Works', the SR-71A Blackbird. This astonishing aircraft, capable of a ceiling of 88,000 feet and a speed of 3.5M, was evolved from the Lockheed A-11, which also gave birth to an experimental interceptor version, the YF-12A. Both the U-2 and the A-11 variants underwent their proving at Edwards.

The lessons of the Korean War also led to the evolution of a new generation of fighter and attack aircraft for the US Navy. The air war over Korea, in which US naval aviation had played a substantial part, had shown that existing naval jet types such as the McDonnell F2H Banshee and Grumman F9F Panther were no match for modern land-based fighters like the MiG-15. The US companies tackled the problem with urgency while the Korean War was still in progress, conscious that the conflict might escalate.

To replace the Panther and its swept-wing version, the Cougar, Grumman conceived the F11F Tiger supersonic fighter, which first flew in 1954. The Tiger's design featured area ruling and other aerodynamic refinements which were then novel, and although the formulae used turned out to be correct, the type experienced some serious technical troubles during early flight testing. These were gradually ironed out by Grumman's design staff on the recommendations of the Edwards' test pilots, and the Tiger, incorporating several major aerodynamic

refinements as a result, eventually entered service in March 1957.

The first aircraft to give the US Navy a true supersonic capability, however, was the Chance Vought F8U-1 Crusader day-fighter, which first flew at Edwards AFB in March 1955. The type was formally accepted by the US Navy in December 1956, only twenty-one months later; the main reason for this rapid development was that virtually no changes were required in production aircraft, which had the same engine as the two prototypes — another clear-cut example of American designers getting it right first time.

Crusaders were used extensively during the Vietnam War, alongside another type that had been born out of the lessons of the Korean conflict. In 1950, having abandoned the XA2D Skyshark as a potential turboprop-powered replacement for the lengendary Skyraider, the Douglas Aircraft Company began design studies of a turbojet-powered shipboard attack aircraft capable of delivering nuclear weapons and performing the wide variety of conventional attack roles undertaken by the Skyraider in Korea. The result was the A4D Skyhawk, the prototype of which flew on 22 June 1954, only eighteen months after the start of detailed engineering design. The first A4D-1 Skyhawks were delivered to the US Navy in September 1956, and equipped some forty USN and USMC squadrons during the 1960s. As well as seeing extensive action in the Vietnam War, it was also the mainstay of the Israeli Air Force's attack squadrons during the Yom Kippur War of October 1973, when about forty per cent of Israel's Skyhawks were lost in combat — and in 1982, in Argentinian colours, it was dealing out severe punishment to the warships of the Royal Navy off the Falklands Islands. Few jet aircraft have seen more action

The Korean War showed that existing naval jet types such as the Grumman F9F Panther were no match for the MiG-15. To improve performance, Grumman gave the Panther swept flying surfaces and it became the Cougar.

The Grumman F11F Tiger was one of the first to feature an area-ruled fuselage. After many teething troubles, it entered US Navy service in 1957.

than the Skyhawk in a career spanning thirty years, and fewer still have shown such amazing development potential.

One American aircraft, however has eclipsed all others in the latter respect. One of the most powerful and versatile combat aircraft ever built, the McDonnell F-4 Phantom stemmed from a 1954 project for an advanced naval fighter designated F3H-G/H. A mock-up was built, and in October 1954 the US Navy ordered two prototypes under the designation YAH-1. This aircraft was to have been a single-seater, armed with four 20-mm cannon and powered by two Wright J65 turbojets, but when the Navy finalised its requirement in April 1955 the design was changed substantially, the aircraft now being fitted with two General Electric J79s, two seats and an armament of four Sparrow missiles instead of the cannon. The designation was also changed, to F4H-1, and then later to F-4.

The Phantom became operational with the United States Navy in December 1960, and was also delivered to the USMC in 1962. The new aircraft's potential was soon apparent; in that same year, twenty-nine F-4Bs were loaned to the USAF for evaluation, and proved superior to any Air Force fighter-bomber. The Phantom's success story needs no re-telling here, except to say that its debut marked a double milestone in aviation history. Not only was it the first multi-role aircraft of the jet age; it was also the first to give the US forces and many of America's allies a Mach Two capability in a wide variety of missions.

The Phantom was a fine example of an aircraft that was originally developed for one job and ending up carrying out a lot of others. Ironically enough, if it had been designed as a tactical fighter-bomber instead of a naval fighter, its story might have had a different ending, for the USAF sometimes appeared slower to recognise the

The Chance Vought F8U-1 Crusader was the first aircraft to give the US Navy a true supersonic capability.

potential of individual combat aircraft than did the USN. The career of the Republic F-105 Thunderchief was a case in point.

Although beset by continual difficulties and delays during its early development career, the Thunderchief eventually was to emerge as the workhorse of the USAF's Tactical Air Command during the 1960s. It was conceived as a successor to the F-84F Thunderstreak at a time when the US Department of Defense was giving top priority to building up the American nuclear deterrent, and consequently the evolution of a supersonic strike fighter came low down the list of considerations. Nevertheless, in March 1953 the Department of Defense ordered an initial batch of 37 aircraft for evaluation, this being reduced to 15 aircraft in February the following year. To add to Republic's problems, the DoD instructed that four of these aircraft were to be powered by Pratt & Whitney J75 engines instead of the planned J57. In September 1954 the number of aircraft ordered was cut still further to three, and it was not until February 1955 that the order was raised to 15 once more.

The first of two YF-105 prototypes flew in October 1955, and a third aircraft in May 1956. During that year the F-105 was evaluated in competition with its main opponent, the North American F-107 (see Appendix 2), and the Republic design proved superior on most counts. As a result, the F-105B was ordered into production in January 1957, deliveries of operational aircraft beginning in May 1958. Only 75 F-105Bs were built, this variant being replaced on the production line in 1959 by the all-weather ground-attack F-105D version.

The latter entered service with Tactical Air Command in 1960, and although it was initially unpopular, mainly because of early snags with its avionics systems, it was soon to prove its worth over Vietnam, where it flew more than 75 per cent of USAF strike missions with an abort rate of less than one per cent.

For the largest and heaviest single-seat fighter-bomber in the world, it also showed an astonishing ability to absorb tremendous battle damage and still get back to base.

Meanwhile, military aircraft development in the Soviet Union had been following closely parallel lines to that in the USA, and during the Krushchev decade, from 1955 to 1964, the Soviet Air Force acquired a stable of first-class fighter, strike and reconnaissance aircraft which, in turn, gave impetus to the development of still more advanced types in the West. The MiG-19 Farmer, which went into series production in 1955 and was the first Soviet fighter with supersonic capability in level flight, was succeeded by the MiG-21 Fishbed, a smaller and lighter aircraft whose delta wing gave it the Russian nickname of Balalaika. The MiG-21 is an outstanding example of how the life of an aircraft can be extended by constant modifications and changes; when first produced, the Fishbed-A was a clear-weather point defence and air superiority fighter, but by the end of the 1950s the follow-on version, the Fishbed-C, had an all-weather multi-role capability. Before the MiG-21 had reached the end of its dozen versions, the NATO designators had gone from Fishbed-A to Fishbed-N.

Pavel Sukhoi, re-instated after the death of Stalin in 1953, contributed greatly to the Soviet air build-up, and his bureau has continued to do so ever since. From it, in 1956, came the Su-7 Fitter-A and the Su-9 Fishpot-A, both single-engined, single-seat types. The Su-7, designed for close air support with the Frontal Aviation, featured 60 degrees of sweep and carried two 30-mm cannon in its

The Douglas A4D-1 Skyhawk was designed as a replacement for the ageing Skyraider after the failure of the XA2D Skyshark. It proved to be one of the most successful attack aircraft of all time.

The McDonnell F-4 Phantom is one of the most versatile combat aircraft ever built, and has eclipsed all others as far as development potential is concerned. An advanced version, the Super Phantom, was being marketed in 1985 – thirty years after the original made its appearance.

wing roots; it also carried a relatively heavy load of ordnance, either rockets or bombs, under the wings. The Su-7B variant, which entered service in 1959, is still used by the Soviet Air Force, the satellite countries and some client States.

The Sukhoi Su-9 Fishpot-A was a delta-wing, single-seat interceptor — to some extent, an Su-7 with a delta wing. It was armed with the first Soviet AAM, the semi-active radar homing Alkali, four of which were carried under the wings. In 1961 a new model, the Su-11 Fishpot-B, was developed from the Su-9 and entered service with the Soviet Air Force, and this was followed by the Fishpot-C with an uprated engine. By the end of the Krushchev regime, the Su-7 Fitter was widely used by the Frontal Aviation as a strike aircraft, while the Su-11 was a key aircraft in the Soviet air defence system.

The first true all-weather fighter used by the Russians was the Yak-25 Flashlight, which entered service in 1954. This twin-engined, two-seat machine was later supplanted by the largest of the interceptors produced in the Soviet Union during the decade in question: the Tupolev Tu-28P Fiddler. Powered by two Lyulka AL-7F turbojets, the Fiddler entered service in the early 1960s and was capable of a speed of 1.65M at 40,000 feet.

The Fiddler was first revealed to the public at the Tushino air display of 1961, together with other advanced types whose appearance showed that Soviet aviation had at last ceased to be dependent on foreign inputs, German or otherwise, and that its airframe and engine design bureaux were well able to hold their own with the West. For the Russians, 1961 marked the beginning of what may best be termed a great leap

Although beset by continual difficulties and delays during its early development career, the F-105 Thunderchief emerged as the workhorse of the USAF's Tactical Air Command during the 1960s, replacing its ancestor, the F-84F Thunderstreak.

forward that was to lose none of its momentum over the next two decades.

In the fighter field, the follow-on to the Su-11 was the Su-15 Flagon, a twin-engined delta-wing interceptor that first flew in 1965 and was in Soviet Air Force service by 1969. Capable of 2.5M and carrying two AAMs, the Flagon was numerically Russia's most important all-weather interceptor by 1974.

The Russians also showed a remarkable talent for developing existing designs to the fullest extent. This was particularly apparent in the case of the Sukhoi Su-7, which was redesigned with a more powerful engine, variable geometry wings and increased fuel tankage; in this guise it became the Su-17/20 Fitter-C, which is unique among combat aircraft in being a variable-geometry derivative of a fixed-wing machine. The development of the Fitter-C was a facet of the Soviet practice of continued development of their aircraft in order to keep them in service for 30 or 40 years and foster long-term standardisation within the Warsaw Pact countries. Also, the use of the same production facilities over a long period of time helped greatly to reduce costs, which is why the Russians are usually able to offer combat types on the international market at far more competitive rates than the West.

There were further revelations at the 1967 Domodedovo air display, when new designs from the Mikoyan bureau were much in evidence. One of these was the MiG-23 Flogger, which entered service with the Frontal Aviation in 1971 as a strike aircraft and by 1973 was being deployed to the Soviet forces in Germany. A VG type with wings sweeping from 23 to 71 degrees, the Flogger was the Soviet Air Force's first true multi-role combat aircraft, and was also configured as an interceptor.

The other Mikoyan aircraft at Domodedovo in 1967 was a twin-engined, cropped, delta-wing interceptor designated MiG-25 and given the NATO code-name Foxbat. The prototype MiG-25 was flown as early as 1964 and was apparently designed to counter the projected North American B-70 Valkyrie, with its Mach Three speed and ceiling of 70,000 feet. The cancellation of the B-70 left the MiG-25 in search of a role; it entered service as an interceptor in 1970, but soon a MiG-25R variant appeared, equipped with cameras and electronic intelligence equipment, and it was in this role that the type found its true value. In September 1976, Lieutenant Viktor Belenko flew a MiG-25 Foxbat-A to Hakodate Airport in Japan, giving US and Japanese experts a golden opportunity to examine the aircraft in detail. This examination produced a number of surprises, the first of which was the use of steel instead titanium in all except such hotspots as the leading edges and tailpipes. Another surprise was the use of vacuum tubes instead of transistors in the electronic systems, an indication that the Russians were well behind the West in avionics when the Foxbat began to come off the production line. Nevertheless, the examiners reported that the vacuum tubes and the steel construction seemed to work very well.

The 1960s saw the Russians beginning to catch up with the West in bomber design, too. The Tushino air display of 1961 saw the appearance of the Tupolev Tu-22 Blinder, the first supersonic bomber to enter service with the

Russia's Tupolev Tu-95 Bear is a good example of an aircraft with long-term potential. Thirty years after it entered service with the Soviet Long-Range Aviation, its latest version is now being developed to carry cruise missiles – following the lead of America's B-52 force.

Although produced in relatively small numbers, the Myasishchev Mya-4 Bison was a good design. This example was pictured on an ELINT mission high over the Faroes Gap.

Soviet Air Force. The first operational version, Blinder-A, was produced in limited quantity only, its range of about 1,400 miles falling short of planned strategic requirements, but the second variant, Blinder-B, was fitted with a flight refuelling probe and was equipped to carry an air-to-surface stand-off weapon (NATO: Kitchen) recessed in the weapons bay. This version, some 200 of which were built, was intended primarily for the Soviet Naval Air Arm in the anti-shipping role, and carried a nose-mounted search radar. The Blinder-C was a maritime reconnaissance version carrying a battery of six cameras in the weapons bay and was also equipped for the ELINT and ECM roles. Between 60 and 70 were in

service with the Naval Air Arm by 1978, by which time a further variant, armed with air-to-air missiles, had begun to replace the Tu-28P Fiddler in the long-range interceptor role. Its task was presumably to deal with Strategic Air Command's B-52s before they were in a position to enter Soviet airspace.

Then, in the autumn of 1969, official US sources stated that the Soviet Union was developing a new supersonic variable-geometry medium bomber, presumably to supplant or complement the Tu-22 Blinder in service with the Soviet Air Forces. In July 1970, intelligence satellite data confirmed that the aircraft existed in prototype form, and it was later identified as a twin-engined

The sleek Tu-16 Badger was one of Russia's most successful bomber designs, and the progenitor of more modern types such as the Tu-22 Blinder and Tu-26 Backfire.

The proximity of powerful Russia has long been of concern to neutral Sweden, and has led to the creation of some of the world's most potent and advanced combat aircraft. Sweden, with a limited defence budget, has mastered the importance of 'getting things right' without wasteful expenditure, as the following photographs show:

The SAAB J21R, Sweden's first jet fighter, flew for the first time in March 1947 and became operational in 1949. It provided Swedish pilots with much experience and laid the foundation for the service debut of more advanced types.

The SAAB J-29 had the distinction of being the first swept-wing jet fighter of European design to enter service after the Second World War. Produced in five different versions, it remained in service until well into the 1960s and was also exported to Austria.

The SAAB A-32 Lansen attack aircraft went into quantity production in 1955 and was still an important item on the Swedish Air Force's inventory in the late 1970s.

Tupolev design. About a dozen machines were flying by the end of 1973, and the type's designation was reported to be Tu-26, although its true identity was the Tu-22M.

The Tu-22M, code-named Backfire, bears some resemblance to a one-off Tupolev supersonic bomber prototype built and flown in the late 1950s under the manufacturer's designation Tu-98 (NATO: Backfin). Tu-22M design requirements called for a maximum over-the-target speed in the order of 2.5M, a maximum unrefuelled range of up to 6,000 miles at high altitude and a low-level penetration capability. Again according to US sources, early production Tu-22Ms (Backfire-As) fell short of the range requirement, but the subsequent model, the Backfire-B, is believed to have met all operational demands. It was this production version that received the designation Tu-26.

The Backfire-B entered service with the Soviet Air Force in 1975, and towards the end of that year some maritime reconnaissance/strike units of the Soviet Naval Air Arm were also re-equipped with the type. A third variant, the Backfire-C, was identified in 1983.

Until the advent of Backfire, the Soviet long-range bomber force had relied on its elderly Tu-95 Bears, Mya-4 Bisons, and Tu-16 Badgers; now it possessed an ultra-modern bomber capable of attacking targets on the North American continent and also one which, in the low-level naval strike role, posed a considerable threat to NATO maritime power. Its appearance gave impetus to the development in the United States of the supersonic Rockwell B-1A bomber, which was originally intended to replace Strategic Air Command's B-52 force; the first of four prototypes flew in December 1974 but the programme was cancelled in 1977.

Two of the four prototypes continued flying until 1981, however, so that when the B-1 was resurrected and ordered into production by President Reagan's administration in 1982 nearly two-thirds of the required flight test programme had been completed. The first of a planned 100 operational B-1B variable-geometry bombers flew on 18 October 1984; deliveries were scheduled to begin in June 1985, with the first squadrons becoming fully operational in 1986. The primary

The SAAB J35 Draken, which replaced the J-29, was designed from the outset to intercept transonic bombers at all altitudes and in all weathers, and at the time of its service debut in 1960 formed part of the first fully integrated air defence system in western Europe. Capable of Mach 2, it was in service before Britain's one and only indigenous supersonic interceptor, the Lightning.

function of the B-1B will be to take over the penetration role from the Boeing B-52H, filling a gap until the advent of the so-called 'Stealth' or Advanced Technology bomber sometime in the 1990s; the B-1Bs will then take over the role of cruise missile carriers from the ageing B-52s.

Meanwhile, the Russians had not been idle. In the late 1960s, the Sukhoi design bureau had begun work on a prototype supersonic strategic jet bomber that bore a strong resemblance to the North American B-70 Valkyrie. The requirement called for long flights at sustained supersonic speed, and the aircraft was designed to reach 2.8M at altitude. The experimental aircraft featured a thin-section trapezoidal-planform wing with a break in the leading edge. The design was tailless, but with a small foreplane. The slender fuselage had tandem seating for the crew, and the aircraft featured a drooped nose like that of the Tu-144 supersonic airliner. The first flight was reportedly made on 22 August 1972, but no further information about the type is available at the time of writing and it appears to have been abandoned.

Then, in 1982, an American reconnaissance satellite detected something new at Ramenskoye air base, Russia's equivalent of Edwards AFB. The satellite's cameras revealed what appeared to be a new strategic bomber, an aircraft similar in configuration to the Rockwell B-1 but considerably larger. Known first by the temporary designation RAM-P and later allocated the NATO code-name Blackjack, the variable-geometry aircraft showed distinctive features of the Tupolev design bureau. According to US estimates, it could be operational by 1987. With an estimated range of 4,000 nautical miles and a speed of Mach Two, Blackjack, armed with cruise missiles, could present a significant threat to the North American continent.

So much for strategic bomber development. In another vital area, military aviation developments in both NATO and the Warsaw Pact have been dominated by the need to achieve air superiority over the battlefield in the event of a conventional war in Europe, and also to strike effectively at the enemy's base areas without recourse to nuclear weapons.

In 1965, the USAF requested funds for the development of a new air superiority fighter, and over the next four years designs were submitted by Fairchild Hiller, McDonnel Douglas and North American Rockwell. By this time the development programme had assumed great urgency, for the USAF possessed no operational aircraft capable of meeting the Soviet Air Force's MiG-25 Foxbat on equal terms. In December 1969 McDonnell Douglas was selected as the prime airframe contractor and an order was placed for twenty development aircraft under the designation F-15A. The first of these flew in July 1972, and the F-15 Eagle was ordered into production the following March. The F-15C became the major production version; the latest variant is the F-15E interdictor/strike aircraft, which can carry up to 22,000 pounds of ordnance.

The second important US fighter development was the General Dynamics F-16 Fighting Falcon lightweight air superiority fighter, which first flew on 2 February 1974 and which has replaced the F-104 Starfighter in service with several air forces. The F-16's contender was the Northrop YF-17; both aircraft underwent an eleven-month evaluation programme in which the General Dynamics aircraft readily attained all its design objectives. The major production version is the F-16C,

which is equipped for all-weather beyond-visual-range air defence and night or adverse weather ground attack.

Over the past decade, the Soviet Union has made great strides in developing aircraft to match, or counter, those in the NATO arsenal. The first significant development of the 1970s was the Sukhoi Su-24 Fencer variable-geometry interdictor/strike aircraft, which was designed to perform roughly the same tasks as the General Dynamics F-111 and has comparable low-level, all-weather terrain avoidance capabilities. The Fencer entered service in 1974 and now (1985) equips units of the Soviet tactical and strategic forces. Fencers based in Eastern Europe could attack targets anywhere in the European theatre, including the United Kingdom. To counter the threat posed by low-level interdictors such as the F-111 and Tornado — and also cruise missiles — the Russians have also deployed the MiG-31 Foxhound, the first Soviet fighter with a look-down/shoot-down capability. The Foxhound, is a development of the MiG-25 Foxbat, and service deployment began in 1983. In the anti-cruise missile role, Foxhound may operate in conjunction with a military version of the Tu-144 supersonic airliner, which is thought to have been developed into a supersonic cruise missile interceptor.

The other ultra-modern Mikoyan design is the MiG-29

One of the most potent combat aircraft of the 1970s, the SAAB 37 Viggen (Thunderbolt) replaced the A-32 Lansen and was designed to carry out the four roles of attack, interception, reconnaissance and training. It will be replaced by the SAAB JAS-39 Gripen, scheduled to enter service from 1992.

Selected in January 1969 as the winner of a US Navy contest for a new carrier-borne fighter, the Grumman F-14 Tomcat was designed primarily to establish air superiority in the vicinity of a carrier task force and also to attack tactical objectives as a secondary role.

The McDonnell Douglas F-15 Eagle air superiority fighter was developed to counter the threat posed by the MiG-25 Foxbat.

The butterfly-tailed Northrop YF-17 underwent an eleven-month evaluation programme in competition with the F-16. The latter won.

The General Dynamics F-16 Fighting Falcon lightweight air superiority fighter has replaced the F-104 Starfighter in service with several air forces. NATO air forces represented in this line-up are those of Holland, Denmark and Belgium.

Until recently the Americans had a strong monopoly in the anti-armour field in the shape of the Fairchild Republic A-10 Thunderbolt II. Now the Russians have their equivalent, the Su-25 Frogfoot.

Fulcrum single-seat, twin-engined air superiority fighter, developed as a counter to its equivalent, the F-16. First deployed early in 1984, the Fulcrum is similar in size to the F-16 and has look-down/shoot-down capability; it may also, like the F-16, be able to undertake multi-role missions. Fulcrum, which has a maximum speed of 2.3M, was first sighted at Ramenskoye in 1979 and allocated the provisional code-name RAM-L.

Russia's equivalent of the F-15 Eagle is the Su-27 Flanker, deployment of which started late in 1984. The Flanker also has look-down/shoot-down capability and can carry up to eight air-to-air missiles, at least four of them medium-range weapons designed to engage low-flying targets. The Su-27, which was first detected at Ramenskoye in the late 1970s and provisionally designated RAM-K, has an estimated maximum speed of 2.3M.

The Russians have also developed considerable close-support and anti-armour potential. Until recently the Americans had a strong monopoly in this field with the Fairchild Republic A-10 Thunderbolt II, the end product of the USAF's A-X programme which was initiated in 1967. The A-10 beat a Northrop contender in meeting the requirement and went into service in the European theatre with the 81st Tactical Fighter Wing at Bentwaters, in Suffolk.

First indications that the Soviet Union might be developing a comparable aircraft came, yet again, from satellite surveillance of Ramenskoye, and was confirmed when the aircraft was seen in action over Afghanistan.

Designated Su-25 and given the NATO code-name of Frogfoot, it is smaller than the A-10 and bears a closer resemblance to the Northrop A-7, which lost the A-X contest.

Perhaps the most significant development in recent years, however, has been the build-up of Soviet seaborne naval aviation. When the then-new Soviet carrier *Kiev* passed through the Mediterranean in the summer of 1976, the aircraft it carried came as a surprise to Western observers. Although it was known that the Russians had been experimenting with V/STOL techniques for sometime — a research aircraft, the Yakovlev Yak-36 Freehand, had flown at Domodedovo in 1967 — it had not been thought that they had succeeded in developing an operational V/STOL type. Yet the *Kiev's* complement of Yak-38 Forgers were undoubtedly operational, and today equip all four Kiev-class carriers. Moreover, the Russians are building a new generation of super-carriers comparable with the US Navy's giants; they will be able to carry aircraft in the same category as the Grumman F-14 Tomcat and the McDonnell Douglas F-18 Hornet.

Whether those new Soviet naval aircraft will be derivatives of existing land-based types remains to be seen. But if the West is to expand its rapidly-diminishing margin of air superiority in all fields, priority must be given to the development of yet another generation of combat aircraft which will assure that superiority into the 21st century. What form those aircraft may take will be discussed in a later chapter.

Chapter Seven
Lightweight Fighter Development

In April, 1954, the increasing complexity of modern combat aircraft, together with a complete reappraisal of tactical air power requirements in Europe, led to the issue of a specification for a new lightweight strike fighter for service with NATO's tactical fighter-bomber squadrons. The specification, drawn up by the technical staff of the Supreme Allied Commander, Europe — at that time General Lauris Norstad — called for a single-seat aircraft of robust construction, easy to maintain under arduous operational conditions, with equipment that included gyro gunsight and rocket sight, DME, IFF, radar homing, UHF radio and cockpit pressurization. It had to carry any one of three different types of built-in armament (four .5-inch machine guns, two 20-mm or two 30-mm cannon) as well as a variety of underwing stores such as two 500-lb bombs and twelve 3-inch rockets. The empty weight of the machine was not to exceed 5,000 lb. It had to be capable of taking off from a grass strip fully laden to clear a 50-foot obstacle within 1,000 yards, and of flying at 0.95M at heights between sea level and 500 feet for one-third of its mission, the remainder of the sortie to be flown at a cruising speed of 400 mph. A rate of roll of at least 100 degrees per second at O.9M was also required.

When the specification was issued, Great Britain enjoyed a substantial lead in lightweight jet fighter development. In 1950, W. E. W. Petter, chief designer of the Folland Aircraft Company, had initiated design studies of just such an aircraft based on the use of a 3,800 lb.s.t. Bristol Saturn axial-flow turbojet, which was originally intended to power a guided missile. In the event the missile project was cancelled and development of the Saturn was abandoned, but Petter persisted in his design work in the knowledge that a suitable powerplant would materialise before long. Development went ahead with a low-powered prototype of the proposed fighter, and on 11 August 1954 this aircraft — the Folland FO.139 Midge, fitted with a 1,640 lb.s.t. Viper 101 engine — flew for the first time from Boscombe Down under the hands of Squadron Leader E. A. Tennant, Folland's chief test pilot.

Most maiden flights are restricted to a few minutes' duration, but after taking the Midge up to 8,000 feet and putting it through various handling checks at speeds of between 120 and 350 knots Tennant felt so confident that he stayed in the air for over half an hour, carrying out several rolls and high-speed turns before returning to Boscombe. During the next five hours he made four successive flights in the little aircraft, culminating in a trip to Chilbolton where the test programme was to be carried out.

The performance of the Midge — which, despite its low power, was later dived at speeds in excess of 0.9M — provided an enormous boost to Folland's morale. The aircraft had been developed as a private venture and a lot of money had been invested in it; it now seemed certain that the operational version, the FO.141 Gnat — which was to have a much more powerful Bristol Orpheus turbojet — would have a high chance of acceptance by both the Royal Air Force and NATO.

Admittedly, the competition was stiff, and so were the conditions imposed by NATO. Whoever received the contract would have to deliver three prototypes and twenty-seven production aircraft by January 1957. Nine designs were submitted, of which five were French and two Italian; apart from Folland, the other British contender was Avro, who proposed the Type 727, a small tailless delta.

It was the French, however, who appeared to have a head start, for the French Air Ministry had for some time envisaged a requirement for just such an aircraft and had issued a complementary specification calling for the development of a twin-jet strike fighter as well as a single-engined one. The twin-engined machine would be heavier than that required by the NATO specification, but this would be offset by greater reliability; it would offer a similar performance and payload as the lighter single-engined type, and a prototype could be built and flown quickly with existing turbojets.

France, therefore, was able to offer alternative configurations based on the same airframe, and the Ministère de l'Air lost no time in awarding development contracts to the two principal companies involved, Avions Marcel Dassault and Louis Breguet. Dassault, who were already engaged in the development as a private venture of their mixed-powerplant MD.550 delta (see Chapter four), received the go-ahead for the Mystere 22 and 26, the former to meet the French requirement and the latter NATO's. Both aircraft used basically the same airframe, but the 22 was designed to take a pair of existing turbojets while the 26 was to be fitted with the Bristol Orpheus.

The first prototype Mystere 22, renamed Etendard II, flew for the first time at Melun-Villaroche on 23 July 1956, powered by two Turboméca Gabizo lightweight turbojets. On the following day a second, scaled-up aircraft, the Etendard IV, made its first flight at Bordeaux-Merignac under the power of a single SNECMA Atar 101E-4 turbojet. A developed version of the Etendard IV was eventually to be produced for the Aéronavale, but the Etendard II was shortlived; trouble was experienced with the Gabizo engines and the Armée de l'Air abandoned the requirement shortly afterwards. The Mystere 26, meanwhile — renamed Etendard VI — was nearing completion, but the Orpheus engine was still not available for installation and so Dassault proceeded, at their own expense, to refit the prototype with an Atar 101. It eventually flew in March 1957, and was evaluated alongside the other contenders later in the year.

The other French company involved in the lightweight fighter contest, Avions Louis Breguet, had approached the twin requirement in similar fashion. Their proposal for the NATO contract was the Orpheus-powered Br.1001 Taon — the name means Horsefly, but is also an anagram of NATO — while to meet the Armée de l'Air requirement they put forward a twin-engined design, the Br.1100.

The Taon was a highly promising design which, on the face of it, enjoyed one major advantage over the other competitors. Design work started in July 1955, but was halted in February 1956 when, as a result of wind tunnel tests with a mock-up in the United States, it was decided to incorporate area rule in the aircraft's fuselage design. Consequently, although there was a considerable delay before construction of the Taon prototype could begin, the aircraft that took shape was aerodynamically more advanced than the other contenders, all of which were flying by then.

The first metal for the prototype Taon was cut in January 1957. Only seven months later, on 26 July, Breguet test pilot Bernard Witt took the aircraft on its maiden flight. This machine, and two more prototypes, were powered by the Bristol Orpheus B.Or.3 turbojet, although it was planned that the definitive version would have the more powerful B.Or.12. The built-in armament selected for the Taon was four .5-inch Colt-Browning machine guns; external armament comprised two or four 500-lb napalm tanks or bombs, two Nord 5103 beam-riding missiles, or two Matra 116c missile pods each containing nineteen 68-mm Brandt SNEB rockets.

BREGUET TAON Br.1001. The Br.1001, flew on 26 July 1957 and was designed to NATO requirements. the aircraft was powered by a single 4,850 lbs. thrust Bristol Orpheus turbojet.

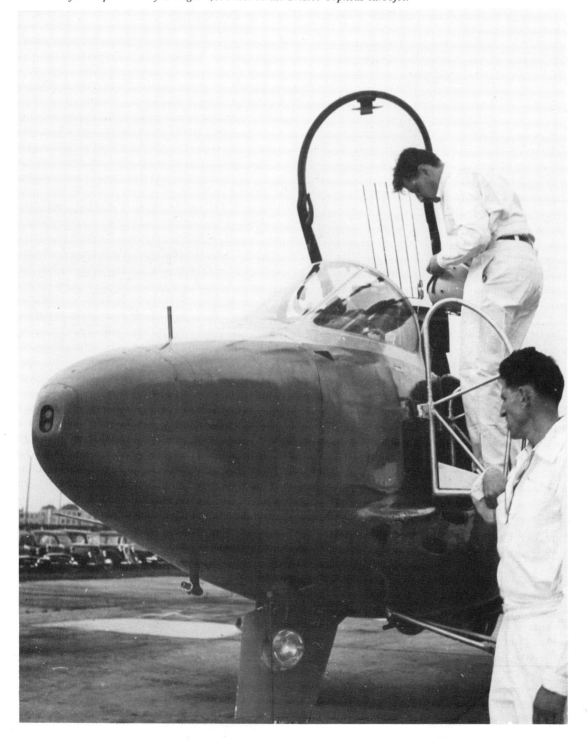

FOLLAND MIDGE.

Preliminary flight trials proved very satisfactory, the Taon meeting every aspect of the NATO requirement, and in September 1957, the first prototype went to the Flight Test Centre at Bretigny for evaluation alongside the other competitors. Meanwhile, the prototype of the Breguet 1100 had also flown on 31 March, powered by two Turboméca Gabizo engines, but the 1100's test programme was halted when the Armée de l'Air requirement for a twin-engined strike fighter was withdrawn.

Of the two Italian companies that submitted designs to the NATO specification, it was Fiat who were destined to win the contest with their G.91, which ultimately went into production as NATO's standard tactical fighter-bomber. It was an ironic choice, for the other design was the work of a man who, for nearly twenty years, had devoted much of his talent as an aircraft designer to perfecting a lightweight fighter — and who had come very close to succeeding.

Sergio Stefanutti, chief designer of the Industrie Meccaniche Aeronautiche Meridionali-Aerfer, had begun studies of a lightweight fighter as long ago as 1939, and after producing some experimental types had designed the SAI.207 Sagittario (Arrow), which weighed only 4,993 lb loaded and carried an armament of two 20-mm cannon and two machine guns. During tests, it was dived at an indicated airspeed of 466 mph at 10,000 feet, and its performance was so promising that 2,000

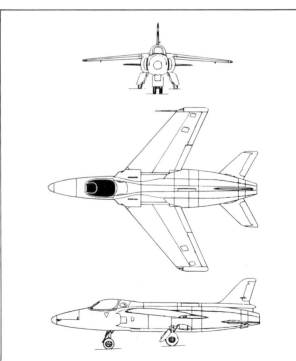

The Folland Midge — prototype of what might have been a generation of British lightweight fighters with enormous export potential — if government support had been forthcoming.

BREGUET TAON. The highly promising Breguet TAON lightweight fighter might have been selected to fill the NATO requirement had the prototype flown earlier. As it was, the Fiat G.91 was selected.

examples were ordered for the Regia Aeronautica; however, only a few had been completed by the time Italy signed the armistice in 1943.

Stefanutti resumed his experimental work after the war, fitting his SAI.7 trainer design with swept flying surfaces and testing this configuration as a first step in the development of a lightweight jet fighter. The next step was simple enough; after amassing a considerable amount of aerodynamic information with the aid of the piston-engined test aircraft — named Freccia — Stefanutti replaced its powerplant with a little Turboméca Marboré II turbojet. Renamed Sagittario I,

the revamped design flew for the first time on 5 January 1953 and was tested extensively, the upper limit of its flight envelope being dictated by its all-wood construction.

Work went ahead on the development of a definitive fighter variant, the Sagittario 2. This was to have been powered by a Bristol Saturn turbojet, but when the Saturn was cancelled Stefanutti opted for a Rolls-Royce Derwent Mk.9. It was this engine which powered the prototype Sagittario 2 on its maiden flight from Practica del Mare, Rome, on 19 May 1956; on 4 December that year, piloted by Colonel Giovanni Franchini, it became

AERFER SAGITTARIO 2. The Sagittario 2, flown on 19 May 1956, was powered by a 3,600 lbs thrust Rolls-Royce Derwent 9 turbojet.

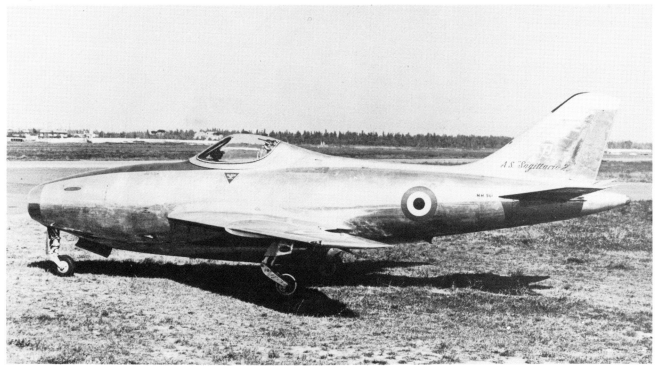

AERFER SAGITTARIO 2.

the first aircraft of Italian design to exceed Mach One, reaching 1.1M in a shallow dive.

Although the Sagittario 2 was highly manoeuvrable, could carry the requisite combination of weapons and was able to operate from grass strips, its overall performance did not match the NATO requirement, so, with the help of US funds, Stefanutti took development a stage further and modified the basic design to include a 1,810 lb.s.t. Rolls-Royce Soar R.Sr.2 auxiliary turbojet in addition to the Derwent.   The configuration of the new prototype fighter, known as the Ariete (Battering Ram), was exactly the same as that of the Sagittario except for the rear fuselage, which was made deeper to house the auxiliary turbojet and was four inches longer. The Ariete flew for the first time on 27 March 1958, and while flight testing continued Stefanutti's design team was occupied with the third and final development, the Leone. This was to have been powered by either a Bristol Orpheus B.Or.12 or a de Havilland Gyron Junior turbojet, with a de Havilland Spectre rocket motor replacing the Soar, but the adoption of the Fiat G.91 by the Italian Air Force and NATO brought further work to an end.

Of the two British contenders in the NATO competition, the Avro 727 was adjudged a 'close runner-up' in the original design contest, but it never left the drawing-board. The other aircraft, the Folland Gnat, was to enjoy at least a partial success story as a combat aircraft, but not within NATO. The prototype of the Orpheus-powered Gnat flew on 18 July 1955 and was followed by a batch of six aircraft for the Ministry of

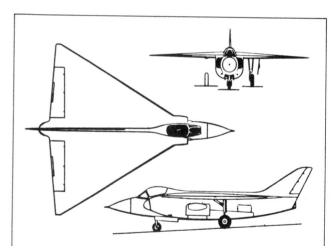

Designation: Avro Type 727.
Role: Lightweight ground-attack fighter.
Engine: One Bristol Siddeley Orpheus turbojet.
Span: 27 ft 3½ in.
Length: 35 ft 9½ in.
Weight: No data.
Crew: 1.
Service ceiling: No data.
Range: No data.
Max speed: 0.95M at sea level.
Weapons: Two 20-mm cannon; two 500-lbs. bombs and twelve 3-in RPs.

Supply, the first of these flying on 26 May 1956. Production Gnat Mk.1s were powered by the Bristol Orpheus 701 turbo-jet of 4,520 lb.s.t. and carried an armament of two 30-mm Aden cannon plus up to 2,000 lb of underwing stores, but despite the promise shown by the diminutive aircraft — which cost far less to manufacture than other combat aircraft of comparable performance — it was not adopted by the RAF or NATO. One hundred Gnat Mk.1s were built under licence in India; the type saw considerable action during the 1971 war between that country and Pakistan and proved quite deadly in high-speed, low-level combat. It therefore adequately fulfilled the role for which it was originally intended years earlier; it was also supplied to Finland and developed into the Gnat T.Mk.1 trainer, a guise in which it became famous as the mount of the Red Arrows aerobatic team.

Perhaps the real irony about the Gnat, however, was that its development potential was never fully appreciated at the right time, at least in its European context. Hindustan Aeronautics Ltd were not slow to realise it, though; the first of ninety-odd examples of an uprated variant, the Ajeet, began to reach squadrons of the Indian Air Force in 1982, and will serve in the light strike role for some time to come.

AERFER ARIETE. The Ariete interceptor, which had an 1,810 lbs thrust Rolls-Royce R.Sr.2 turbojet as well as the Derwent and flew on the 27 March 1958.

Chapter Eight
Variable Geometry:The Uphill Path

Despite the lack of government interest in the Gnat, as described in the previous chapter, Folland Aircraft — now part of the Hawker Siddeley Group — had initiated design studies into a supersonic variant, the Gnat Mk.5, which in its two-seat configuration would have provided a logical follow-on to the T.Mk.1 advanced trainer then in production for the RAF and, as a single-seater, would have given valuable additional firepower to Fighter Command's interceptor force. At that time — in 1959 — the Lightning had yet to enter service, and no other supersonic fighter was envisaged.

The Gnat Mk.5 was to have been powered by two RB.153R engines mounted in the rear fuselage. Estimated performance included a maximum speed in excess of Mach Two, an operational ceiling of 60,000 feet and a zoom climb ceiling of 73,000 feet; combat radius on internal fuel only was to have been 400 nautical miles, and time to 50,000 feet three minutes. Assuming that the Gnat Mk.5 prototype flew in 1962, which was not unrealistic, Folland estimated that a production version could be in service by 1967.

In the event, the Gnat Mk.5 received no official backing. Had such backing been forthcoming, Britain would have been in a position to offer for export a low-cost supersonic combat aircraft with a performance better, in many respects, than that of the Northrop F-5.

The Gnat Mk.5, however, was not quite dead. In 1960, the new Director and Chief Engineer of Folland Aircraft Ltd, Maurice Brennan, was asked by Hawker Siddeley to investigate the variable geometry concept and the possibility of applying it to a future multi-role combat aircraft. Brennan took the basic Gnat Mk.5 design and adapted it to carry a variable-geometry wing, designing two variants, one with a large tailplane and pointed wings and the other a tailless version with wingtip controls and a rotating retractable foreplane. The new type was designated FO.147, and its variable sweep arrangement was quite ingenious; the wings were mounted on tracks, so that in the fully-swept position the leading edge moved several feet forward, close to the engine air intakes, while in the fully-spread position the leading edge was roughly at fuselage midpoint.

The FO.147 was designed to use the same engines as the Gnat Mk.5, and estimated maximum speed was Mach Two plus. The design, however, never left the drawing board, and plans for a definitive version, the FO.148, were stillborn. As far as the Ministry of Aviation was concerned, variable geometry was something to be tinkered with, but not approached too seriously; it was certainly not an area that merited the allocation of substantial development funds.

Yet the story of British research into the variable-geometry concept, on a practical level, was at that time fifteen years old — and the concept was proven.

Early experiments had been carried out in 1945 by Dr. Barnes Wallis of Vickers, who received sufficient government funds to initiate a series of tests with models

featuring VG wings. Early experiments involved hand-launched models, but from the beginning of 1950 power launches of the test vehicles, known as Wild Geese, were carried out at Thurleigh in Bedfordshire. The vehicles were launched from a rocket-powered trolley and then radio-controlled in gliding flight. After three early rocket-boosted trials, all of which ended with the crash of the Wild Goose, Wallis modified both the model aircraft and the launch trolley and moved the test site to the old disused RAF airfield of Predannack, in Cornwall, where aerodynamic models of the ill-fated Miles M.52 had also been tested. Between January 1950 and May 1952 eleven rocket-boosted flights were made with Wild Geese, and not until the end of this series of tests did the vehicles make a successful flight. After that, the tempo of success picked up somewhat, and thirty-one further powered tests were made between July 1952 and October 1954. Plans were made to fly a piloted VG test aircraft, and a contract was actually placed with Heston Aircraft Ltd for the building of a small piston-engined type known as the JC-9; its sections were taken to the Vickers plant at Weybridge, but it was never assembled and was eventually broken up. (It should be remembered that, by this time, the Americans had already built and flown two VG types, the Bell X-5 and the Grumman XF10F-1 Jaguar!)

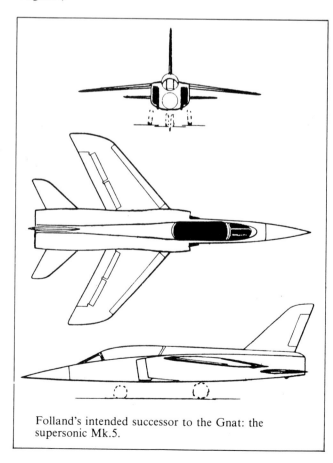

Folland's intended successor to the Gnat: the supersonic Mk.5.

The eventual goal Barnes Wallis aimed to reach was a variable-geometry airliner, capable of flying non-stop to Australia at subsonic speed and an altitude of 50,000 feet. Funds for the further development of the project, known as Swallow, were forthcoming from the Ministry of Supply. Following wind tunnel tests, a model of the design was successfully flown in November 1955. By this time, Vickers were having to support fifty per cent of the R and D costs, so with a view to procuring more funds Wallis adapted the basic Swallow design to meet Operational Requirement 330 for a supersonic bomber, issued in 1954. The engines were mounted in pairs one above the other in wingtip pods that rotated as the angle of sweep changed, and the aircraft was designed to carry a single nuclear weapon that was to be ejected rearwards from a bay in the tail cone. Wallis also argued that the design could be readily adapted to the early warning role or as a high-altitude interceptor; with wings fully spread it would be able to loiter for very long periods high above the weather, yet with wings fully swept it would be capable of a fast supersonic dash to intercept any incoming threat.

In the event, the 1957 White Paper brought an end to the military development of the Swallow project after about £1 million had been spent on it and fourteen free flights had been carried out with models. Nevertheless, further research continued for a time under the joint sponsorship of Vickers and the Royal Aircraft Establishment, with five more free flights undertaken between October 1958 and June 1959.

It was now apparent that no British Government funding would be available for the development of a full-size Swallow, and so Wallis approached the Paris office of the American Mutual Weapons Development programme. The Americans were interested, because although they had compiled a fair amount of technical experience with their two subsonic VG types the Wallis project took the whole field of variable sweep into the realms of supersonic flight. In 1959, therefore, Vickers and NASA embarked on a joint research programme under which all the research material assembled by Vickers was handed over to NASA, who initiated wind-tunnel testing of the Swallow configuration at Langley Field. Results were disappointing: NASA reported that, in the wind tunnel at least, the tailless arrowhead shape of the Swallow was aerodynamically unstable at subsonic speeds. NASA's recommendation was that a future VG aircraft should be far more conventional, with a tailplane and with engines buried in the fuselage.

Meanwhile, the British Naval and Air Staffs had issued a joint operational requirement, OR.346, for a multi-role combat aircraft to form the standard equipment of both Services in the 1970s. The requirement was very complex, and made more so by the fact that the RAF and the Royal Navy were thinking along completely different lines in terms of performance and principal combat role. Nevertheless, a specification, ER.206, was issued to BAC and Hawker Siddeley, inviting tenders for the design of a research aircraft as a preliminary step.

De Havilland, as part of Hawker Siddeley, proposed a conventional design, the DH.127, which had a shoulder-mounted delta wing and was designed to carry a variety of nuclear and conventional stores, or alternatively four AAMs. Main propulsion was to be provided by two Rolls-Royce Spey engines, with two lift engines mounted in the nose. At BAC, on the other hand, the Vickers design team pursued the variable-geometry idea,

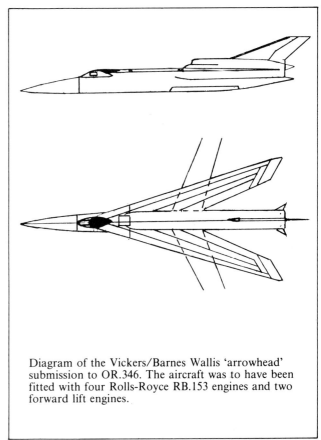

Diagram of the Vickers/Barnes Wallis 'arrowhead' submission to OR.346. The aircraft was to have been fitted with four Rolls-Royce RB.153 engines and two forward lift engines.

submitting a tailless arrowhead design based on the Swallow; Barnes Wallis and his men were clearly not convinced that the results of NASA's wind tunnel tests were valid. The Vickers design was much more ambitious than de Havilland's; the team was already talking of an aircraft which, with development, would be capable of a speed of 3.0M at altitudes of over 80,000 feet.

OR.346, in the event, was killed stone dead by the escalating development costs of TSR-2, and so was any hope that Wallis's arrowhead VG aircraft would ever fly. Nevertheless, the research undertaken so far was by no means wasted, and in 1962 BAC submitted VG designs to meet two separate requirements, one for an interceptor/strike aircraft (the Type 583) to replace the Sea Vixen with the Royal Navy, and the other for a land-based multi-role aircraft (the Type 584) to meet NATO Specification NBMR.3 At Hawker Siddeley, the de Havilland team also submitted their own design to meet the naval requirement; this was the DH.128, a navalised version of the earlier DH.127 delta-wing combat aircraft. At the same time, as mentioned at the beginning of the chapter, another Hawker Siddeley company, Folland Aircraft, embarked on studies of a variable-geometry version of the Gnat Mk.5.

None of these proposals came to anything, but the volume of research undertaken by BAC, or more specifically Vickers, into variable-geometry had given that company design leadership in the field, so in 1964 the design team at Warton, on which BAC's variable-geometry work was now centred, was in a strong position to propose a VG project to meet an RAF requirement for a small strike and training aircraft. The requirement arose originally out of Air Staff Target 362, which was for an advanced jet trainer only, but as time passed it was realised that such an aircraft could be readily adapted for the short-range strike and interception roles — probably even produced in two versions, one single — and the

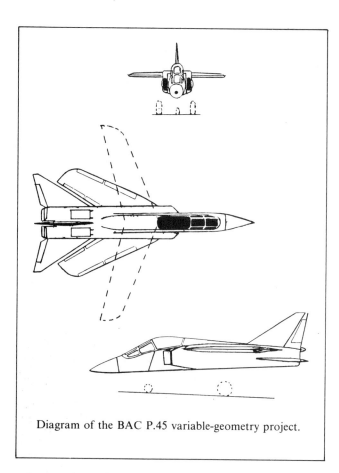

Diagram of the BAC P.45 variable-geometry project.

RAF and the Armée de l'Air. The result was the Jaguar, which was developed from the Breguet Br.121 and traced its ancestry back to the Br.1100; and as far as BAC was concerned, design leadership was handed to the French on a plate.

The go-ahead for Jaguar was given by a Memorandum of Understanding, signed on 17 May 1965 by the Defence Ministries of France and Britain. At the same time, it was agreed that the two countries should begin collaborative design work on a larger variable-geometry multi-role combat aircraft, to be known as the AFVG. Airframe design was to be undertaken by BAC and Dassault, while Bristol Siddeley and SNECMA were made responsible for development of the powerplant, designated M45G. The AFVG's specification called for a two-seater with a maximum speed of 800 knots at sea level and 2.5M at altitude; operational ceiling was to be 60,000 feet plus, and combat radius 500 nautical miles. A carrier-borne version was envisaged for service with the French and Royal Navies.

BAC went ahead and built a full-scale mock-up at Warton, but the days of AFVG were already numbered. The British and French requirements, particularly with regard to the land- and carrier-based variants, were incompatible with one-another. In the summer of 1967, on the grounds of cost, the French Government announced its intention to withdraw from the AFVG programme.

Only a year earlier, the 1966 White Paper on Defence had stated that AFVG was to be the core of Britain's future defence and industrial programmes. Small wonder that the British Government was thrown into complete confusion by the French desision, or that the Commons announcement by Mr Denis Healey, the Secretary of State for Defence, to the effect that urgent consideration was being given to the new situation and that while investigating the possibility of collaboration with other countries the Government was authorising British firms to carry out a project study on a VG aircraft to a modified specification, had a rather lame ring to it.

other twin-engined. BAC's design to meet this requirement took shape as the P.45. Had government backing been forthcoming immediately, a prototype could have been flying in 1968 and Service deliveries initiated in 1972. However, with a Labour Goverment in power, collaboration with Europe was the order of the day, and early in 1965 BAC and Avions Louis Breguet joined forces to produce a supersonic light strike fighter/trainer to meet the common requirement of the

ANGLO-FRENCH VARIABLE-GEOMETRY AIRCRAFT. Model of the Anglo-French variable-geometry aircraft. The operational machine was to have had a speed of 2.5M at altitude.

DASSAULT MIRAGE G.8. Two prototypes of the Dassault Mirage G.8 variable-geometry aircraft were built, the first flying in May 1971. Dassault also built another prototype VG fighter, the Mirage G, which flew in November 1967, but this was destroyed in a crash. Neither type went into production.

An editorial in that excellent magazine *Air Pictorial* (August 1967) summed up the position perfectly:

"The AVFG project owes its existence to the cancellation of TSR-2 coupled with the totally unwarranted conclusion. . . that this country could never again embark by itself on a major military aircraft project. Originally the RAF was to have had 150 TSR-2s as Canberra replacements. TSR-2, having been brought successfully to the stage of prototype testing, the whole project, including jigs, tools and everything connected with it, was destroyed. In its place the RAF was offered the American F-111, still ostensibly as a Canberra replacement; but by that time there seemed to be less emphasis on STOL and more on long range, owing to the announced policy of scrapping our aircraft carriers, most of whose tasks would (it is hopefully imagined) then be carried out by shore-based aircraft of F-111 range and speed. The 1966 White Paper revealed that the number of F-111s to be bought was only fifty, and that the balance of effective air power in the relevant category would be made up by the projected AFVG.

"In effect, therefore, the Canberra replacement will now comprise fifty F-111s, and that will be all until we have devised ways of producing the AFVG as an all-British project, or found for it a substitute acceptable to the RAF, and available in time. Time

is becoming the over-riding factor, because we have lost the whole of the eight years since TSR-2 was initiated."

As things turned out, the RAF never got its Canberra replacement in the form of the F-111. In January 1968, the Labour Government announced its plans for the

BREGUET/BAC JAGUAR. Model of the Breguet/BAC Jaguar. This picture was released soon after the signing of the agreement between the British and French defence ministries in May 1965 authorising Jaguar development to proceed.

BAC P.45. The BAC P.45 variable-geometry project was shelved in the mid-1960s, but some of its design features were incorporated in the fixed-wing Hawk – one of Britain's notable aviation success stories, seen here on a demonstration flight over Egypt.

JAGUAR. The first two Jaguar prototypes under construction. The cancellation of the Anglo-French Variable Geometry Aircraft meant that Anglo-French combat aircraft collaboration rested solely with Jaguar – but design leadership was handed to the French.

TORNADO F.2. The Tornado F.2, interceptor version of the Anglo - German - Italian VG aircraft. It is probably the finest aircraft in its class to be found anywhere – but it owes its existence to the demise of TSR-2 and, in turn, the AFVG.

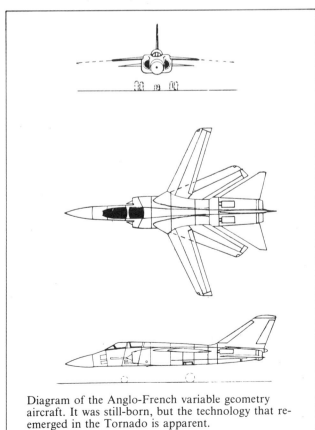

Diagram of the Anglo-French variable geometry aircraft. It was still-born, but the technology that re-emerged in the Tornado is apparent.

progressive withdrawal of British forces from the Far East and the Arabian Gulf by 1971; there would no longer be a requirement for a long-range tactical strike and reconnaissance aircraft, and so the decision was taken — at a cost of nearly £50 million — to cancel the F-111 order.

The RAF received its 'acceptable substitute' in the shape of the Buccaneer Mk.2, and in the meantime BAC continued design work on a wholly-British variable geometry combat aircraft, the UKVG, while discussions went on with various NATO member countries on the possibility of collaboration. In July 1968, representatives of the governments of the United Kingdom, the German Federal Republic, Italy and the Netherlands indicated that they had a mutual requirement for a supersonic strike and reconnaissance aircraft for service in the 1970s, to be known as the MRCA — Multi-Role Combat Aircraft. The Dutch subsequently dropped out, and it was left to the British, Germans and Italians to set up the machinery for the development and eventual production of MRCA. Today, the operational version of that aircraft, the variable-geometry Tornado, is in service with the air forces of all three countries. In terms of combat effectiveness, it is probably the finest aircraft of its class in the world — but in the shadow of every Tornado flies the ghost of TSR-2, twenty years dead.

Chapter Nine
Military V/STOL Projects Since 1945

The story of the vertical take-off application to air combat really begins in 1945, when Germany, as a desperate last-ditch measure, had plans to mass-produce a rocket-powered target defence interceptor known as the Bachem Ba 349 Natter (Viper). Armed with a battery of 73-mm rockets in the nose and powered by a Walter 509 bi-fuel rocket, the diminutive Natter was designed to be launched vertically from a ramp under the power of four auxiliary rocket boosters; the main rocket would then take over and thrust the Natter to an altitude of 7½ miles. After attacking his target, the Natter's pilot would pull a lever, detaching the nose of the aircraft and leaving him exposed to the slipstream; another lever activated a drogue parachute attached to the rear of the Natter, and the sudden deceleration ejected the pilot, who was then supposed to make a normal parachute descent. However, only one manned test flight was carried out, and that ended in disaster when the Natter dived into the ground seconds after launch. Other wartime German VTOL projects, which never flew, were the Focke-Achgelis Fa 269 carrier-based fighter that was designed to use thrust-vectoring — a single BMW radial engine in the fuselage driving two large-diameter propellers aft of the wing, which could be rotated downwards to provide vertical thrust and rearwards for horizontal flight — and the Focke-Wulf Triebflugel, a jet-powered coleopter fighter project. The Triebflugel's small jets were mounted at the end of three long arms which, in turn, were mounted at about the mid-section of the design's fuselage; the idea was that when the arms rotated they would act like a helicopter's rotor blades and lift the device, which sat on its tail.

The main problem confronting designers researching the vertical take-off concept was to find a foolproof means of ensuring stability during the critical transition phase between vertical and horizontal flight. However, in 1951, when the US Navy issued a requirement for a small fighter aircraft capable of operating from platforms on merchant ships for convoy protection, Convair and Lockheed both launched into a research programme that was to produce surprising results in the long run.

Each company developed an aircraft with a broadly similar configuration, a 'tail-sitter' using a powerful turboprop engine with large contra-rotating propellers to eliminate torque. The idea was that the aircraft, using a simple two-axis auto-stabliser, would be flown vertically off the ground and then bunted over into horizontal flight; during landing, it would hang on its propellers, which would then perform the same function as a helicopter's rotor and lower it down to a landing on its tail castors.

The US Navy specification was finalised in 1950, and in March 1951 contracts were issued for the building of two prototypes, the Convair XFY-1 and the Lockheed XFV-1. The latter aircraft was the first to fly, beginning normal horizontal flight trials with the aid of a stalky fixed undercarriage in March 1954. For these tests the XFV-1 was fitted with an Allison T40-A-6 turboprop, although plans were in hand to re-engine it with the more powerful YT40-A-14 when this powerplant had completed its full series of trials. For vertical take-off and landing the XFV-1 stood on small wheels attached to the tips of its cruciform tail unit, an arrangement that would almost certainly have proved unstable on a pitching deck. Projected armament for the XFV-1 was two 20-mm cannon mounted in wingtip pods, or forty-eight 2.75-inch unguided folding-fin rockets. The XFV-1 made a number of transitional flights before the test programme was concluded in 1955, but its full performance was never evaluated. Performance figures registered during trials, however, together with wind tunnel data, gave the type an estimated maximum speed of 580 mph at 15,000 feet and an initial climb rate of 10,820 feet per minute.

The Convair XFY-1 was generally a better design. Its flying surfaces were of delta configuration, the wings having a leading edge sweep of 57 degrees, and the castor-

LOCKHEED XFV-1. Designed to the same requirement as the Convair XFY-1, the Lockheed XFV-1 was an experimental VTOL fighter intended to take off in an upright position from an aircraft carrier. The XFV-1 began horizontal flight trials in March 1954, powered by an Allison T40-A-6 turboprop.

CONVAIR XFY-1. Of radical design, the Convair XFY-1 was an experimental VTOL carrier-borne fighter. Powered by a 5,850 eph Allison T40-A-6 turboprop driving contra-rotating propellers, the prototype made its first vertical take-off on August 1, 1954.

type undercarriage was of much wider track than that of the XFV-1, enabling the aircraft to remain stable on its take-off platform at angles of up to 26 degrees from the vertical. It carried fifty gallons more fuel than the XFV-1, and proposed armament was four 20-mm cannon in wingtip pods or forty-six 2.75-inch rockets. Like the XFV-1, the XFY-1 was fitted with a gimbal-mounted ejection seat that rotated 45 degrees for vertical flight, then slipped into conventional position for flying horizontally. The XFY-1 initially flew in a series of 69 tethered test flights that began in April 1954, with cables attached to the nose and tail allowing the aircraft to rise and descend but limiting lateral movement. The first free flight took place at Brown Field, south of San Diego, in November; the XFY-1 rose slowly to 200 feet, gradually nosed over into a horizontal position, and flew in level flight for twenty minutes, after which test pilot Skeets Coleman brought it down for a perfect vertical landing. It was the first successful VTOL fighter flight in history, and it brought Coleman the award of the Harman Trophy.

The XFY-1 underwent a much fuller test programme than the XFV-1, achieving a performance that included a maximum speed of 610 mph at 15,000 feet and 592 mph at 35,000 feet. Climb to 20,000 feet and 30,000 feet was 2.7 and 4.6 minutes respectively, somewhat better than the estimated figure for the XFY-1, and operational ceiling was 43,700 feet. In 1956, however, the US Navy withdrew its requirement and abandoned the VTOL programme; reasons given were technical ones, such as instability

during the transition phase, but the real reason was that a powerful lobby of senior officers in the US Navy saw the development of the VTOL concept as a threat to the production of newer and larger aircraft carriers. It was to be many years before the VTOL concept returned to the US Navy as an operational reality.

It was the Ryan Aeronautical Company of San Diego who first showed a real interest in the development of pure-jet VTO, in 1947, carrying out initial research with an Allison J33 turbojet suspended in a vertical test rig. Later, equipped with a rudimentary cockpit, reaction controls and two-axis auto-stabliser, this made a series of tethered flights. In 1953, as a consequence of these early experiments, Ryan received a USAF contract to build a prototype VTOL jet aircraft, the X-13 Vertijet. This was intended to be launched from its own self-contained servicing trailer which incorporated an hydraulically-operated inclining launch ramp. The X-13 prototype first flew on 10 December 1955, fitted with a temporary undercarriage for normal take-off and landing trials, and its first vertical take-off was made on 28 May 1956. A second aircraft was built, and this went on to make the full sequence of vertical take-off, transition to horizontal flight and transition back to the vertical for a landing on 11 April 1957. Both aircraft were powered by a Rolls-Royce Avon turbojet, and although they carried just enough fuel for about twelve minutes' flying they had proved that vertical take-off was a feasible enterprise, provided the engine thrust exceeded the weight of the aircraft by a substantial margin.

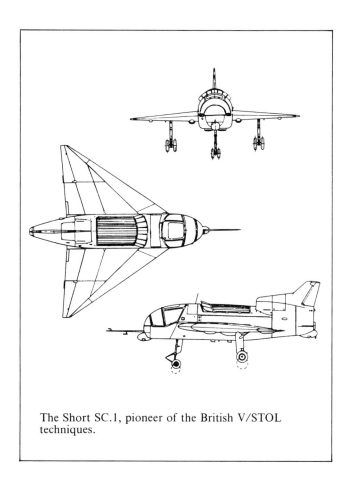

The Short SC.1, pioneer of the British V/STOL techniques.

SHORT SC.1. The Short SC.1, pioneer of the British V/STOL techniques.

Meanwhile, vertical take-off experiments had also been progressing in other countries. In Britain, Rolls-Royce commenced tethered flights of a Thrust Measuring Rig (known more popularly as the 'Flying Bedstead') which had two Rolls-Royce Nene turbojets installed horizontally at opposite ends of the assembly, their tailpipes directed vertically downwards near the mass centre. In France, SNECMA mounted an Atar turbojet in a special test rig fitted with a four-wheeled undercarriage; after unmanned trials, a piloted version — the C.400P-2, or Atar Volant — made its first tethered hovering flight on 8 April 1957, followed by a free flight on 14 May. The next step was to enclose the Atar in a fuselage, surrounded by an annular wing to allow the aircraft to change from vertical to horizontal flight; the machine, known a the C-450 Coleoptere, flew for the first time on 17 April 1959, but on 25 July it went out of control as its pilot (who ejected safely) was trying to stabilise it for a vertical descent, and was totally destroyed. In 1958, the Russians also flew an experimental bedstead-type rig known as the Turbolet, which featured a single vertically-mounted turbojet surrounded by a spidery structure and equipped with a fully-enclosed cockpit.

Such was the state of the art in 1958. Four countries were involved in VTOL development; one of them, the United States, had already carried out trials with 'tail-sitter' aircraft, and another — Great Britain — was about to start flight testing of a VTOL research aircraft mounted on a conventional tricycle undercarriage. Its name was the Short SC.1.

In 1953, when the Rolls-Royce Thrust Measuring Rig was beginning its vertical flight trials, the Ministry of Supply issued Specification ER.143 for a research aircraft which could take off vertically by jet-lift and then accelerate forward into normal cruising flight. Short Brothers' preliminary design, the PD.11 — a small tailless delta aircraft with five RB.108 engines, four for lift and one for forward propulsion — was judged to be the most promising, and in August 1954 Shorts received a contract to build two prototypes, XG900 and XG905.

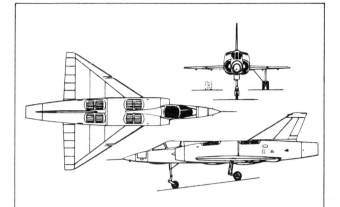

Designation: Dassault Balzac V.

Role: VTOL research aircraft.

Engines: One 4,400 lb.s.t. Bristol Siddeley Orpheus B.Or.3 turbojet for propulsion; eight 2,160 lb.s.t. Rolls-Royce RB.108-A turbojets for lift.

Span: 27 ft.

Length: 45 ft.

Weight: Loaded 14,300 lb.

Crew: 1.

Operational ceiling: No data.

Range: No data; endurance approx. 20 minutes.

Max speed: 686 mph at sea level.

Weapons: None.

The first of these, XG900, was shipped to Boscombe Down in March 1957, and on 2 April test pilot Tom Brooke-Smith took it on its maiden flight, which involved a conventional take-off and landing. XG900 was not fitted with lift engines at this stage, and it was the second Short SC.1, XG905, which began hover trials on 23 May 1958. There followed five months of tethered trials over a raised platform with open-grid decking, and the initial free hovers were also made over this platform, but in November 1958 Brooke-Smith landed away from the platform on a football pitch, which was undamaged

MIRAGE III-V. The Mirage III-V supersonic VTOL fighter prototype flew in February 1965. The second prototype, which reached a speed of 2.04M, was destroyed in an accident in November 1966.

apart from a slight scorching of the grass. In September 1959 XG905 made its first public appearance at Farnborough, where it was intended to demonstrate vertical and horizontal flight; however, the demonstration was cut short in rather embarrasing circumstances when the debris guard over the lift engines' intake became clogged with newly-mown grass, causing a sudden power loss that compelled Tom Brooke-Smith to make a rapid descent.

On 6 April, 1960, Tom Brooke-Smith achieved the first complete transition from level flight to vertical descent and vertical climb following a conventional take-off from Bedford in XG905. That summer, XG900 rejoined the test programme, complete with its five RB.108 lift engines, and the two aircraft were used to develop rolling take-off techniques from unprepared surfaces, the object being to avoid erosion and also to increase the take-off weight when a short, but not vertical, take-off was permissible.

In April 1961 XG900 was handed over to the RAE at Bedford, while XG905 went back to Belfast to be fitted with a new auto-stabilisation system designed to compensate for gusts. More than 80 flights were made with the new system, starting in June 1963, the development pilot being J. R. Green, who had joined Shorts from the RAE. On 2 October, Green was returning for a landing when the gyros failed, producing false references which caused the auto-stabliser to fly the aircraft into the ground. The failure occurred at less than thirty feet, giving Green no time to revert to manual control. XG905 went into the ground upside down, and Green was killed. The aircraft itself was repaired and flew again in 1966, carrying out trials with the Blind Landing Experimental Unit.

At no time was the Short SC.1 intended to lead to the development of a more advanced combat aircraft; indeed, when the SC.1 began its trials in 1958 the Air Ministry was showing little or no interest in the concept.

The general feeling in the United Kingdom (and, for that matter elsewhere) was that the use of four or five engines solely to provide lift would result in a prohibitive weight penalty, effectively cancelling out the combat potential of VTOL.

It was a French engineer, Michel Wibault — whose company had built a range of commercial aircraft during the 1930s — who came up with a possible solution. Wibault's idea was for a turbojet using vectored thrust, whereby rotating nozzles could be used to direct exhaust gases either vertically downwards or horizontally aft. Seeking funds to develop his theme, he approached the Paris office of the Mutual Weapons Development Team, which at that time was headed by Colonel Bill Chapman. This was in 1956, at the time when Bristol Siddeley was working on the Orpheus engine to power NATO's lightweight fighter, so Chapman approached Dr. Stanley Hooker, Bristol's Technical Director, and sought his views on the Wibault project. Hooker was enthusiastic, and one of his project engineers, Gordon Lewis, was briefed to investigate the possibilities. After preliminary studies, Wibault and Lewis applied for a joint patent covering the design of a vectored-thrust engine known as the BE.52 in January 1957; this was further developed into the BE.53 Pegasus 1, which was based on the Orpheus.

In the summer of 1957, details of the proposed engine were passed to Sir Sydney Camm at Hawker Aircraft, who made a preliminary design for an aircraft to go around it. The design was allocated the project number P.1127. It bore no resemblance, at this stage, to the amazing combat aircraft that was ultimately to be developed from it — the Harrier — but it was a firm beginning.

In June 1958, the Mutual Weapons Development Team agreed to pay 75 per cent of the development costs of the Pegasus engine. Funding the airframe, however, proved a tougher obstacle, for research funds had been

DORNIER DO 31E. One of Federal Germany's ambitious V/STOL projects was the Dornier Do 31E experimental transport, which first flew in July 1967. The aircraft was extensively evaluated in the USA as well as Germany, but the programme was abandoned in the early 1970s.

eaten up by other projects — notably the abortive Swallow VG design — and whatever remained was being channelled into the development of TSR-2. Hawker had no alternative but to proceed as a private venture while the Air Staff set about drafting an operational requirement to cover the concept. This emerged in April 1959 as GOR.345, and Specification ER.204D was issued to cover the P.1127, but it was not until October 1959 that Hawker recieved a preliminary contract and a niggardly £75,000 to enable further design work to be carried out, and not until 22 June 1960 did the company receive a contract for the building of two prototypes. It was fortunate that Hawker recognised potential when they saw it, or there might never have been a Harrier — with appalling operational consequences in the South Atlantic over twenty years later.

In Hawkers' eyes, the P.1127 was the ideal design to meet a new NATO specification, NBMR-3 (NATO Basic Military Requirement No.3) which was issued in 1961 after several revisions and called for a VTOL strike fighter with a sustained capability of 0.92M at low level and supersonic speed at altitude. The P.1127 was not supersonic, but it had a vast amount of development potential ahead of it and so Sir Sydney Camm proposed a modified version, the P.1150, which was to have a thin wing and an advanced Pegasus engine using plenum chamber burning. Hawkers could have progressed with the building of a prototype almost immediately, but yet another revision to NBMR-3, requiring greater range and load-carrying capacity, meant that the 1150 would have been too small. Camm and his team therefore set about designing a scaled-up version, the P.1154, which was to have a BS.100 engine of 33,000 lb.s.t. and was to be equipped with plenum chamber burning.

However, the P.1154 had a formidable challenger, at least in theory, in the shape of the Dassault Mirage III-V, whose forerunner, the Balzac VTOL research aircraft, was then under construction. The Balzac used the wings and tail surfaces of the Mirage III-001, married to a fuselage that was completely redesigned except for the main frames and the cockpit section. French research into VTOL, in fact, pre-dated both the Hawker P.1127 and NBMR-3, having been initiated to meet an Armée de l'Air requirement, but the French chose to pursue their experiments with a combination of lift jets and propulsion engine, rather than vectored thrust. Even then, the engines they chose to power the Balzac were British, consisting of eight lightweight Rolls-Royce RB.108 lift engines and a Bristol Siddeley Orpheus B.Or.3 turbojet for forward propulsion. Ironically, the use of British engines of proven design led to a strong lobby in both the Ministry of Aviation and the RAF that favoured concentrating on the development of the Balzac/Mirage III-V as the standard NATO strike fighter at the expense of the P.1154.

The Balzac made its first tethered flight on 12 October 1962, in the rig once used by the ill-fated Coléoptère at Melun-Villaroche, and initial tests were made with a non-retractable landing gear. The aircraft made its first free vertical take-off on 18 October 1962 and the first transition to horizontal flight on 18 March 1963. The test programme continued until 10 January 1964, when the aircraft suffered a critical divergent lateral oscillation during hovering descent and crashed, killing its pilot. However, it was repaired and trials were resumed at a later date.

Meanwhile, the first flight of the Mirage III-V had been delayed because of problems in selecting an appropriate

HAWKER P.1154. The cancellation of the Hawker P.1154 supersonic V/STOL project gave life to the Harrier and the later Sea Harrier, seen here, with subsequent dramatic results in combat over the Falklands.

HARRIER. *Prototype for a supersonic V/STOL fighter? A Harrier PCB-1 fitted with a Rolls-Royce Pegasus engine equipped for plenum chamber burning being tested on a special rig at Shoeburyness in 1984.*

propulsion engine. The prototype eventually flew on 12 February 1965, when hovering trials began; at that time the aircraft was fitted with a SNECMA TF-104 turbofan, but this was subsequently replaced by a more powerful TF-106. The lift engines were eight Rolls-Royce RB.162-1 turbojets.

During flight testing, the first prototype Mirage III-V reached a speed at high altitude of 1.35M. The second prototype, which flew for the first time on 22 June 1966, was fitted with a Pratt & Whitney TF-30 turbofan rated at 11,330 lb.s.t. (18,520 lb.s.t. with afterburning), and on 12 September 1966 the aircraft reached a speed of 2.04M. However, it was destroyed in an accident on 28 November that year, resulting in the cancellation of plans to build further prototypes and develop the aircraft to production standards. In fact, the Mirage III-V programme had been under critical review for some time, not only on grounds of escalating costs but also because the programme had slipped badly. Originally, it had been expected that the prototype Mirage III-V would fly late in 1963, and that the first squadron would form in 1966, if trials were successful. Ironically, another Dassault design, the Mirage F, which had been built solely to test the Mirage III-V's armament system and the TF-306 engine that was to have powered the operational version of the VTOL fighter, was found to have enormous potential in its own right as an operational strike fighter. It eventually entered service as the Mirage F-1, and did everything the Mirage III-V was expected to do except take off vertically.

In Federal Germany, the design teams of Bölkow, Heinkel and Messerschmitt had joined forces in 1959 at the suggestion of the German Defence Ministry to develop a Mach Two VTOL interceptor. The design they adopted involved an aircraft of conventional configuration, but with turbojet engines mounted in swivelling wingtip pods to provide both lift and control in vertical and low-speed flight, together with fuselage-mounted lift engines. A bedstead-type test rig was built and made 126 flights by April 1965, fitted with a single RB.108 lift engine. The consortium, known as the Entwicklungsring Süd Arbeitsgemeinschaft, produced two prototypes of an experimental single-seat VTOL aircraft, the VJ-101C, which were fitted with six RB.145 engines developed jointly by Rolls-Royce and MAN Turbomotoren. Tethered trials of the VJ-101C X-1 began in December 1962, the first free hover being made on 10 April 1963. The aircraft made its first horizontal take-off on 31 August, 1963, and its first transition on 20 September that year. During further trials the following spring the VJ-101C X-1 exceeded 1.0M in level flight on several occasions, proving the viability of the concept; unfortunately, the aircraft crashed after a normal horizontal take-off on 14 September 1964, the pilot escaping thanks to his Martin-Baker Mk.GA7 zero-zero ejection seat.

Hovering trials of the second prototype, the VJ-101C X-2, began in the spring of 1965, and it made its first free flight on 12 June that year. By this time Heinkel had dropped out of the consortium, and the resources of Bölkow and Messerschmitt were being channelled into other programmes, so plans to produce an operational version of the VTOL research aircraft, the VJ-101D, were never implemented.

Nevertheless, the two VJ-101Cs had provided a wealth of knowledge about VTOL techniques, and it formed a

LOCKHEED XV-4A HUMMINGBIRD. Originally designated VZ-10, the Lockheed Model 330 Hummingbird VTOL research aircraft was built as part of a US Army Transportation Research Command Programme. Powered by two 3,000 lb thrust Pratt & Whitney JT12A-3 turbojets.

sound basis for other German companies involved in the field. Foremost among them was the former Focke-Wulf company, which had produced a design study to meet a German Defence Ministry Requirement — VAK 191B — for a subsonic VTOL tactical fighter to replace the Fiat G.91. The initial design study was designated FW 1262, and in 1964 VFW and Fiat agreed to collaborate in development work under a Memorandum of Agreement signed by the German and Italian Defence Ministers. The Italians later dropped out of the programme, but VFW (Vereinigte Flugtechnische Werke, created by the almalgamation of Focke-Wulf and Weser Flugzeugbau) found another partner in Fokker of Holland, and Fiat agreed to carry on as sub-contractor.

A hovering rig was built to assist in development work, and it was planned to build three prototypes of the proposed VAK 191B fighter. These were to be powered by two Rolls-Royce/MAN RB.162 lift jets and one RB.193 vectored-thrust turbojet. Fiat, who had already made advanced design studies of their own VTOL fighter project, the G.95/4, was responsible for building major components of the prototypes.

Work proceeded with Federal German Government funding, and the first VAK 191B was rolled out in April 1970. It made its first conventional flight on 10 September 1971, and this was followed by a period of tethered hovering trials. By this time the other two prototypes had also joined the test programme, and on 26 October 1972 one of these made the type's first vertical-to-horizontal transition. During this test the aircraft reached a speed of 276 mph, and its RB.162 lift jets were shut down and restarted in flight for the first time. At the end of 1972, however, German Government funding of the VAK 191B was terminated, and no further development was undertaken. By this time, Royal Air Force Harriers were being deployed to Germany, and their presence more than adequately filled the VTOL requirement in NATO's front line. Hawker's earlier faith had paid dividends, and the Harrier remained Western Europe's only operational VTOL combat aircraft.

The story might have been very different, had Hawker Siddeley been allowed to proceed with the development of the Harrier's supersonic derivative, the P.1154. But the P.1154's fortunes had been clouded right from the start. Even though the design had been declared the outright winner in the NBMR-3 design contest, thanks in large part to the experience already gained by Hawker Siddeley with the P.1127, its rival, the Mirage III-V, was more of an international project and therefore politically favoured. The crunch came when France declared her intention to pursue a unilateral development course with the Mirage III-V, notwithstanding the greater technical merit of the P.1154; the upshot was that NATO, faced with little prospect of a truly collaborative VTOL fighter project becoming a reality, withdrew the NBMR-3 requirement altogether.

It was not all the fault of the French; the British Air Staff had shown little interest in the progress of the NBMR-3 contest or the possible development of P.1154 to fit the European requirement, being preoccupied with Britain's own air defence needs. Nevertheless, P.1154 was a very viable project, and in August 1962 Hawker, at the instigation of the Air and Naval Staffs, submitted draft proposals for a P.1154 variant that would meet the requirements of both Services. It was an enormously difficult task, for the requirements were greatly different; they differed, in fact, on fourteen major points, starting with the Royal Navy's insistence on a two-seater as opposed to the RAF's single-seat aircraft.

Nevertheless, Hawker Siddeley worked hard to produce a firm plan. The company had decided to adopt the Bristol Siddeley BS.100/8 engine — provided that a development contract was forthcoming in mid-1963 — and was looking for the first prototype flight in the summer of 1965, followed by initial Service deliveries in 1968. Early in 1963, however, an unexpected complication arose when Rolls-Royce came forward and offered two Spey engines as an alternative to one BS.100; the Naval Staff, who preferred a twin-engined configuration anyway, thought the Rolls-Royce proposal a sound one, especially as the Spey was already available in its civil form and would be ready in a vectored-thrust version far sooner than the BS.100. In the event it was decided to go ahead with the latter engine, but the Rolls-Royce representation, sound though it might have been, had served to reinforce growing doubts about the P.1154 programme.

Despite these complications, authorisation was given for a development programme costing some £750 million. It involved several development aircraft, followed by 700 production machines for the RAF and Fleet Air Arm, and in 1964 Hawker Siddeley embarked on the construction of the first single-seat and two-seat prototypes. There was little likelihood now that the first operational examples would be in service before 1969, and so the Admiralty decided to withdraw from the P.1154 programme altogether and seek the purchase of F-4 Phantoms from the United States instead. Hawker Siddeley persevered with the development of the P.1154 for the RAF and with the design of a V/STOL transport, the HS 681, but in November 1964 the Air Staff was informed by representatives of the newly-elected Labour Government that there were insufficient funds to support the continued development of the P.1154, HS.681 *and* TSR-2. Two would have to go, and so the RAF opted for TSR-2, the aircraft in the most advanced stage of development and on which so many hopes were pinned. The hopes were forlorn, for TSR-2 was cancelled in its turn a few months later.

In retrospect, and with regard to the enormous development potential of the P.1127 — development that is still going on today — the P.1154 was a costly red herring in the main stream of British VTOL combat aircraft development. It would have proved a complex aircraft, and development problems that were not envisaged at the time might have set back the programme by a considerable margin.

The history of aviation has its ironies, and nowhere more so than in the VTOL story. The Harrier serves today with the RAF, the Royal Navy and three other air forces, and is combat-proven; the Harrier II is in service with the Royal Air Force and US Marine Corps, and development is in progress of a possible supersonic version featuring plenum chamber burning. The demise of P.1154 effectively gave life to the Harrier, and one wonders whether, had the P.1154 reached fruition, its success story would have been any greater than that of the aircraft which fought with such distinction over the Falklands.

Chapter Ten
Prototype 2000

Tracing the course of military aircraft research and development is a fascinating exercise. It is possible to follow the development of fighter or bomber aircraft, say, in a fairly straight line up to the early 1960s, but after that things become more complex as the hardware becomes more complex. After 1960, not even the most powerful nations were in an economic position to hand out prototype development contracts to several companies for aircraft designed to the same specification, and companies certainly could no longer afford — except in exceptional circumstances — to develop military prototypes as a private venture.

The objective now was to get design exactly right on the drawing board, something that could increasingly be achieved with the aid of computer technology, so that the non-starters might be weeded out at this stage and the most promising design selected for funding. Only exceptionally during the past twenty years, in the Western world at least, have prototype contracts been awarded to two rival companies and the contenders 'flown off' against one another.

The unexpected has sometimes happened. Only a few years ago, this book would have dealt at length with the Rockwell B-1 as an advanced bomber project that failed to reach production status, yet now the pendulum has

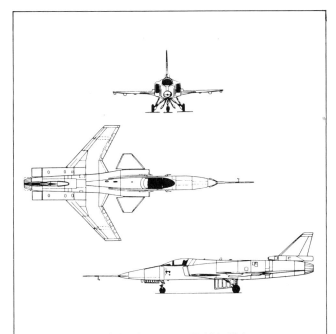

The purpose of the Grumman X-29A flight demonstrator is to prove that forward-sweep technology is a viable alternative to conventional sweep, offering improved aerodynamics for tomorrow's combat aircraft.

swung the other way and the B-1 is in production for Strategic Air Command. This is one example of a case where politics, and not the design itself, dictated the course of events. The B-1 was fortunate in being reprieved; many other promising combat aircraft in the Western world have not been so fortunate.

Almost all of today's successful combat aircraft are the result of groundwork laid twenty years ago, which is really why the bulk of this history deals with military prototypes up to that point in time. For example, the F-15 Eagle and the F-16 Fighting Falcon both originated in concepts formulated in the mid-1960s, and both types have shown so much development potential — in common with other combat aircraft originating at about the same time — that a new generation of military prototypes has been much slower to gestate than was previously the case. After all, it would have made little sense to devote enormous funds to the development of new military aircraft for specific roles when existing types had potential enough to enable them to carry out those roles over a span of two decades or more.

Only now (in 1984) are the leading aerospace agencies once again beginning to investigate the development of new combat aircraft for service well into the next millennium. In the United States, the USAF has launched a ten-year development programme that will ultimately lead to an Advanced Tactical Fighter (ATF), while at the same time investing heavily in improvements that will extend the lives of the current F-15 and F-16 and possibly keep them in the front line until the turn of the century. And perhaps the most classic example of all to illustrate the enormous development potential of a sound design is McDonnell Douglas's Super Phantom, which if all goes well will be around for the next quarter of a century and which traces its lineage in an unbroken line to the first flight of the XF4H-1 Phantom in 1958.

The requirement for the Advanced Tactical Fighter is enormously demanding. It must have a range up to 100 per cent greater than that of the F-15, be capable of short take-off and landing from damaged airfields and of engaging multiple targets at once, beyond visual range. While doing so, it must be able to survive in an environment filled with hostile weaponry, both in the air and on the ground — and all this under the command of a single pilot. It is a requirement born of dire necessity, for since January 1979, when the USAF's last fighter the F-16 — entered service, the Russians have introduced new fighter aircraft which in some respects are better than anything NATO has to counter them.

The Sukhoi Su-24 Fencer, for example, has the ability to strike deep into NATO territory at low altitude in all weathers, whereas the previous generation of Soviet fighters possessed only a limited combat radius and restricted all-weather capability. The MiG-31 Foxhound, a greatly enhanced variant of the MiG-25 Foxbat, is the Soviet Union's first look-down/shoot-down interceptor

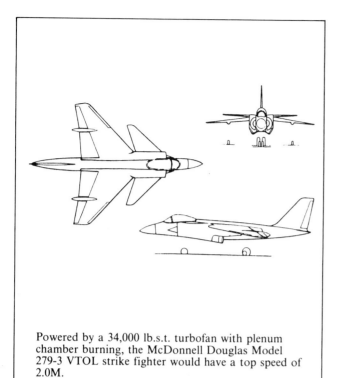

Powered by a 34,000 lb.s.t. turbofan with plenum chamber burning, the McDonnell Douglas Model 279-3 VTOL strike fighter would have a top speed of 2.0M.

and is equipped with a long-range pulse-Doppler radar that can possibly illuminate targets at a greater distance than any Western AI radar with the exception of the Tornado F.2's AI.24 Foxhunter. The Su-25 Frogfoot, deployed operationally in Afghanistan, is the equivalent of the Fairchild A-10 Thunderbolt II and by all accounts is an excellent close air support fighter.

And this is not all. As this is being written the Soviet Union is on the point of deploying two new air superiority fighters, the MiG-29 Fulcrum and Su-27 Flanker, both of which are equipped with new medium-range AAMs that will enable them to engage targets beyond visual range. The MiG-29 is roughly comparable with the F-18 Hornet, the Su-27 with the F-15 Eagle.

The Soviet Union is rapidly closing the combat aircraft technology gap that has hitherto permitted NATO to enjoy a lead in quality, if not quantity, and in some areas may even have established a margin of superiority. The need for ATF is therefore pressing, and the multi-stage improvement programmes initiated by the USAF on the F-15 and F-16 to fill the gap until ATF comes along have assumed high priority.

The technology that will be applied to the Advanced Tactical Fighter has already been around for some time. Since the late 1970s several test aircraft have been flown, incorporating advances in aerodynamics, control systems and avionics. They include the YF-16 control-configured vehicle, the HiMAT highly manoeuvrable remotely piloted research vehicle, the integrated flight and fire control F-15, and the advanced fighter technology integration F-16. Still to fly, at the time of writing in late 1984, are the X-29 forward-swept-wing demonstrator, the mission-adaptive-wing F-111 and the F-15 STOL and manoeuvre technology demonstrator.

Out of these experiments will emerge a fighter aircraft that can skid sideways, turn without banking, climb or descend without changing its attitude, or point its nose left or right, up or down without changing its flight path. It will be capable of a sustained 8g turn at high subsonic

speeds on the edge of the stratosphere, at altitudes of 30,000 feet or more — almost twice that possible with existing aircraft. With its integrated flight and fire control system, in which an optical sensor/tracker pod supplies target trajectory data direct to the flight control system, it will be able to make accurate head-on gun attacks against supersonic targets. To improve manoeuvrability, range and structural life it will have a wing whose camber varies continuously throughout the flight to produce the maximum aerodynamic benefit; this is the mission-adaptive wing which is to be tested on an F-111.

So much for the USAF and ATF, a prototype of which is likely to fly before 1995. The US Navy, for its part, is thinking along somewhat different lines in that its next-generation multi-role fighter, as well as incorporating advanced technology, will also feature V/STOL performance. The trend is logical, for the proven performance of the AV-8 Harrier in US Marine Corps service has more than vindicated the concept. Unlike the USAF, the US Navy is prepared to accept a slight blunting of overall performance in return for an aircraft than can operate equally well from an aircraft carrier or a jungle clearing.

General Dynamics, McDonnell Douglas, Rockwell and Vought are currently exploring the aerodynamic design of a single-engined supersonic V/STOL naval fighter/attack aircraft for service at the end of the century. The requirement is for an aircraft with a sustained speed of 1.6M or better, good STOL performance and high manoeuvrability, with a take-off weight varying between 20,000 lb for VTO to 40,000 lb for STO carrier-based strike.

The McDonnell Douglas design, the Model 279-3, is based on the well-tried Harrier/Pegasus concept, using a single bypass-ratio turbofan with rotating nozzles. The project is a wing/canard design with a Pegasus-type engine fitted with plenum chamber burning, and will have a gross weight of 48,000 lb for ski-jump operations. Rockwell International's proposal, on the other hand, is based on thrust augmentation and is a development of the XFV-12A project, which never flew. A lot of work remains to be carried out on this concept, in which engine exhaust is diverted to ejector channels and, in theory, energises a larger mass flow of freestream air. In practice, the only aircraft to have used this principle was the Lockheed XV-4A Hummingbird, which was limited to very short duration hovering flights during testing.

The General Dynamics design is also based on thrust augmentation, but uses an improved type of ejector developed by de Havilland Aircraft of Canada. The proposal offers two different wing planforms, one of delta and the other of cranked-arrow configuration. In theory, the latter should be capable of lifting off at an all-up weight of 37,000 lbs from a 6-degree ski-jump following a 400-foot take-off run.

Vought's proposal, the TF120, is the most ambitious of the four and is aimed for a maximum speed of 2.4M, making it by far the fastest. It is based on the tandem-fan concept, in which a core engine drives two widely separated fan stages via a single shaft. Between them lies a transition stage, with a flow diverter, dorsal inlet and ventral exhaust nozzle. For cruising flight, the transition-stage inlet and exhaust are closed, the diverter retracted, and the assembly operates as a conventional low-bypass turbofan; for VTOL, the transition stage is opened and the diverter blocks the duct, the rear fan breathing through a dorsal inlet and the front fan through a normal

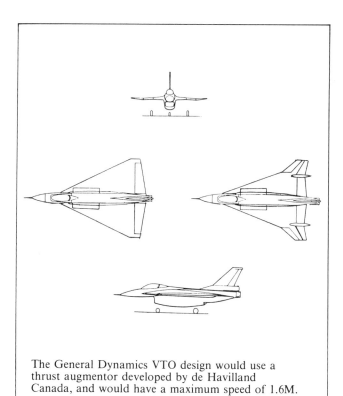

The General Dynamics VTO design would use a thrust augmentor developed by de Havilland Canada, and would have a maximum speed of 1.6M.

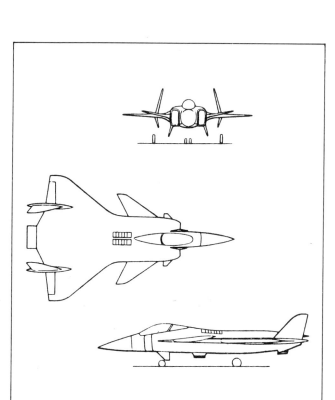

Vought's submission for a US Navy fighter for the 21st century — the TF120.

intake. In 1984 all these projects were at the wind-tunnel testing stage, and with all the attendant problems and new technology involved it is unlikely that a supersonic VTOL strike fighter for the US Navy would be operational much before the turn of the century.

In Western Europe, the hopes of five air forces are pinned on the development of a Future European Fighter Aircraft. FEFA's story goes back to 1969 — another example of the length of time involved in setting the development of a new combat aircraft in motion — when the RAF issued Air Staff Target 396 for an all-weather, supersonic, STOL ground-attack aircraft to replace the Jaguar and Harrier. The resulting scheme was too complex, and too like the Tornado to warrant development, so it was simplified and Air Staff Target 403 — calling for a relatively uncomplicated ground attack aircraft that could also defend itself in air combat — was written around it. The requirement had by now dispensed with the STOL clause, and in 1979 Air Staff Requirement 409 was issued to cover a subsonic V/STOL Harrier replacement; this has reached fruition as the AV-8B/Harrier GR.5.

This left AST 403 as a Jaguar replacement only, which meant that the project was not financially viable unless it involved international co-operation. The ideal was a European Combat Aircraft, or Eurofighter, for service in about 1990; it would be developed jointly by Britain, France and Federal Germany.

There were problems right from the start, not the least of them being that Germany's requirement was completely different from that of France and Britain. But in the end it was shortage of funds that killed the European Combat Aircraft, in 1981. As far as Britain was concerned, the role of the Jaguar would be assumed by the Tornado GR.1 and the Harrier GR.5 from the late 1980s.

However, the need for a new single-seat agile combat aircraft still existed, and studies proceeded independently in Britain, France and Germany. British Aerospace, as a private venture, took the European Combat Aircraft a stage further and developed it into the P.110 project, and in September 1982 this became the Agile Combat Aircraft, with B.Ae's Tornado partners — MBB and Aeritalia — joining in. At the same time, the UK Ministry of Defence announced the initiation of a programme, costing £70 million, to build and fly an 'agile demonstrator' in 1986. France had clearly been thinking along the same lines, because in 1983 it was revealed that Dassault-Breguet also planned to fly an experimental fighter prototype, the ACX, in 1986. The difference is that ACX will be just that — a fighter prototype. Britain's agile demonstrator will not, although its configuration will be similar to that of the fighter that is expected to be developed from it.

Development of the new agile fighter must be rapid if it is to succeed. Ideally, it ought to be in production by 1990 if it is to capture export orders from Third World countries who will otherwise turn to France and the United States to fulfil their requirements, just as they did in the 1960s as a result of Britain's muddled aviation policies. France is clearly interested in FEFA, but the emergence of ACX is proof that Dassault-Breguet are determined to pursue their own path if FEFA fails.

What comes after FEFA, and America's ATF, is anybody's guess. The quest is now to discover the formula for the ultimate fighter aircraft for the 21st century. Such an aircraft must come, and it is economy,

The McDonnell Douglas Model 279-3 is designed for Mach 2 and features plenum chamber burning.

R.McM.

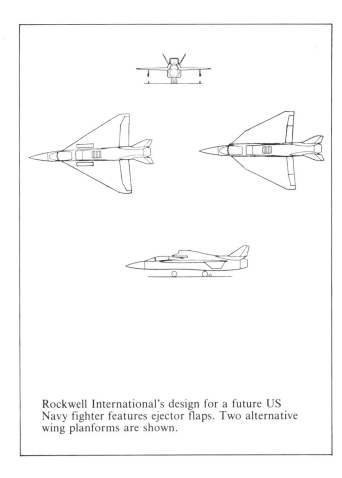

Rockwell International's design for a future US Navy fighter features ejector flaps. Two alternative wing planforms are shown.

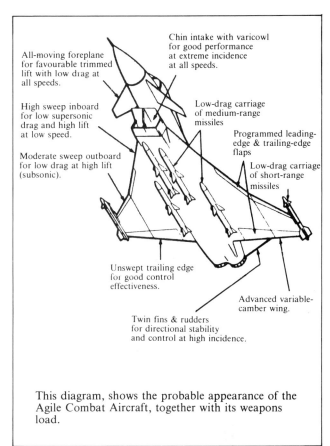

All-moving foreplane for favourable trimmed lift with low drag at all speeds.

High sweep inboard for low supersonic drag and high lift at low speed.

Moderate sweep outboard for low drag at high lift (subsonic).

Chin intake with varicowl for good performance at extreme incidence at all speeds.

Low-drag carriage of medium-range missiles

Programmed leading-edge & trailing-edge flaps

Low-drag carriage of short-range missiles

Advanced variable-camber wing.

Unswept trailing edge for good control effectiveness.

Twin fins & rudders for directional stability and control at high incidence.

This diagram, shows the probable appearance of the Agile Combat Aircraft, together with its weapons load.

General Dynamics future Naval V/STOL fighter design uses thrust augmentors.

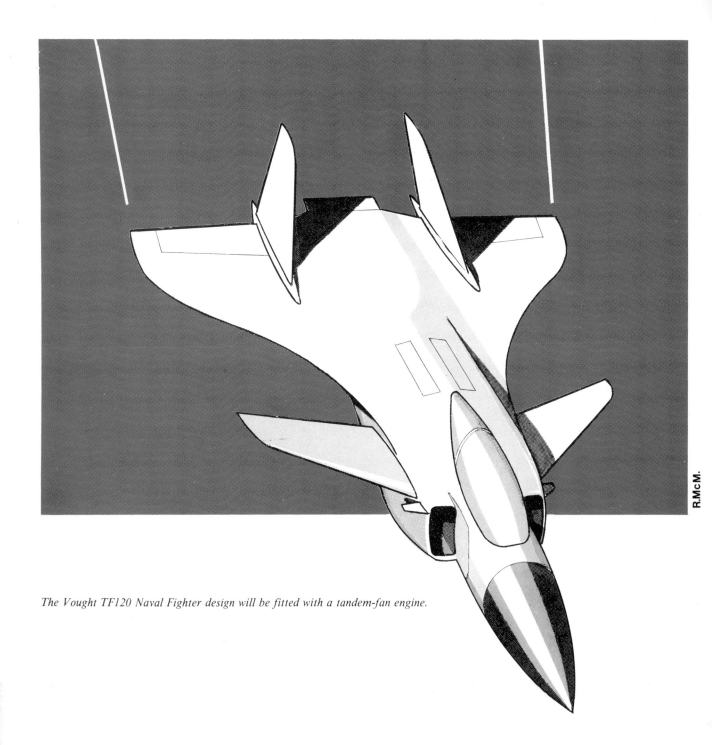

The Vought TF120 Naval Fighter design will be fitted with a tandem-fan engine.

R.McM.

rather than technological barriers, that will eventually draw the stop line across the upward curve of advancement.

It is a sobering thought that, as has been suggested, the entire Gross National Product of the United States will not be sufficient, by the middle of the next century, to buy a single example of a new fighter aircraft if the present upward spiral of development costs continues.

Appendix 1
Combat Flying Boats: The Lost Cause.

Although the years of the Second World War witnessed great strides in the development of flying-boats for the long-range maritime reconnaissance role, little attention was paid to the use of seaplanes to fill other combat requirements until the closing months of the Pacific War, when the British Air and Naval Staffs issued a joint specification, E.6/44, for a single-seat twin-jet water-based fighter.

In 1944, preparations were under way to send a Royal Navy task force formed around a nucleus of five fleet carriers — the *Illustrious, Formidable, Indomitable, Implacable* and *Indefatigable* – to the Pacific Theatre to support the United States' effort there. This was to be followed, late in 1945, by Tiger Force, comprising several squadrons of Lancasters, Lincolns and Mosquitos of the RAF. At this stage, no-one knew for certain how long the Pacific War might drag on; the atomic bomb was still in the future as an operational weapon.

Because of the vast distances involved, the aircraft carrier — and the long-range B-29 bombers of the USAAF — remained the only means of carrying the war to the Japanese homeland. Aircraft carriers, however, were vulnerable to air attack, as were the bases on newly-captured islands that would be used in the final assault on Japan; the extent to which Japan's offensive capability was becoming depleted was not yet known, and the

British, with bitter memories of campaigns lost in the early days of the war because air bases were knocked out by enemy air attack, were determined to take out some kind of insurance against the possibility of it happening again. The result was E.6/44.

After some preliminary studies, a team led by Henry Knowler of Saunders-Roe Ltd submitted a design for a jet fighter flying boat intended for operation from sheltered coastal waters such as the bays and lagoons that were a feature of many Pacific islands. With no advanced flying boat design data to draw upon, Knowler and his team decided to go for a conventional hull, with a length-to-beam ratio of approximately 6:1, even though this would result in an aircraft with a maximum level speed considerably lower than that of a land-based counterpart. Fortunately, the nature of the specification, which did not envisage operation in open waters, made it unnecessary to raise the engine air intake to height where there would be no possibility of flooding in rough seas, so the designers were able to keep hull depth to a minimum.

The aircraft's twin turbojets were mounted side by side in the hull, sharing a common nose intake but exhausting through individual jet pipes. These were angled outwards at 5 degrees to keep the efflux clear of the rear fuselage. The wing was conventional, employing a high-speed section and shoulder-mounted, its leading edge just

SAUNDERS ROE E6/44. The first prototype that flew for the first time at East Cowes in July 1947.

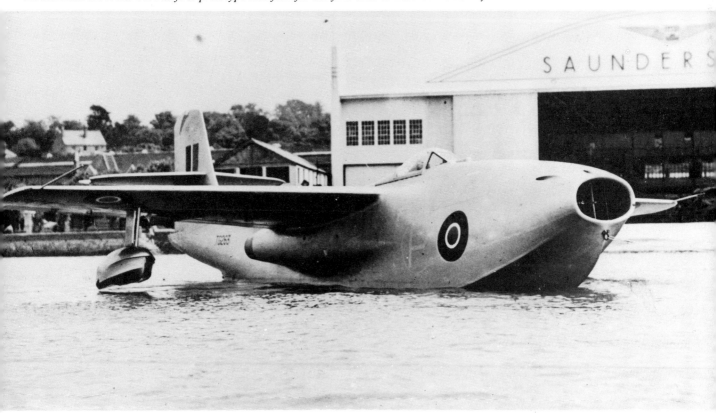

below the cockpit. The stabilizing floats retracted inwards, rotating through 90 degrees in the process to form an aerodynamically clean bulge under the wing when fully retracted. The cockpit was fully pressurized, the pilot seated under a sliding canopy and having a Martin-Baker ejection seat.

Three prototypes of the fighter were ordered under the designation SRA/1, and it was decided to continue building them for evaluation even after the end of the Pacific War. The first prototype, TG263, flew for the first time at East Cowes on 16 July 1947 under the power of two Metropolitan-Vickers F.2/4 Beryl axial-flow turbojets, the test pilot being Geoffrey Tyson. The aircraft was already close in design to meeting the operational requirement, provision being made for four 20-mm cannon above the air intake, and there were points for two flush-fitting auxiliary fuel tanks under the inboard wing sections.

The first four test flights revealed very few snags, and Saunders-Roe felt confident enough to demonstrate the SRA/1 before representatives of the RAF, Royal Navy and the Royal Aircraft Establishment late in July; the aircraft was also shown to the public at Farnborough in September. The other two prototypes, TG267 and TG271, joined the test programme in 1948; the former was fitted with an acorn-type fairing at the junction of the fin and tailplane and had a strengthened cockpit canopy. It was powered by uprated Metrovick Beryl MVB 2 engines of 3,500 lb.s.t.; the third aircraft had the fully operational version of the turbojet, the Beryl Mk.1, and it was this machine that was demonstrated at the 1948 SBAC Show.

The second and third SRA/1 prototypes were both involved in accidents, causing serious delays to the test programme, but testing was resumed with the first prototype in 1951. By this time it was clear that the SRA/1, although a surprisingly manoeuvrable aircraft, was inferior on every other count to contemporary land-based fighters, and that it had little development potential. The prototype went to the College of Aeronautics at Cranfield and was later acquired by the Skyfame Museum at Staverton, where it may be seen today.

In the United States, there had been a drift away from flying-boat development by 1944, with long-range maritime patrol tasks increasingly undertaken by land-based aircraft such as the Liberator and Privateer. In the immediate post-war years, however, research into new hydrodynamic shapes, coupled with jet propulsion, led to a re-awakening of interest in the belief that many of the previous seaplane limitations could now be overcome. The lion's share of the research was carried out by the US Navy Bureau of Aeronautics, the National Advisory Committee for Aeronautics and Convair's Hydrodynamic Research Laboratory, and it was Convair who received a Bureau of Aeronautics contract to develop a flying-boat configuration that would result in a water-borne fighter with a performance comparable to that of land-based aircraft.

The Convair design team, under the direction of Ernest Stout, set about proving their theories in practical fashion by devising a series of scale models. The climax was the top-secret Project Skate, which involved some of the most advanced aerodynamic designs to be tested in the late 1940s. The later models employed 'blended hulls', the idea being that the aircraft rode so low in the water that its wings aided buoyancy. In these models, wing and hull blended in unprecedented aerodynamic cleanness;

CONVAIR XF2Y-1 SEA DART. A transonic, delta-wing seaplane fighter, the XF2Y-1 (originally Y2-2) Sea Dart flew for the first time on 9 April 1953, powered by two Westinghouse XJ46-WE-2 turbojets.

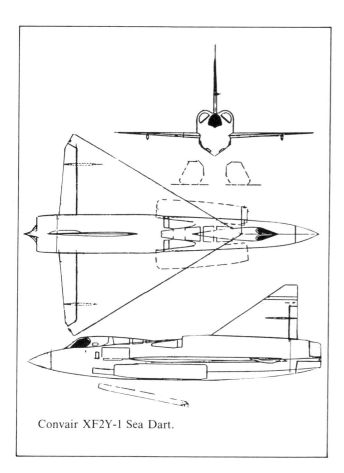

Convair XF2Y-1 Sea Dart.

spray dams were fitted on either side of the fuselage nose to speed take-off by deflecting the spray downwards, keeping it clear of the air intakes. Some models were taxied, taken off, flown and landed under radio control; others were catapult-launched, and yet others were towed behind high-speed motor launches to test spray and aerodynamic characteristics. At the same time, the NACA carried out extensive tests to find an acceptable form of undercarriage that would do away with conventional floats and improve hydrodynamic characteristics.

The configuration that seemed most acceptable was the hydro-ski. In this arrangement, twin hydro-skis, fitted flush against the under-surface of the hull, extended like flat seaplane floats under the water, and as the aircraft gathered speed the action of the skis pushed up its fuselage until it was clear of the surface, the machine skimming the waves until take-off speed was reached. When safe flying speed was attained, the skis were retracted, leaving the aircraft aerodynamically clean.

By early 1984, the Convair blended hull concept and the NACA hydro-skis had reached an advanced stage of development, and this led to a BuAer requirement for a full-scale seaplane fighter prototype. The requirement called for an aircraft with a maximum speed of 0.95M and an ability to operate in a five-foot swell. A design contest was initiated on 1 October 1948 and two designs were submitted, one by the NACA and the other by Convair; the former embodied hydro-skis and the latter the blended hull principle. The Convair design, which offered a better rate of climb and high-altitude performance, was accepted, but the project went ahead on a relatively low budget; the US Navy's emphasis was on the development of carrier-borne jet fighters.

At this stage, further development concentrated on comparative tests between the hydro-ski and blended hull

concepts. By 1950, hydro-ski development had undergone considerable advances, and as a result the Navy's requirement changed; what was now wanted was a faster aircraft fitted with skis, and smaller in overall dimensions than the original Convair proposal. This had envisaged a large twin-engined fighter with swept flying surfaces, based on the later series of Project Skate models; to meet the new requirement, Convair now evolved a smaller delta-wing design, the Y2-2, equipped with twin hydro-skis.

The new design was aerodynamically similar to the Convair F-102 delta-wing interceptor, then being developed for the USAF. Estimated performance figures included a maximum speed of 1.5M and an initial rate of climb of 30,000 feet per minute. Power was to be provided by two Westinghouse XJ46-WE-2 turbojets rated at 4,080 lb.s.t., but by the time Convair received a letter of intent on 19 January 1951 it had been decided to install 3,400 lb.s.t. Westinghouse J34-WE-32 engines, the XJ46 development programme having been subjected to some delays.

In August 1951, the Y2-2 was redesignated XF2Y-1, and on 28 August 1952, with work on a prototype well advanced, Convair received a BuAer contract for twelve pre-series F2Y-1s.

In January 1953, the completed prototype XF2Y-1, now known as the Sea Dart, began taxying trials in San Diego Bay, and it was during these that unexpected problems were encountered with the hydro-skis. The skis worked adequately at speeds of up to 60 mph, but beyond that they were susceptible to a phenomenon known as ski-pounding, with severe vibration that threatened to damage the airframe. Some modifications were carried out to the shape of the skis and to the shock absorbers between the skis and the hull, and the Sea Dart eventually made its first true flight on 9 April 1953 — although it had

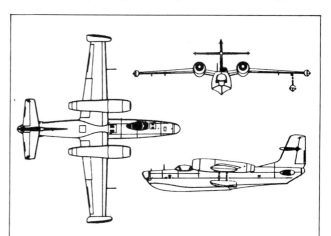

Designation: Beriev Be-R-1.
Role: Maritime patrol.
Engines: Two 6,040 lb.s.t. Klimov VK-1 turbojets.
Span: 66 ft.
Length: 64 ft.
Weight: Loaded 38,000 lb.
Crew: 3.
Service ceiling: 37,950 ft.
Range: 1,250 miles.
Max speed: 500 mph at 16,400 ft.
Weapons: Various offensive stores; two 23-mm cannon.

BERIEV Be-R-1. A twin-jet, high-wing flying-boat, the Be-R-1 flew in 1949, powered by two 6,040 lb thrust Klimov VK-1 engines. Flight testing continued until 1951, but the type was not adopted for service with the Soviet Naval Air Arm.

already made a 300-yard hop during a taxi run on 14 January.

Meanwhile, problems had been experienced with the proposed XJ46 powerplant, which, during test runs, had failed to develop the envisaged thrust. This fact, together with some aerodynamic deficiencies which had been belatedly revealed, meant that the Sea Dart would be unlikely to exceed 1.0M. It was therefore proposed to adopt a single Wright J67 or Pratt and Whitney J75 turbojet, but then the designers realised that this would lead to an unacceptable amount of fuselage redesign and the idea was dropped.

By the autumn of 1953, with the hydro-skis still causing problems, the future for the Sea Dart looked anything but rosy. Development of one of the XF2Y-1 prototypes was abandoned in October, and in November the order for ten production F2Y-1s was cancelled. The order for the other two production aircraft was also cancelled in March 1954, leaving Convair with an order for four YF2Y-1s for evaluation by the US Navy.

During 1954, more than a hundred hydro-ski modifications were tested, using both single-and twin-ski configurations, and it was found that the single-ski arrangement was the more satisfactory. Ski-pounding was reduced, although stability on take-off left much to be desired and there was a tendency to porpoise.

The Navy evaluation programme began on the first day of November, 1954, and was attended almost

MARTIN SEAMASTER XP6M-1. The XP6M-1 prototype which first flew on 14 July 1955 and completed seventy-nine hours of taxying and flight testing before it crashed on 7 December 1955 following a control malfunction. It was powered by four Allison J-71 turbojet engines with take-off after-burners.

immediately by disaster. On 4 November, the first of the three YF2Y-1s to be built broke up during a public demonstration over San Diego Bay when test pilot Charles E. Richbourg inadvertently exceeded the airframe limitations. Richbourg was fatally injured, and the evaluation programme was postponed until May 1955. Testing continued with the two remaining YF2Y-1s and the XF2Y-1 prototype, but ski difficulties persisted and the Sea Dart programme was abandoned in 1956.

In parallel with the development of the Sea Dart, the US Navy had also shown considerable interest in the potential of a jet-powered bomber/reconnaissance flying-boat, and in October 1952 the Martin Aircraft Company was awarded a contract for the development of such an aircraft, the Model 275 (XP6M-1) SeaMaster. The development programme called for the construction of two XP6M-1 prototypes and six YP6M-1 evaluation aircraft, all of which were to be powered by four Allison J71-A-4 turbojets. They were to be followed by an initial production batch of twenty-four P6M-2s, powered by 15,000 lb.s.t. Pratt and Whitney J75-P-2 engines.

The XP6M-1 prototype flew on 14 July 1955 and completed seventy-nine hours of taxiing and flight testing before it crashed on 7 December 1955 following a control malfunction. The second SeaMaster flew on 18 May 1956, but that also crashed on 9 November 1956 following a failure in the hydraulic system. The first YP6M-1 evaluation aircraft, with modifications to prevent the recurrence of the disasters that had overtaken the two prototypes, flew on 20 January 1958, and this was followed by the first production P6M-2 on 17 February 1959. In all, as well as the two prototypes, six YP6M-1s and four P6M-2s were completed, but by the spring of 1959 the US Navy's research and development budget was being allocated to other programmes which were thought to be more important. Testing of the SeaMaster had revealed numerous technical problems — water seepage throught the rotary weapons bay door in the hull was one, although this was later solved — and the cost of the programme had risen to three times the original estimate.

By this time, the number of P6M-2 SeaMasters on order had been reduced to eight, which were to have formed a single US Navy squadron. Only three P6M-2s, however, were taken on charge, and these were eventually broken up for scrap at the Patuxent River Naval Air Test Centre, Maryland. Basically, the SeaMaster's biggest drawback had been its advanced concept. It was potentially a very versatile aircraft with a high performance; maximum speed, for example, was 654 mph (0.92M) at 21,000 feet, and unrefuelled range was 1,500 miles with a 30,000-pound payload. With its ability to carry mines, bombs, torpedos or a camera pack, the SeaMaster would have been capable of undertaking a variety of roles, but its operational use would have needed considerable logistical support and most of the tasks it was designed to carry out could be done equally as well by a new generation of advanced carrier-borne

aircraft. The demise of the SeaMaster was the final nail in the coffin of combat flying-boat development in the United States.

The Russians, too, did not enjoy much success with jet-powered flying-boats, although one design, the Beriev Be-10, briefly attained operational status.

After the end of the Second World War, the Russians concentrated all flying-boat and seaplane research and development under Georgii M. Beriev's design bureau, and priority was given to the design of a modern maritime patrol aircraft with a long endurance. The design evolved by the Beriev team was the LL-143, the 'LL' standing for Letayushchaya Lodka, or flying-boat. It was a large gull-wing monoplane powered by two 2,000 hp Shvetsov ASh-72 radial engines, and was armed with a 23-mm cannon in the bow and paired 23-mm cannon in dorsal and tail turrets. In its definitive version, the LL-143 was ordered into production as the Be-6 (NATO code-name: Madge).

Meanwhile, Beriev had been working on an advanced jet-powered flying-boat, the Be-R-1. It was a good design from both the aerodynamic and hydrodynamic points of view, with a length-to-beam ratio of 8:1 and a long, narrow planing bottom that greatly reduced drag, both in the air and on the water. Moreover, the Be-R-1 was designed for operation in rough seas. The aircraft was powered by two Klimov VK-1 turbojets mounted above the shoulder-mounted gull wing, their long nacelles projecting a considerable distance forward of the leading edge. Wing and tail surfaces were conventional and unswept. Everything in the Be-R-1's design reflected Beriev's desire to keep aerodynamic drag to a minimum; the pilot was seated under a fighter-type blister canopy, offset to port, the stablizing floats were retracted in flight to lie flush with the wingtips, and defensive armament comprised two 23-mm cannon in a streamlined tail barbette.

The Be-R-1 underwent flight trials at Taganrog from 1949 to 1951, but although its performance was promising, including a maximum speed at sea level of 478 mph, the aircraft was not accepted for service, and it was the turboprop-powered Be-12 Tchaika (code-name: Mail) that succeeded the Be-6 in service with the Morskaya Aviatsiya.

Nevertheless, the Be-R-1 provided the Beriev team with invaluable experience in high-speed flying-boat design, and the Be-R-1's ancestry was apparent when, in 1961, a twin-jet flying-boat with sharply swept flying surfaces was publicly revealed for the first time at the Tushino air display. This was the Be-10 (Mallow), which subsequently established a number of FAI-approved records for seaplanes. A small number of Be-10s entered service with the Morskaya Aviatsiya, but the type's career was brief and its operational use was confined to a development and evaluation unit. Like the Americans before them, the Russians had discovered that the pure-jet flying- boat was not the ideal vehicle for the maritime task.

Appendix 2: Military Aircraft Prototypes not mentioned in Main Text.

The following aircraft have been selected for inclusion in an Appendix primarily because they do not readily fit into the 'main stream' of combat aircraft development as described in the main text. Nevertheless, some of them — Avro Canada's CF-105 Arrow and the North American XB-70 Valkyrie, for example — have made a significant contribution to aviation technology, while others, such as Switzerland's FFA P-16 and Argentina's Pulqui II, represent valiant efforts on the part of smaller nations to break free of the combat aircraft monopolies enjoyed by their larger counterparts. Every aircraft described briefly here has its part to play in the overall fabric of the book.

AVRO CANADA CF-105 ARROW
Country of Origin: Canada
The CF-105 delta-wing all-weather interceptor flew for the first time on 25 March 1958, powered by two P&W J75 turbojets. Four more aircraft were built, designated CF-105 Mk.1, and four more — designated Mk.2, with 22,000 lb thrust Orenda PS-13 engines — were almost complete when the project was cancelled in February 1959. Span: 50 ft. Max Speed: Mach 2.3. Eight Sparrow AAMs.

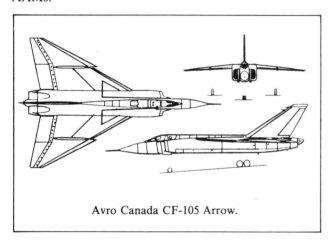

Avro Canada CF-105 Arrow.

BLACKBURN Y.A.1 FIRECREST
Country of Origin: Great Britain
Designed to specification S.28/43 as a successor to the Firebrand, the Blackburn B.48 Y.A.1 flew in March 1947, three and a half years after design work was begun. Engine was a 2,825 hp Bristol Centaurus radial. Three prototypes were built. Span: 44 ft 11½ in. Max Speed: 323 mph at sea level. Provision for two .5-in machine guns, one torpedo, two 500-lb bombs and RPs externally.

CONVAIR XP-81
Country of Origin: USA
Flown for the first time on 2 February 1945, the Convair XP-81 prototype long-range escort fighter was the first combat aircraft designed to use a combination of turboprop and turbojet, power being supplied by a GE XT31-GE-3 turboprop and a GE J33-GE-5 turbojet, the latter installed in the rear fuselage and fed via intakes aft of the cockpit. A second prototype was built, but the type was not adopted and an order for 13 pre-production aircraft was cancelled. Span: 50 ft 6 in. Max Speed: 484 mph at sea level. Proposed armament: Six .5-in machine guns or six 20-mm cannon.

AVRO CANADA CF-105 ARROW.

AVRO CANADA CF-105 ARROW.

DASSAULT MIRAGE G8

Country of Origin: France

In October 1965, Avions Marcel Dassault received a contract to build a prototype variable-geometry fighter known as the Mirage G. This was flown on 18 November 1967, but was destroyed after completing about 400 flying hours. Two prototypes of a smaller, twin-engined VG aircraft, the Mirage G8, were subsequently ordered by the French Government; the first flew on 8 May 1971 and reached Mach 2.03 four days later, powered by two SNECMA Atar 09K-50 engines. The type was not adopted. Span (Mirage G): 49 ft 2½ in spread, 22 ft 11½ in swept. Max Speed: 1,650 mph at 40,000 ft. Two 30-mm cannon.

BLACKBURN YA-1 FIRECREST.

CONVAIR XP-81.

DASSAULT BALZAC/MIRAGE III-V
Country of Origin: France
Employing part of the airframe of the original Mirage III-001 prototype, the Balzac VTOL research aircraft flew for the first time on 12 October 1962, powered by a Bristol Siddeley Orpheus B.Or.3 turbojet and eight Rolls-Royce RB.108 Stage 1A lift jets. It was, in fact, a scale model of the experimental Mirage III-V VTOL strike fighter, which began hovering trials on 12 February 1965. The Mirage III-V used a SNECMA TF-104 (later TF-106) turbofan and eight Rolls-Royce RB.162-1 lift engines, and the second prototype, which flew on 22 June 1966, was fitted with a Pratt & Whitney TF30. Span: 28 ft 7¼ in. Max Speed: Mach 2+.

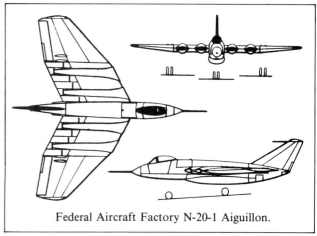

Federal Aircraft Factory N-20-1 Aiguillon.

FAIREY SPEARFISH
Country of Origin: Great Britain
Designed to specification 0.5/43 as a Barracuda replacement, the first of four prototype Spearfish flew on 5 July 1945, powered by a Bristol Centaurus radial

engine. Forty production Spearfish TBD.1s were ordered, but cancelled in 1946. Span: 60 ft 3 in. Max Speed: 292 mph at sea level. Proposed armament: two forward-firing .5-in machine guns, two .5-in guns in a barbette aft of the cockpit, underwing rockets and up to 2,000 lb of bombs.

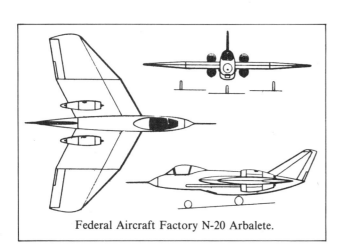

Federal Aircraft Factory N-20 Arbalete.

FEDERAL AIRCRAFT FACTORY N.20
Country of Origin: Switzerland
A prototype 'flying-wing' fighter for the Swiss Air Force, the N.20 Aiguillon (Sting) was powered by four 3,300 lb thrust SM-01 by-pass engines, which were basically adapted Armstrong Siddeley Mamba I turboprops with the propeller reduction gear removed and a low-pressure compressor installed. A three-fifths scale model, the N.20 Arbalete (Crossbow) flew on 16 November 1951, powered by four 242 lb thrust Turboméca Piméné I turbojets, but although the prototype N.20-01 Aiguillon made a few 'hops' during taxi trials in April 1952 it never made a proper first flight and the project was abandoned. Span (Arbalete): 24 ft 10 in. Max Speed: 466 mph.

FFA P-16

Country of Origin: Switzerland

Designed for operations in Alpine terrain, the P-16 single-seat strike fighter flew in prototype form on 31 August 1955, designated P-1604 and powered by an 11,000 lb thrust Armstrong Siddeley Sapphire A.S.Sa.7 turbojet. Several prototypes were completed, but the type was not adopted for service use. Span: 36 ft 6½ in. Max Speed: 710 mph at sea level. Two/four 30-mm Oerlikon cannon, MATRA air-to-air rockets and 24 8-cm Oerlikon air-to-ground rockets.

HISPANO HA-300

Country of Origin: Spain (Egyptian-Developed)

Originally designed in Spain in the late 1950s by a German-Spanish team led by Prof. Willy Messerschmitt, the HA-300 delta-wing fighter project was transferred to Egypt in 1961. Four prototypes were completed, the first flying at Helwan on 7 March 1964, powered by a Bristol Siddeley Orpheus 703 turbojet. Span: 19 ft 4 in. Max Speed: Mach 1.1

HUGHES XR-11

Country of Origin: USA

Designed specifically for photo-reconnaissance, the XR-11 (formerly XF-11) twin-engined, twin-boom monoplane flew for the first time on 7 July 1946, but crashed when it lost a propeller. A second aircraft flew on 5 April 1947. Both machines were powered by Pratt & Whitney R-4360 radial engines driving eight-blade contra-rotating propellers. Span: 101 ft 4 in. Max Speed: 400 mph.

I.Ae.27 PULQUI I

Country of Origin: Argentina

Designed by Emile Dewoitine, the I.Ae.27 Pulqui (Arrow) single-seat fighter flew for the first time on 9 August 1947, powered by a Rolls-Royce Derwent 5 turbojet. The type's performance, however, was disappointing and it was abandoned. Span: 36 ft 11 in. Max Speed: 447 mph at sea level. Four 20-mm cannon.

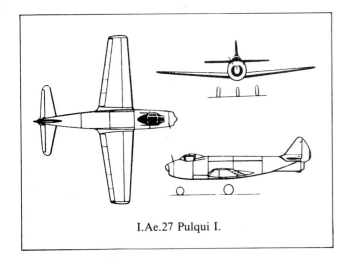

I.Ae.27 Pulqui I.

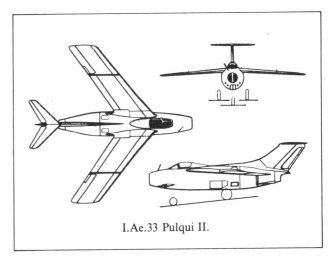

I.Ae.33 Pulqui II.

I.Ae.30 NAMCU

Country of Origin: Argentina

A single-seat, twin-engined all-metal fighter monoplane, the I.Ae.30 Namcu was flown for the first time in July 1948, powered by two Rolls-Royce Merlin 134/135 engines. A very promising design, in the same class as the de Havilland Hornet — and bearing a strong resemblance to the British machine — it nevertheless did not progress beyond the prototype stage. Span: 49 ft 2 in. Max Speed: 435 mph at sea level. Six 20-mm cannon.

I.Ae.33 PULQUI II

Country of Origin: Argentina

Designed by Dr. Kurt Tank, of Focke-Wulf 190 fame, the swept-wing Pulqui II (which bore no relationship to the earlier Pulqui I) owed much to the wartime Focke-Wulf Ta 183 project. Powered by a Rolls-Royce Nene II turbojet, the aircraft flew on 27 June 1950 and three more prototypes were built, the last flying in 1959. The project was abandoned when Dr. Tank and his team left Argentina. Span: 34 ft 9 in. Max Speed: 652 mph at 16,400 ft. Four 20-mm cannon.

IKARUS TYPE 451

Country of Origin: Yugoslavia

A small, twin-engined prone pilot research aircraft, the Ikarus Type 451 flew in 1951 and was a development of the pre-war Ikarus B-5 Pionir. The Type 451 was powered by two 160 hp Walter Minor 6-III engines. Span: 21 ft 11¾ in. Max Speed: 208 mph at sea level.

IKARUS TYPE 452-M

Country of Origin: Yugoslavia

The Ikarus Type 452-M, which flew for the first time on 23 July 1953, was an experimental light jet aircraft powered by two 330 lb thrust Turboméca Palas turbojets. The aircraft had swept wing and tail surfaces, an unusual feature being twin booms supporting the vertical tail surfaces. The tailplane was supported by a centrally-mounted third fin. Span: 17 ft 2½ in. Max Speed: 485 mph at sea level.

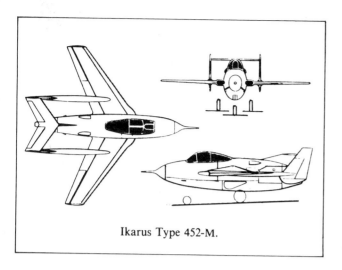

Ikarus Type 452-M.

LOCKHEED XV-4A HUMMINGBIRD
Country of Origin: USA

Originally designated VZ-10, the Lockheed Model 330 Hummingbird VTOL research aircraft was built as part of a US Army Transportation Research Command Programme. Powered by two 3,000 lb thrust Pratt & Whitney JT12A-3 turbojets, the first of two prototypes flew in August 1962. Span: 25 ft 8 in. Max Speed: 518 mph.

LTV XC-142A
Country of Origin: USA

Designed as a V/STOL military transport for all three US services, the tilt-wing XC-142A was developed jointly by LTV, Hiller and Ryan. Five prototypes were built, the first flying on 29 September 1964. During the test programme, the XC-142As carried out successful carrier trials, flew at speeds between 35 and 400 mph and reached heights of up to 25,000 feet. Despite the XC-142A's promise and versatility, the project was abandoned for economic reasons. the type was powered by four GE T64-GE-1 turboprops. Span: 67 ft 6 in. Max Speed: 409 mph at sea level.

MILES STUDENT
Country of Origin: Great Britain

Designed as a private venture jet trainer, the Miles M.100 Student flew for the first time on 14 May 1957, powered by an 880 lb thrust Turboméca Marboré II turbojet. Although highly manoeuvrable and pleasant to fly, the Student was overshadowed by types such as the Jet Provost and was subsequently used for experimental work at the Royal Aircraft Establishment, Bedford. In 1974, it participated in a noise suppression research programme. Span: 28 ft. Max Speed: 289 mph at sea level.

MYASISHCHEV M-52
Country of Origin: USSR

First flown in 1958, the mighty M-52 (NATO code-name: Bounder) was an attempt by its designer to produce an aircraft, which by combining a low-drag airframe with powerful unreheated engines, would be able to operate over intermediate ranges at speeds some 50 per cent higher than existing heavy bombers. Powered by four podded D-15 turbojets of 28,660 lb thrust, the aircraft established several FAI records in various payload classes under the designations 103-M and 201-M, but its performance apparently fell far short of expectations because of the severity of the transonic drag rise, and it never entered production. Span: 83 ft. Max Speed: 680 mph.

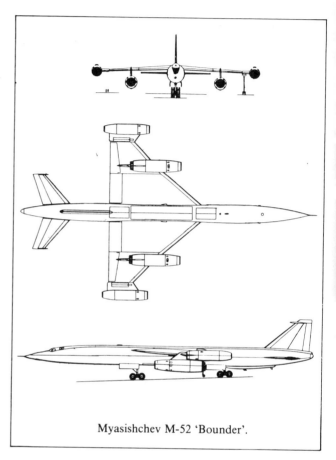

Myasishchev M-52 'Bounder'.

NORTH AMERICAN B-70 VALKYRIE
Country of Origin: USA

Originally designed as a supersonic bomber to replace the B-52, the large, delta-wing B-70 was in fact produced only as a research aircraft, the first of two prototypes flying on 21 September 1964. The second XB-70A flew on 17 July 1965 and flew at Mach 3 for more than thirty minutes in January 1966. On 8 June that year, it was lost when an F-104 chase aircraft collided with it. The first XB-70A continued to serve as a high-speed aerodynamic research vehicle in connexion with the US supersonic transport programme until the latter was abandoned. Both XB-70As were powered by six General Electric YJ93-GE-3 turbojets rated at 31,000 lb thrust each. Span: 105 ft. Max Speed: Mach 3+.

NORTH AMERICAN XB-70 VALKYRIE.

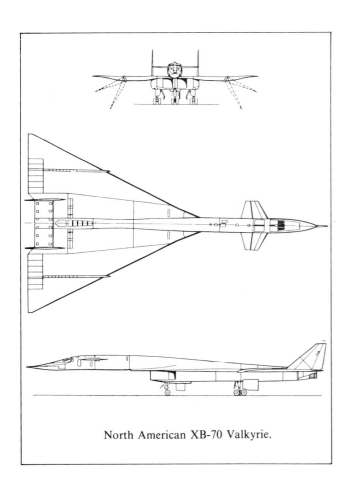

North American XB-70 Valkyrie.

NORTH AMERICAN XF-107
Country of Origin: USA

Designed in competition with the F-105 Thunderchief, the XF-107 was a much modified and updated variant of the F-100 Super Sabre. Powered by a Pratt & Whitney J75 turbojet, the first of three prototypes flew in September 1956. The turbojet air intakes were mounted on the upper fuselage, immediately aft of the cockpit. Span: 38 ft. Max Speed: Mach 2 at altitude.

NORTHROP F-15 REPORTER
Country of Origin: USA

Developed from the prototype XP-61E Black Widow, the XF-15 Reporter high-altitude photo-reconnaissance aircraft flew in June 1945. A contract for 175 aircraft was placed by the USAF, but only thirty-six had been built by the end of the war with Japan. The F-15, which saw no operational service, carried a battery of six cameras in the nose and all defensive armament was deleted. Span: 66 ft. Max Speed: 440 mph at 33,000 ft.

NORTH AMERICAN XF-107.

REPUBLIC XR-12.

REPUBLIC XR-12
Country of Origin: USA
Originally designated XF-12, the Republic XR-12 was designed specifically as a photographic reconnaissance aircraft. The first of two prototypes flew on 7 February 1946, powered by four Pratt & Whitney R-4360-31 Wasp Major radial engines developing 3,000 hp. Six production aircraft were ordered under the designation F-12A, but later cancelled. Span: 129 ft 2 in. Max Speed: 450 mph.

RYAN XV-5A
Country of Origin: USA
The Ryan XV-5A Vertifan V/STOL aircraft was designed as the forerunner of a two-seat battlefield surveillance machine, the first of two prototypes flying on 25 May 1964. The aircraft was powered by two General Electric J85-GE-5 turbojets of 2,650 lb thrust, gases from these being diverted to drive large lift fans buried in the wings. Span: 44 ft 6 in. Max Speed: 550 mph at sea level.

Photographic Acknowledgements

Aerospatiale
Page 84, 85, 90, 91, 92.

Armand Agababian
Page 146.

Bell Aerospace
Page 27, 33.

British Aerospace
Page 39, 40, 52, 57, 60, 101, 103, 104, 108, 109, 110, 138, 140, 141, 147.

Dassault/Breguet
Page 90, 93, 95, 131, 133, 139, 140, 145.

Fairchild Republic.
Page 22, 114, 115, 120, 129.

General Dynamics.
Page 20, 21, 143, 157.

Grumman
Page 34, 117, 118.

Handley Page
Page 41, 42.

Ann Harrington
Page 19, 50, 53, 54, 58, 133, 134, 135, 144, 156, 159.

Mike Jerram
Page 10, 11, 12, 13, 14.

Lockheed
Page 23, 101, 116, 142.

McDonnell Douglas
Page 16, 17, 18, 24, 25, 31, 32, 35, 37, 119, 120.

R. McManners.
Page 153, 154, 155.

North American Rockwell
Page 30.

Ministry of Defence (RAF)
Page 121, 122.

Musée de l'Air.
Page 82, 83, 86, 87, 88, 89, 94, 96.

Pilot Press
Page 64, 66, 67, 68, 69, 70, 72, 73, 74, 75, 76, 77, 78, 79, 159.

Rolls-Royce
Page 148.

Royal Navy
Page 59.

Short Brothers
Page 43, 102.

Short Brothers, via Alan Todd
Page 43.

SAAB
Page 123, 124, 125, 126.

Alan Todd
Page 43, 44, 45, 49, 55, 56, 127, 128, 132.

USAF
Page 9.

Vought Corporation
Page 28, 29, 118.

Westland
Page 98, 100.

Index